EMPATH NARCISSIST

How a Super Empath Can Destroy a Narcissist! Increase Your Confidence, Overcome Toxic Relationship and Understand How to Recognize Him to Learn to Deal with His False Power

Rose Hoskins

Rose Hoskins © Copyright 2023

All rights reserved.

It is not permitted in any way to reproduce, duplicate, or transmit any part of this document in digital or printed form. Dissemination of this publication is strictly prohibited, and any use of this document is not permitted without the prior written con-sent of the publisher. All rights reserved.

The accuracy and integrity of the information contained herein is guaranteed, but no responsibility of any kind is assumed. It is in fact, in terms of misinterpretation of the information through carelessness, or through the use or misuse of any policies, processes, or instructions contained within the book, the sole and absolute responsibility of the intended reader. Under no circumstances may the publisher be legally prosecuted or blamed for any damage done or monetary loss incurred as a result of information contained in this book, either directly or indirectly.

Rights are held by the respective authors and not the publisher.

Hide these books

Legal Note: This book is copyrighted. It is for personal use only. No part of the contents of this book may be modified, distributed, sold, used, quoted, or paraphrased without the specific consent of the author or copyright owner.

Any violation of these terms will be sanctioned as provided by law.

Disclaimer:

Please note that the contents of this book are exclusively-for educational and entertainment purposes. Every measure has been taken to provide accurate, up-to-date, and completely reliable information. No warranties of any kind are expressed or implied. Readers acknowledge that the author's opinion is not to be substituted for legal, financial, medical, or professional advice.

TABLE OF CONTENTS

Narcissistic Abuse and Codependency 19

Introduction 19

FIRST PART: RECOGNISE A NARCISSIST 21

Chapter 1: Who is the narcissist? (identikit) 21

Narcissism: a possible definition 21

Narcissism in psychoanalysis 22

Narcissism as a mental disorder 22

A brief history 23

Narcissism: a typical personality issue 25

Pathological narcissism 26

The complexity of the phenomenon: the various types of narcissists............... 27

Healthy narcissism 27

Malignant narcissism 27

Worst of all: the malicious or perverted narcissist 28

Overt and covert narcissism 28

Causes of pathological narcissism 30

Differential diagnosis 31

Narcissism and society 31

Conclusions about narcissism definition 31

Chapter 2: How to recognize a narcissistic personality? 34

Healthy narcissism sings 34

Psychological characteristics of Narcissistic Personality Disorder 35

Symptoms of the narcissistic personality 37

Diagnostic criteria 39

How to recognize a narcissist? 7 foolproof signs 40

1. The conversation is like a soliloquy 40

2. Show open contempt for others 41

3. Aim to be admired 41

4. Shows a fleeting interest in people 41

5. Seeks attention through negative emotions 42

6. He perceives himself as having a great personality 42

7. Tends to manipulate others 42

How to recognize the covert narcissist? 43

Consequences of Narcissistic Personality Disorder 44

SECOND PART- NARCISSISTS AND RELATIONSHIPS 46

Chapter 3: The relationship between codependency and narcissism 46

What is codependency? 46

Difference between codependency and love addiction 47

Features and signs of codependency 47

Origins of codependency 49

The narcissist and his relationship of codependency with his partner 50

Narcissistic and codependent 51

Building a codependency relationship 52

A summary outlines 53

Chapter 4: How a narcissist sees love 57

Narcissism and love: are a possible duo? 57

What is love for a narcissist? 58

Origins of the narcissist's inability to love 59

But does the narcissist fall in love? 59

Chapter 5: How a narcissist submits in relationships and what their goal is? 61

The goal of the narcissist: the so-called narcissistic supply 61

How does the narcissistic supply work? 62

What are the functions of narcissistic supply in narcissistic pathology? 64

The other side: narcissistic extension 65

How the narcissist seeks to achieve their goals through relationships? 66

Narcissists relationships: a way to achieve their goal 67

The narcissist and the victim role: another way to achieve the goal 68

The stages of the relationship with narcissists 69

Stage 1 – Seduction, Love bombing, or the golden age 69

Phase 2 – Intrusion 71

Stage 3 – Discard or Destruction of the other 72

THIRD PART- SOME WARNING FOR THE POTENTIAL VICTIM 74

Chapter 6: Long-term effects on your psyche 74

The immediate consequences for the narcissist's victim 74

Long term effects 75

Post-trauma psyche effects 77

To recap: all the effects and consequences of the relationship with the narcissist 79

Conclusions regarding the psychic effects on the victims 79

Chapter 7: 9 signs of a narcissistic partner 81

How do we know if we are dealing with a pathological narcissist? 81

9 irrefutable signs of a narcissist partner 81

1.   Talk about himself or herself 82

2.   He or she knows no rules and limits...and respect! 82

3. Apparent splendor 83

4. You feel anger and humiliation in their presence 83

5. They change their minds; they deny and seem the same charming 84

6. Control and fear of abandonment 84

7. They are envious of your relationships with others 85

8. Superficiality...sounds familiar? 85

9. And finally... love bombing: you must be more careful about this! 85

FOURTH PART- COMING OUT OF A RELATIONSHIP WITH THE NARCISSIST 88

Chapter 8: First solutions on what to do once you realize you have a narcissistic partner ... 88

A premise 88

What can I do? 89

The First Step to Healing: It Starts with You 91

Bottom line: it's about taking back your life 92

Chapter 9: Do's and Don'ts of a Toxic Relationship 94

Types of toxic relations 94

Toxic love relationship 95

Toxic friendship relationships 95

Toxic family relationships 95

Toxic relationships work 95

Toxic relationship: the warning signs 96

Lack of support 96

Toxic communication 96

Controlling behaviors 96

Resentment 97

Dishonesty 97

Constant stress 97

Ignore your needs 97

Lost relationships 97

What happens in toxic relation with a narcissist? A small verification questionnaire 98

Dos in a toxic relationship 99

Cultivate self-esteem 99

Give up having his esteem 100

Indulge his narcissism 100

Try to mortify him 100

So, think of yourself and make yourself desired 101

Indifference 101

But the best do's is always the same: silence 101

And finally: ask for some help 101

Don'ts in a toxic relationship 102

Don't let it get to the point where it sucks all your vital energies 102

Avoid becoming completely addicted 102

Never think you can change him or her 102

Never justify the narcissist 103

Avoid blaming yourself 103

No stalking 103

No anger 104

If you have decided to leave him, avoid any contact 104

Chapter 10: The 5 steps to get away from your toxic partner (practical methods) 105

Some general defense strategies 105

5 important steps to get away from the narcissist 107

1. Gather energy and avoid traps 107

2. Develop an action plan 107

3. Action 108

4. Keep as little contact as possible 109

5. Metabolize the breakup 110

The importance of no contact 111

No contact: what it is not 112

No contact rules 113

The difference between no contact and ghosting 113

Chapter 11: How to manage your psychological side during the transition 115

Now it's over: what can I do? 115

Tips for the transition phase 117

Recognize what happened and what role you played during the relationship 117

Improvisation 118

Always the dear no contact 118

Self-esteem 118

Release your anger 119

Detox 119

See a therapist 119

Contact your support group 119

Don't think you'll be alone forever 120

Do not regret the past 120

Make your physical health, emotional and mental health 120

Healing 121

Surround yourself with positivity 121

Stand firm in the decision 121

Forgiving yourself after a toxic relationship 121

FIFTH PART: HOW TO MOVE ON AND BE HAPPY AGAIN 123

Chapter 12: What you need to do to avoid falling into this trap again (practical methods) 123

First things first: what not to do to prevent your current toxic partner from coming back 123

How to deal with a returning narcissist? 125

How to avoid narcissists in the future? A general reflection 127

Prevention is better than cure: tips to avoid falling into the narcissistic trap 128

How to avoid manipulations like love bombing, gaslighting or emotional abandonment? 131

Chapter 13: How to live happily in a new relationship 132

A small premise: listen to yourself 132

Living happily with a new partner is possible! 132

The key is doing better choices 133

Learn from the past and think love it's still real! 133

Get smarter... and you'll be happy! 134

And finally: 6 ways to return to love after a toxic relationship 134

Conclusions 136

EMPATH IN RELATIONSHIP 137

Introduction 137

FIRST PART-RECOGNISE EMPATHY AND EMPATH 140

Chapter 1: Understanding Empathy 140

What is empathy? 140

Empathy: historical notes 141

Ancient Greece 141

Feel inside 141

Meaning of empathy: definition by Edith Stein 142

Meaning of empathy today 142

Empathy theories 143

Empathy: psychology theory 143

A double theory: mind and heart 144

Mirror theory 145

Empathy and psychotherapy theory 146

Empathy: social theory 147

Empathy and Development: Martin Hoffman's Theory 147

Different types of empathy: get to know them 148

Positive and negative empathy 148

Difference between female and male empathy 149

Empathy and mentalization 150

Empathy and emotional intelligence 151

Empathy in medicine 151

Empathy in love relationships 152

The Dark Side of Empathy: Disorders and Degeneration 152

Empathy and Psychopathology 153

Empathy in the dark triad 154

What are the characteristics of empathy in the dark triad? 155

So, who is the dark empath? 156

Chapter 2: Are You an Empath? (Typical signs and how to recognize if you are an empath)
.... 159

Who is an empath? 159

Doubts about the subject empath 160

Do all human beings have the same capacity to be empathic? 160

Are there people who are not empathetic? 160

Why do we become more Empaths? 160

Signs that you are an empath 161

1. You are a woman, and you may probably be empathic by nature 162
2. You can feel the emotions of others, even when they are not present 162
3. The "vibe" of a room matters to you, a lot 162
4. In the evening you are often tired for no reason 163
5. You understand where people come from 163
6. People come to you for advice 163
7. Tragic or violent events on TV can completely knock you out 163
8. You cannot contain your love for pets, animals, or children. 164
9. You may also perceive people's physical illnesses, not just their emotions ... 164
10. You can get overwhelmed in love relationships 164
11. You have a strong sixth sense and you recognize people who lie 165
12. You fail to understand why a leader wouldn't put their team first 165
13. You have a calming effect on other people and the power to heal them 165
14. You can't see someone in pain without wanting to help them 166
15. You are too good 166

Chapter 3: 12 signs you need to recognize an empath 167

What does it mean to feel empathy? 167

The importance of recognizing empathy in the others 167

1. Basic empathy 168
2. Mutual empathy 168
3. Intersubjective empathy 168

12 signs of an Empath 170

1. Empaths are very sensitive people 170
2. They feel the emotions of others, and feel their own pain 170
3. Empaths are very introverted people 171
4. They are loners and spend a lot of time alone 171
5. They have excellent intuition and problem-solving skills 171
6. They are a favorite "target" of energy vampires 172
7. They love nature and animals 172
8. They hate lies 172
9. They are creative and dreamers 173
10. They can't stand violence 173
11. They are free spirits 173
12. They have a mighty heart 174

Chapter 4: The different types of empaths there are and how to classify them 175

How many types of empaths? 175

1. Emotional empath 176
2. Medical empath 176
3. Empath from places 176
4. Intellectual empath 176
5. Environmental empath 177

How to classify different kinds of an empath? 177

SECOND PART- EMPATH AND RELATIONSHIPS 179

Chapter 5: Empaths in relationships and how it behaves 179

The different types of relationships for the empath 179

Empaths in love relationships 179

Empath: relationship with parents 180

Empath in friendship 181

Empath at work 182

How an empath sets relationships 182

Basic empathy 182

Mutual empathy 182

Intersubjectivity 183

Learning empathy day after day 183

Friendship empath behavior 184

The ability to listen 184

Another great relational skill of the empath: accepting differences 184

How the empathy relationship is established between parents and children .. 185

Empath and the couple relationship: how she or she behaves 187

From falling in love to love 188

Double blade in a couple of relationships? 188

Mutability 188

Chapter 6: Why Do Empaths Usually Attract Narcissists? 190

Empath and narcissist: a sad combo 190

Why this attraction? 191

Why empathetic people are attracted to narcissists? 193

How do narcissists make their empathetic partner codependent? 194

The 11 stages of a toxic relationship between a narcissistic person and an empath 194

Phase 1: the Attraction 194

Phase 2: the Illusion 195

Phase 3: Manipulation 195

Phase 4: The Game of "Victim" and "Perpetrator" 195

Stage 5: Failure 195

Phase 6: the Trap 195

Stage 7: The "Suffocation" 195

Stage 8: The Empath's Escape 196

Phase 9: Acknowledging the truth 196

Phase 10: the Painful Awakening 196

Stage 11: The End of the Relationship 196

THIRD PART-ABOUT EMPATH POWERS 197

Chapter 7: "Power" of empaths. Let's know better 197

What does mean empath power? 197

The power of empathy: what mirror neurons are and how they work 197

Mirror neurons and relationships 198

Being an empath is already a superpower 198

The other powers of the empath 199

Chapter 8: How to defend your fears and feed your power 201

What are the fears that hinder empaths? 201

Dear empath: defend your fears 201

The courage of empathy 203

Feed your powers: some good tips to "train" your empathy 205

Can empathy be trained? 205

Feed your empath power in a love relationship 205

1.   Awareness 207

2.   Emotional sharing 207

Increase the educational power of the empath 208

Train a Culture of Empathy in a work environment 209

Step 1: Train empathy like a muscle 210

Step 2: Connect consistently 210

Step 3: Take action 210

Step 4: Develop an ecosystem of empathy 210

How to enhance the power of empathy and use it for relationships in general 211

- ✓ Understand your own emotions 211
- ✓ Ask people to talk about their feelings 211
- ✓ Interact with various types of people, even with those you don't like 211
- ✓ Try to see things from another point of view 212
- ✓ Recognize (and accept) the perspectives of others 212
- ✓ Don't advise unless it's asked for 212
- ✓ Give attention to others in a sincere way 212
- ✓ Smile and encourage people 212
- ✓ Learn to listen 213
- ✓ Don't be afraid to appear vulnerable 213

FOURTH PART- DEFEND YOURSELF FROM NARCISSIST 215

Chapter 9: How a narcissist approaches an empath to submit 215

A Trap for the Empath: The Narcissist's Approach 215

How a narcissist subdues the empath: from the traumatic bonding to hoovering technique
.... 216

Chapter 10: How to protect yourself from a narcissist (practical methods) 220

Let's summarize the situation 220

Protect yourself from narcissist: how to do it 220

Counter-manipulation 221

Emotional avoidance 221

Indifference: always the best weapon 222

If you recognize it, you avoid it 222

Prepare yourself right 222

Turn inward to support yourself 223

If we reveal what we lack, we will be at the mercy of others 223

Resist the narcissist's nastiness 224

Don't try to have a conversation with him/her 224

No-contact is key to leaving a narcissist 225

Let go 225

Healthy self-esteem 226

Ask for help 226

Give yourself time 226

Chapter 11: How to govern your emotions and keep them at bay 227

Some good ways to govern your emotions 227

Emotional regulation 227

So, this is all about you 229

Stop handing over power 229

Detox Your Life 230

A good emotional cleansing 230

Give strength to your life 232

Keep your emotions at bay: how to do it 233

From fear to self-confidence 233

Strong borders 233

Communicate your needs 234

Take your time and space 234

Pay attention to what you throw out 234

Cleaning 234

Protect yourself from future energy implications. 235

Chapter 12: How to Repel Narcissists' Evil and Vampire Emotions 236

How to Avoid Absorbing the Evil Energies of Others 236

Find out if you're touchy. 236

Look for the source 237

Move away from the possible source 237

Focus on your breathing 237

Protect yourself 237

Manage emotional overload 237

Look for positive people and situations 238

Create and maintain a refuge to disconnect.. 238

Let a "kitty" choose you as your owner. 238

Neutralizing a narcissist or an emotional vampire: 5 tips 239

1. No, the magic word that can neutralize an emotional vampire 239

2. "I don't believe you, prove it to me!"... 240

3. "You are not superior to others" 240

4. I don't fear you!" 240

5. "Don't change the topic of discussion!" 240

FIFTH PART- WHAT IS IMPORTANT TO ENHANCE YOUR POWER 242

Chapter 13: What to Focus on? Family or relationships 242

The importance of empathic communication... 242

Family or relationship: what and how to focus on? 243

Tips and exercises to train empathic listening 245

Chapter 14: 10 practical ways to release all the power while avoiding narcissists 248

Release Your Power While Avoiding Narcissists: Ways to Protect Your Own Energy 248

10 best ways to enhance your empath powers 250

1. Recognize that you are an empath 251
2. Recognize and avoid toxic people 251
3. Trust your intuition 251
4. Don't play the victim 251
5. Set boundaries 251
6. Meditate 251
7. Breathe 252
8. Transmutes negative energy 252
9. Love yourself 252
10. Australian Flowers 252

Conclusions 254

Narcissistic Abuse and Codependency

Introduction

This is an ultimate guide that will talk about narcissism. It is a psychological phenomenon that many people fail to come out of every day.

We are talking specifically about narcissism and codependency in general. Yes, because for every perpetrator there is always a victim. In the case of a victim of narcissism, a person who indulges it in a very dangerous way, precisely creating an unhealthy codependency relationship.

But before even talking about these two psychological phenomena of our day, let's give some definitions. In general, one can speak of a narcissistic personality, or a person affected by narcissistic personality disorder when ideas of grandiosity, a constant need for admiration and control, and a total lack of empathy, from which derive the belief that one's needs come before anything else. And to fully express these characteristics, a narcissist needs a person who plays a secondary role, indulging all these toxic needs.

It will be with this person, the victim, that he (or she) will create a relationship of codependency. But this passage is fundamental: codependence does not fall only on the victim. Even the narcissist depends on a second person to satisfy this constant need for admiration. In other words, the narcissist is fundamentally dependent on others for the sense of security he lacks, he doesn't get very far without someone to please him. A compliant partner accepts and helps him to perpetrate, his abusive behavior while being a victim of it.

Those who fall into a relationship with a narcissist often become complacent gradually without realizing the situation and are confused by the ambiguous messages from him. Complacent partners may delude themselves into thinking that they are the only ones able to understand and support the narcissistic partner, deeming him intelligent and attractive, and deserving of their dedication. Complacent adults accept the abusive dynamics of a relationship with a narcissist because they grew up with demanding, selfish, abusive parents.

In many cases, they come from narcissistic families or have experienced other dysfunctional family environments and have always learned not to consider their needs.

All these aspects will be discussed in a very detailed way in the course of the book. We aim to make you understand who the narcissist is, what the typical behaviors are, and, above all, for you who will have stumbled upon this book, how to get rid of a narcissistic partner and avoid toxic relationships in the future.

We therefore invite you to continue reading, hoping that from now on it will be useful in your life.

FIRST PART: RECOGNISE A NARCISSIST

Chapter 1: Who is the narcissist? (identikit)

In this first chapter, we will deal with defining both the narcissist and the person affected by this disorder. It is, as the title of the chapter says, the complete identikit of the narcissistic person.

Narcissism: a possible definition
Let's start this guide by defining what actual narcissism is. However, before trying to provide a global definition, it must be premised that narcissism is not a term with a univocal meaning but which has a vast range of meanings, depending on whether it is used to describe a personality trait, a concept of the theory psychoanalysis, a mental disorder, a social or cultural problem.
Narcissism is a very complex personality disorder, in which one of the few things that unite it is that the subject who suffers from it develops a real obsession with his image.
In everyday language, however, narcissism is mostly synonymous with self-centeredness, selfishness, vanity, and presumption.
In popular culture, a narcissist is someone who is in love with themselves. It is no coincidence that the term "narcissus" refers directly to the famous character of Greek mythology who falls in love with his image reflected in a stream.
If instead, we wanted to propose the term in a more "technical" way, in psychology, the term is used both to describe healthy self-love, i.e., normal self-love, and unhealthy self-centeredness caused by a disorder of the sense of self, which is reflected in relationships with oneself and with others. Applied to a social group, narcissism sometimes indicates elitism or indifference to the status of others. But if we are here to talk about narcissism, the reason is another: if we talk about problematic love relationships, the narcissist is now public enemy number one, and we hear more and more often about pathological narcissism. In reality, hardly anyone knows the true meaning of narcissism, and too often it is spoken of with great superficiality to the point of labeling a pathological narcissist as someone who may have behaved badly, but who to be honest does not have a pathology. In other words, narcissism is a tendency and psychological attitude of those who make of themselves, of their person, of their physical and intellectual qualities, the exclusive and pre-eminent center of their interest and the object of a pleased admiration, while remaining more or less indifferent to others, whose value and works he ignores or despises. The term was introduced in 1898 in sexology by the German psychiatrist H.

Ellis (1859-1939) to designate a pathological attitude of sexual life, whereby the subject enjoys admiring his own body, i.e. treats his own body as a sexual object, as a source of desire and pleasure, like the young Narcissus in the Greek myth.

Below, we will make a further small distinction which concerns one the definition universally recognized by psychoanalysis, the other instead which intends narcissism as a mental disorder:

Narcissism in psychoanalysis

According to psychoanalysis, narcissism can be, within certain limits, a normal state, but it can sometimes take on pathological dimensions and meanings that seriously interfere with social life. In the essay "Introduction to narcissism" (1914), S. Freud distinguished a primary narcissism, typical of the first stage of existence and prior to the formation of the ego, in which any kind of object relation and investment is absent (intrauterine life would be the best example of this state), and a secondary narcissism, in which there is a withdrawal from libidinal object-cathexes and the libido is reinvested in the ego.

Narcissism as a mental disorder

Narcissism is a personality trait and can be considered, within certain limits, a normal state. However, if this psychological attitude seriously interferes with interpersonal relationships, daily commitments, and quality of life, it can take on pathological dimensions and significance.

In psychiatry, in fact, narcissism is indicated among personality disorders (narcissistic personality disorder). People with this disorder tend to exaggerate their abilities and talents, are constantly absorbed in fantasies of unlimited success, and show an almost exhibitionistic need for attention and admiration. Unable to recognize and perceive the feelings of others, they tend to exploit others to achieve their goals or to be able to grow themselves. Narcissism is a personality trait that can be considered, within certain limits, an absolutely physiological state. In some respects, it is also functional in some contexts of daily life. However, if this psychological attitude seriously interferes with interpersonal relationships, it can assume proportions typical of pathological narcissism. In psychopathology, within the Diagnostic Statistical Manual (DSM-5), the narcissistic picture is indicated among personality disorders. People with these characteristics may tend to exaggerate their own abilities. They place themselves at the exclusive and pre-eminent center of their own interest and thus become the object of pleased admiration.

People who are affected by this make themselves the exclusive and pre-eminent center of their interest, becoming the object of smug admiration. Individuals who manifest a narcissistic personality are constantly absorbed in fantasies of unlimited success and show an almost exhibitionistic need for attention and admiration. Furthermore, these people are unable to recognize and perceive the feelings of others, tend to exploit others to achieve their goals, or despise the value of their work.

Behind this mask, however, the narcissist has a fragile self-esteem that makes him vulnerable to the slightest criticism. If he encounters a failure, due to his high opinion of himself, he can easily manifest extreme anger or depression.

A brief history

Let's see, after trying to define the term narcissism, how this concept has briefly evolved in history.

As already mentioned above, the word "narcissism" comes from the Greek myth of Narcissus.

The etymological origin of the term narcissism derives from the Greek narkào which means to stun, about the intense perfume of the relative flower.

The term narcissus derives from the Greek myth described in Ovid's Metamorphoses, in which a handsome young man named Narcissus rejects a long line of suitors, among whom is the wood nymph Echo, known for her great conversational and persuasive skills. She had been commissioned by Zeus to entertain her wife Hera during her amorous encounters; the latter, realizing her deception, punishes her nymph by depriving her of her word. When the nymph Echo meets the beautiful Narcissus, she falls in love with him and follows him everywhere, her silent presence irritates Narcissus who will brusquely reject her until she dies of love. The Goddess Artemis when discovers what happens condemns Narcissus to fall in love without ever being able to satisfy his passion and accompanies him near a source of clear and transparent waters. Narcissus notices his image reflected in the water, falls madly in love with it, and, in an attempt to embrace his image, dies transforming into a flower, the narcissus, which usually grows along the edges of watercourses. Another version of the myth has it that Narcissus, realizing that he cannot reach his beloved image of him reflected in the water, dies of pain so that the Narcissus flower is born from his body.

In both versions of the myth, if we think about it, falling madly in love with one's own image or becoming narcissistic is interpreted as a form of punishment for the inability to love and recognize the other, depriving most interpersonal relationships of balance and reciprocity.

In the clinical and psychopathological fields, this term has been used over time to refer to various phenomena passing from a perversion to a socio-cultural phenomenon: from the psychotic functioning of very serious patients to the normal one, to phases of psychosexual development, to defenses against anxieties of paranoid-schizoid and depressive and a definite Personality Disorder. The concept of excessive self-love has been recognized and examined throughout history. In ancient Greece, narcissism can be included in the concept of hubris. It is just in recent times has narcissism has been defined in psychological terms.

Let's briefly see the stages that have marked narcissism understood as we see it today.

- ✓ In 1898, Havelock Ellis, an English sexologist, used the term "narcissus-like" in reference to excessive masturbation, whereby the person becomes his own sexual object.
- ✓ In 1899 Paul Näcke was the first to use the term "narcissism" in a study of sexual perversions.
- ✓ In 1911 Otto Rank published the first psychoanalytic paper specifically concerned with narcissism, linking the latter to vanity and self-admiration.
- ✓ Sigmund Freud published a document exclusively devoted to narcissism in 1914 called Introduction to Narcissism,
- ✓ In 1923, Martin Buber published the essay Ich und Du in which he pointed out that our narcissism often leads us to relate to others as if they were objects rather than our equals.
- ✓ Since 2002, on tests designed to detect narcissism, the scores of US residents have steadily risen. Psychologists have suggested a link with the phenomenon of social network services.

Today narcissism, and more specifically the framework of narcissistic personality disorder, despite Greek myth, is defined as a very complex personality structure. The subject who suffers from it develops a real sort of fixation for the image that refers to others. In fact, pay enormous attention to the feedback on it from the people with whom the narcissist has more or less close relationships.
So, borrowing from the Greek myth of Narcissus, the term 'narcissism' has been used by psychoanalysis to describe a pathological condition. Today the term is used to refer to a concern or interest in the self that runs on a continuum from normality to pathology, i.e., Narcissistic Personality Disorder.

Narcissism: a typical personality issue

According to psychologists, pathological narcissism is not hereditary, but it is a structuring of the personality that originates in childhood, more precisely from what is called a "narcissistic wound", generally associated with feelings of shame and resentment.

Typically, the child who will be an adult narcissist has had a family with very high ambitions, which has led him to believe that he is "special" and, at the same time, has ridiculed or severely blamed his fears and failures. The negative messages became the internal discourse of the child, who developed low self-esteem. In this type of family, authentic feelings, especially if deemed negative or inappropriate, have been ignored, censored, or repressed, leaving a sense of shame in the child; on the contrary, the infant, when he managed to do some "performance" well, to respond to expectations, was praised to excess. He, therefore, grew up "hungry" for recognition and praise, and as an adult, he tends to see others without nuances: either as "perfect" or, conversely, as "worthless", in case he discovers the slightest defect or witnesses it manifests itself of any failure.

Another possible cause of narcissism occurs when, for some reason, the relationship between parent and child turns upside down, and the child is empowered to the point where he must protect his own parents, or even take the role of father or mother. This is the case, for example, of the children of sick parents, with psychiatric disorders or addiction problems, for whom the child takes care, while at the same time being ashamed of it. Yet another possible cause of narcissism occurs when a family, instead of pushing for excellence, discourages the legitimate ambitions of the children, possibly accusing them of ingratitude and selfishness. This can generate resentment.

Resentment arises from the impression that one has suffered injustice and that one could not prevent it from happening. If the child feels that he has been the victim of big injustice, he may harbor resentment as a defense mechanism, and thus arrive at adulthood with high expectations of what life should bestow upon him as compensation.

These people become extremely demanding and judgmental with themselves and with others, but are intolerant of criticism, which they experience as a judgment of their personality; they tend to conceive human relationships essentially as based on power and control (in a relationship, in an argument, one "wins" or" loses" they can use seductive and manipulative techniques). Indeed, bullying can be included in this dynamic, and comorbidities are frequent. These subjects could (very often) have a depressive disorder too (major depressive disorder, persistent depressive disorder), anorexia nervosa, a substance use disorder (especially cocaine), or another personality disorder (that could be one of these three; histrionic, borderline, paranoid).

Pathological narcissism

Individuals who exhibit pathological narcissism tend to be preoccupied with fantasies of unlimited grandeur and success. They often show an almost exhibitionistic need for attention and admiration from others. Furthermore, these people are unable to recognize and perceive both the evaluations and feelings of others (reading others' minds and empathy). They tend to exploit others to achieve their own goals, as well as to despise the value of the work of others.

Perhaps the defining characteristic of pathological narcissism is precisely the lack of empathy. From this comes the belief that one's needs come before anything else. Narcissists can argue as well that their way of seeing things is the only one that is universally right and no other could be taken into consideration.

People with narcissistic personality disorder can also get turned on by a competitive situation. The belief "I must be better than others" is activated by the urge to demonstrate their superiority. The narcissistic person also feels the urge to increase his status, as soon as possible.

Those individuals usually come to therapists because they have received social ultimatums, a financial upset, or other threats of humiliation, such as perceived or actual loss of employment status, disciplinary sanctions for the irresponsible, exploitative, aggressive, or abusive behavior of power, loss of relationship with partner or child, or negative outcomes such as license suspension, or other infractions that stem from the "the rules don't apply to me" grandiosity.

Less frequently, they turn to the therapist to show themselves, seeking attention and admiration and essentially lacking the will to change.

The keyword for narcissistic personality disorder is "impulsivity and instability."

Prevalence estimates of narcissistic personality disorder in the general population are 1% and mainly affect males and Western capitalist countries.

Behind this mask, however, the pathological narcissist usually has a fragile self-esteem that makes him vulnerable to what he perceives as criticism. Often, narcissists believe that others envy them, but are hypersensitive to criticism, failure, or defeat. The dimension represented by the tendency to grandeur, uniqueness, and superiority is therefore contrasted with feelings of inferiority, fragility, vulnerability, and fear of confrontation.

When faced with an inability to satisfy their high opinion of themselves, narcissists can become angry. Sometimes they develop panic attacks, become deeply depressed, or even attempt self-harm. This is usually the moment in which it usually comes to the attention of a clinician (symptoms related to anxiety, depression, and excessive worries are reported).

The most typical characteristics, reported to clinicians, which we will thoroughly explore in the course of the next chapters of the guide, are in fact a sort of sense of emptiness and dissatisfaction, but also depression or hypomania, until suicidal ideation, derealization, or dysphoria.

The impact of pathological narcissism can be significant in many areas of life, such as relationships, work, and school: it is obvious that the consequences of the narcissist's behavior can also play a central role in psychotherapeutic work, in which a relationship is established of attachment par excellence.

The complexity of the phenomenon: the various types of narcissists

As we said before, narcissistic disorder is something more complex that, as anticipated, can be considered along a continuum and cannot be enclosed within a single category. At one end of the spectrum we find, for example, healthy narcissism. We will talk specifically about the different categories below.

Healthy narcissism

A narcissist could be "safe". Could be healthy! In fact, narcissists are those charismatic, assertive, and self-confident people who, galvanized by compliments and praise, often obtain fame and recognition in the community they belong to. They are highly determined men and women, self-possessed and capable of engaging and empathetic leadership. Often these personalities have become like this after overcoming a stormy and turbulent past through therapy or a lucky meeting with a teacher, friend, or mentor. Some successful people fall into the category of healthy narcissism, alongside the ambitious and rampant overt or overt narcissists, who have no qualms walking over the corpses of their enemies.

Malignant narcissism

At the opposite end of the spectrum, we find what Kernberg (1992) defines as malignant narcissism, which corresponds to the psychopathic and paranoid personality described by Lowen (1983).

So, another subcategory of narcissists often cited (even inappropriately) is that of the malignant narcissist or perverse narcissist. This type of person combines the basic characteristics of pathological narcissism with a dose of sadism and aggression. These are people who don't just lack empathy, but who take pleasure in hurting others. Often these traits are recognized in people who commit crimes related to domestic violence and abuse.

The malignant narcissist has characteristics that place him in a hybrid area between narcissism and antisocial personality disorder. Some typical characteristics of narcissism reach the maximum degree of expression in the malignant narcissist:

grandiosity, lack of feelings, loss of contact with the self and the body, lack of contact with reality, sense of omnipotence, distrust of others, expressed anger, sadism (even towards himself) and cruelty. Usually, the malignant narcissist, especially when it is severe, has been the victim of strong parental aggression in early childhood. He often had a strongly sadistic and punitive parent (usually his father) and gradually became identified with him.

In adulthood, his mantra becomes: 'I can do what I want', 'No one can hurt me', in a dichotomous and split vision of life (seen as a jungle) and of others, seen or as completely good (therefore weak and to be subdued) or completely evil (to be attacked or escaped based on perceived strength). The most dramatic development of the disorder, therefore, is observed when the patient's grandiosity is combined with a high degree of aggression.

Worst of all: the malicious or perverted narcissist

The pathological narcissist, as we have seen, is an individual focused exclusively on his own self, who is in constant need of the admiration of others, and who overestimates himself in almost everything he does.

Even if to appear better he tends to devalue others, a pathological narcissist does not necessarily lead to actual physical or psychological violence.

It is the malignant or perverse narcissist who combines the typical characteristics of the pathological narcissist with a certain amount of manipulation and violence.

If the manipulation is exclusively psychological and emotional, the violence can also be physical and even sexual. The pathological/malignant narcissist will have no problem resorting to actual violence to subjugate and control another person and transform him into a being completely dependent on his influence and control.

Even more so than the pathological narcissist, the malignant/perverted narcissist is particularly skilled at manipulation. It can also be defined as a manipulative narcissist. In addition to being very good at choosing victims, he can use his charm and persuasive skills to convince the other person that they cannot do without him.

Dealing with an abusive or perverted narcissist or figuring out how to free yourself from an abusive or perverted narcissist is even more difficult than dealing with a pathological narcissist, as in this case, it is much easier to trigger violent reactions that could even endanger your safety.

Overt and covert narcissism

There are many nuances between benign narcissism and malignant narcissism ranging from covert or hidden narcissism to overt or overt narcissism (Wink, 1991).

The covert narcissist is a sort of "sub-category": this expression indicates a type of narcissist that is particularly difficult to recognize and identify. Here too - since it is a complex subject - we will explain in an extremely simplified way. The main characteristic of the covert narcissist is that of being able to give others an impeccable, respectable, and even benevolent self-image. Only rarely does it reveal much more disturbing characteristics such as inflexibility, lack of empathy, and aggression.

The covert narcissist is inhibited, vulnerable, hypersensitive to criticism, afraid of rejection, often feels ashamed and embarrassed, and always feels an enormous distance between himself and others ('I always see others as if from behind a mirror, I feel them far away, as if I were an alien').

But, contrary to superficial observation, the covert narcissist is not a sweet and affectionate kitten, but a sleeping lion. He shares with his overt counterpart the attitude of exploitation and manipulation towards others, the absence of empathy, a certain amount of aggression (albeit generally lower than the overt narcissist), and the presence of grandiose fantasies (despite these, unlike what happens to the overt narcissist, are covert and less aware). The fear of failure and of not realizing their fantasies of greatness often determines in these people the tendency to avoid situations in which they may find themselves at the center of attention (Kohut & Wolf, 1978). Covert narcissists often feel shame and anger, a sense of failure and defeat, rejection, and expulsion.

He is fascinated by the strong and independent people he decides to bond with to obtain care, protection, and advantages of all kinds. To achieve his goals, use a passive-aggressive type of emotional manipulation, trying to generate feelings of guilt towards you for not loving him enough and not taking care of him enough.

In reality, this type of narcissism is more typical of women, but there are not a few males who adopt this type of behavior.

The overt narcissist appears superior, self-reliant, dominant, euphoric, triumphant (or alternately cold and detached). He feels that he does not belong to the rest of humanity or is part of a higher elite (Dimaggio et al., 2007). The overt narcissist looks similar to the narcissistic character described by Lowen, whereby: "As I walk, I have the feeling that people step aside to let me pass. It seems the division of the waters of the Red Sea to allow the passage of the Jews. I'm proud of it". It, therefore, appears more correct to speak of a narcissistic spectrum than of narcissism. A continuum that goes from healthy to malignant narcissism, from covert to overt narcissism, based on the degree of grandiosity, loss of contact with reality, lack of feelings, and lack of contact with one's needs, one's bodily sensations, and emotions. And narcissists are somewhere on this continuum.

Causes of pathological narcissism

We must say that the causes of pathological narcissism are not defined clearly and unambiguously. Often, this picture results from the combination of several social and biological factors that intervene during the development of the individual. For being more specific, you should know that the development of the disorder could be favored more by growing up in a disabling family environment. This environment is usually characterized by behavioral inhibition by two hyper-demanding parents.

So, the causes of narcissism are therefore not defined clearly and unambiguously; often, this picture results from the combination of several factors, social and biological. In particular, the development of the disorder can be favored by growing up in a disabling family environment, characterized by behavioral inhibition by demanding parents.

These elements would intervene during the development of the individual, influencing his behavior and thoughts. In particular, the clinical picture can be favored by parents who believe in the superiority of the future narcissist and attach great importance to success, excessively criticizing fears and failures.

Narcissistic personality disorder can also result from growing up in a family environment incapable of providing the child with the necessary attention; over time, in response to this attitude, the subject would resolve the continuous threat to his self-esteem, developing a sense of superiority and behavior that demonstrates the need for constant admiration.

Usually, narcissistic personality disorder appears in the teen years or early adulthood.

During childhood, children may show a narcissistic attitude, but this may simply represent a transitory character of their age and does not mean that they will develop a real pathological picture. Estimates of the prevalence of narcissistic personality disorder range between 2 and 16% in the clinical population, while they are less than 1% in the general population, and 50-75% of individuals who receive this diagnosis are male.

The impact of pathological narcissism, as we have said before, can be significant in many areas of life, such as relationships, work, school, or financial affairs.

Narcissistic personality disorder (or high narcissism in general) can also result from growing up in a family environment incapable of providing the child with the necessary emotional attention and the consequent satisfaction of her needs. Over time, in response to this attitude, the subject would resolve the continuous threat to his self-esteem, developing a sort of sense of superiority.

Differential diagnosis

Narcissistic personality disorder must be distinguished from the following:

1. Bipolar Disorder: Patients with a narcissistic personality disorder often present with depression and, due to their grandiosity, may be misdiagnosed as having bipolar disorder. Such patients may suffer from depression, but their persistent need to rise above others distinguishes them from those with bipolar disorder. Also, in narcissistic personality disorder, mood changes are triggered by self-esteem insults.
2. Antisocial Personality Disorder: The exploitation of others to promote oneself is characteristic of both personality disorders. However, the reasons are different. Often, people with antisocial personality disorder exploit others to get material gain; those with narcissistic personality disorder try always to exploit victims to maintain their self-esteem.
3. Histrionic Personality Disorder: Attention-seeking from others is characteristic of both personality disorders. But patients with narcissistic personality disorder, unlike those with histrionic personality disorder, act in disdain for anything cute and silly to get attention; they want to be admired.

Narcissism and society

The narcissistic disorder is widespread today as well as a very strong narcissistic tendency in our society and culture. The theme of appearing is dominant and is successful compared to that of being in a society increasingly characterized by the image and the use of social media as extensions of our identity. We can safely say that we live in a narcissistic society and that this problem deeply affects each of us.
Both millennials and the older generations make profuse use of social media and suffer the imperative to appear and be worth only based on their appearance. On the other hand, the elderly are cut off from this, and often experience all this as a sense of discomfort, rejection, and isolation. To each his discomfort and difficulty. However, the most fragile is the very young who now build their identity through social media, irreparably incurring narcissistic problems that deeply mark them.

Conclusions about narcissism definition

We have explained in an extremely concise way who the pathological narcissist is. Remember that it is a serious pathology that must be diagnosed by a specialist and that it is not as common as we might think. Precisely for this reason, it would be advisable not to use words such as "pathological narcissist" too lightly.

Instead, what is much more common are people with a narcissistic character: we are not dealing with pathology, but with simple character traits that can be more or less accentuated. Traits that in some situations can even be functional, and in others (for example relationships) are less so.

Today, when we speak of "narcissism" it tends to refer to an interest or concern relating to the self on a continuum that goes from health to pathology (Ronningstam, 2001); in fact, let us remember that narcissistic aspects affect all of us.

On the other hand, our socio-cultural context also has important narcissistic dimensions, in fact the purpose of our main vital activities is the immediate achievement of personal gratification and enrichment. Precisely because we live within a cultural orientation aimed at extreme enhancement of the Self, the term "narcissist" is used in various ways and meanings and consequently, it is sometimes difficult to make a distinction between healthy narcissism and pathological narcissism or between the adaptations of socio-cultural demands of our society and narcissistic pathology.

We are in the presence of healthy narcissism, when there is a certain amount of self-respect and egocentrism essential for the health and psychological balance of each of us, it represents the extreme of a continuum at the opposite of which we find instead the so-called pathological narcissism characterized from an abnormal need for affirmation, appreciation, and attention (Gabbard, 2015). Healthy or normal narcissism is an essential component of human functioning as it affects our self-preservation, self-regulation, and self-affirmation activities (Ronningstam, 2001). Indeed, in this we find not only interpersonal empathy and social concern but also a regular dimension of vanity and exhibitionism.

On the other hand, when there is a narcissistic pathology, there is a certain rigidity, persistent insensitivity towards others, a general tendency to exploit, and a lack of reciprocity in interpersonal relationships (ibidem). Indeed, individuals with a narcissistic pathology seem to be incapable of loving, they do not perceive others as people who have a separate existence or specific needs but as "objects" necessary for the satisfaction of their needs.

In conclusion, we can say that a useful strategy to distinguish the two forms of narcissism can be to evaluate the quality of the individual's interpersonal relationships, having seen the differences and characteristics and remembering that the various phases of the life cycle are also an essential point in this assessment, think of the understandable and functional healthy share of narcissism during the developmental phase of adolescence.

For convenience, from here on we will refer to these people with the word "narcissist", specifying that we are not referring to those affected by the pathology that we described in the previous paragraph. So let's try, in the next chapter, to understand the meaning of being a narcissist and to learn to recognize him by analyzing his most frequent characteristics and behaviors.

Chapter 2: How to recognize a narcissistic personality?

To protect ourselves in everyday life, it is better to learn to recognize a narcissist, to avoid him. Having a conversation with a narcissist can initially feel like a rewarding experience. However, he won't be slow to reveal his true intentions, which are to make others feel inferior and take advantage of those around him (or her). In this second chapter we will analyze what are the various aspects that characterize the attitude towards oneself and others, but also the typical behavior of a person affected by the narcissistic disorder.

Healthy narcissism sings
Let's start, before talking about narcissism in its worst form, about healthy narcissism. We already talked about it in the last chapter.
The idea of healthy narcissism was first coined by Paul Federn and gained importance in the 1970s thanks to the research of Otto Kernberg and Heinz Kohut as well.
"Healthy narcissism" is a positive sense of self that is aligned with the greater good. According to Heinz Kohut, the characteristics of healthy narcissism are:

- ✓ Strong self-esteem.
- ✓ A sense of empathy and recognition of the needs of others.
- ✓ Authentic self-concept.
- ✓ Self-respect and self-love.
- ✓ Being able to tolerate criticism from others while maintaining positive self-esteem.
- ✓ Confidence in setting and pursuing goals and realizing one's hopes and dreams.
- ✓ Emotional resilience.
- ✓ Healthy pride in oneself and one's results.
- ✓ The ability to admire and be admired.

More recently, Andrew P. Morrison (1989) recalls that a certain amount of narcissism allows one to balance one's needs in relation to others. Also, according to Craig Malkin (2016), a too low level of healthy narcissism is not positive for the person. In so-called extreme or pathological narcissism, on the other hand, this balance is broken.

Psychological characteristics of Narcissistic Personality Disorder

It is useful, before talking about real signs, to analyze the psychological characteristics of individuals with narcissistic personality disorder in terms of views of themselves and others, intermediate and core beliefs, and coping (coping) strategies.
So, let's see some common features:

- ✓ Self-view: They see themselves as flawed, and vulnerable to abuse, betrayal, and neglect.
- ✓ View of others: They can see others as warm and loving but still find them untrustworthy because "they are strong and might be supportive, but after a while, they change to hurt or abandon me".
- ✓ Intermediate and deep beliefs: "I must ask for what I need", "I must respond when I feel like I'm attacked", "I have to do it because the only thing important to me is feeling better", "If I'm alone, I won't be able to deal with the situation", " if I trust someone, sooner or later they will abandon me or abuse me and I will feel bad", "if my feelings are ignored or neglected, I will lose control".
- ✓ Coping strategies: submission, alternating inhibition with dramatic protest, punishing others, releasing tension with self-harming actions.
- ✓ Narcissistic personality disorder manifests itself with an exaggerated sense of superiority: those who suffer from it tend to consider themselves better than others, they exalt their abilities and successes and exaggeratedly believe in their worth. This behavior makes narcissists conceited, arrogant, selfish, and show-off. A direct consequence of this conduct is the constant need for admiration from others, who are idealized or devalued depending on whether or not they recognize their status as unique and special people.
- ✓ Criticism. After seducing his or her partner, the narcissist tends to be very critical of the woman, making her insecure, weak, and not up to her, but at the same time lucky because she has him by her side. Even when there is no need, it always has a ready critique, from the dress that doesn't fit to "that thing" said badly.
- ✓ In most situations it has to try to be the best, often stepping on others. He is so sure of himself that all people who don't think like him will be judged badly. Gradually the partner will become dependent on the narcissist because he will consider himself incapable of doing anything without his advice.
- ✓ Another peculiar characteristic is the lack of empathy, from which derives the belief that one's needs come before anything else. Because they see themselves as superior to others, narcissists believe they are entitled to having their needs met without waiting, so they can exploit others whose needs and opinions they deem of little value. So, the narcissist cannot put himself in other people's shoes.

Consequently, the narcissist's partner has no priority: his needs and his problems will always take second place. Furthermore, narcissistic people argue that their way of seeing things is the only one that is universally right.

- ✓ Often, people with narcissistic personality disorder believe that others envy or admire them, but are hypersensitive to criticism, failures, and defeats. The dimension represented by the tendency towards grandeur, uniqueness, and superiority is therefore contrasted with feelings of vulnerability, insecurity, fragility, and fear of confrontation. When faced with an inability to satisfy their high self-esteem, narcissists may react with anger or contempt, develop panic attacks, become deeply depressed, or even attempt suicide.

These just described are the typical and accepted characteristics of narcissistic behavior. There are, however, some aspects on which not everyone agrees.

Indeed, according to some specialists, narcissism is not characterized so much by the feeling of grandiosity as by the fear of emptiness and lack of meaning. For a form of "altruistic guilt", the narcissist typically feels at fault when they enjoy life without worries: the presence of a powerful "inner judge" would deprive them of the pleasure of living and enjoying their interests and would force them to lead their existence with the only commandment to "excel", otherwise they will be considered completely incapable. The fact of having early renounced his authentic feelings and interests, for fear of this "judge", made the child and therefore the adult unaware of his emotions and desires for him/her.

The feeling of shame leads the narcissist to see himself and others without nuances, as a person "of value" or "worthless": at the slightest mistake, the narcissist sees his whole person questioned and can fall into a spiral of self-hatred.

For this reason, a characteristic sign of narcissistic people is fits of anger or tears when what they do is not, in their eyes, perfect enough, or something happens that calls into question their pride and self-esteem. Heinz Kohut first coined the term "narcissistic rage" to refer to these fits of anger, usually out of proportion to why they occur, which are motivated by wounded pride.

Resentment can lead narcissists to experience themselves as an unfortunate and persecuted victim, by others and by life in general. This attitude of victimhood (victim playing) has been described, among others, by Eric Berne (The Games People Play, 1964), and Ronald Laing (Self and Others, 1969). An example could be the mother who accuses her son of having "ruined her life" by coming into the world. Typically, the narcissist, since he lives as a victim, feels authorized to claim some favorable treatments (entitlement) and manipulate his interlocutors to get what he wants.

Being sensitive to the feeling of shame, the narcissist tends not to take responsibility for his actions and can go so far as to deny the evidence. For example, he can deny having said or done a certain thing, insinuating that his interlocutor has memory lapses, that he makes things up, or that he is too stupid to understand what he "really" meant to say. This defense mechanism is technically called gaslighting and is considered a form of psychological manipulation.

An important characteristic of narcissists is that they project onto other weaknesses or defects that they fear they have. The narcissist who for some reason experiences a negative feeling, such as shame or envy, immediately "transfers" it to others: he can criticize someone else who is "worse than him", or he attributes his own state of mind to another person ("It's not me who envies him, it's he who envies me", etc.). This allows the narcissist to judge others negatively rather than themselves. Another form in which projection manifests itself is the narcissist's tendency to want to correct another person whom he considers "defective". For example, a narcissistic parent can be hypercritical and controlling with his child, to whom he attributes the weaknesses he fears he has. In this way, the narcissist is taking care of himself but is not listening to the other person's needs. This tendency, called projective identification, according to Melanie Klein, is common to other psychopathologies.

Symptoms of the narcissistic personality

To understand if a person has a narcissistic personality disorder, five or more of the following symptoms must be present:

- ✓ Grandiose self-images are summarized in the belief that one deserves special treatment, that one has particular powers, and unique talents, that one is brilliant or attractive, and that one should associate with equally special or high-status people. Grandiosity, in fact, is feeling superior to others. From a narcissist's point of view, all of his accomplishments and abilities are superior to his, and he uses them to make people around him feel inferior. Narcissists tend to talk and act as if they are the most important people on the planet.
- ✓ He's a megalomaniac: At first, you will seem to have met the man of your dreams, to live a splendid love story, you will have the perception that everything is wonderful. The "prey" will feel the center of attention and will be considered unique and special. This idealization will soon be followed by devaluation: as soon as the narcissist feels secure in the relationship (after a marriage, coexistence, etc.) the partner will become a part of himself that has neither need nor his own individuality.

- ✓ Fantasies of unlimited success, power, charm, beauty, or ideal love. Narcissistic people have one constant concern: to achieve success. Their greatest aspiration is to attain unlimited power and success, exuberant beauty, and a sharp mind.
- ✓ He (or she) is charming and charismatic: the narcissist is endowed with irresistible charm, knows how to seduce, and conquer a woman. At first, the woman will have the feeling that she is special.
- ✓ He (or she) loves to feel the center of attention and to be gratified. For this reason, he or she never really closes on his exes. When a story ends, he will try to give hope to the ex. Precisely because of his insecurity, he has a continuous need for confirmation and will try to feed the interest to prevent someone from forgetting about him.
- ✓ Many women or men will think that he (or she) is still interested in them, but it is yet another form of manipulation to continue to obtain gratification.
- ✓ The narcissist doesn't accept that everyone doesn't like him, and he will make sure to achieve this. When he does a great deed, he does it only to impress others, to feel admired and praised: he uses people to get gratification. The masks worn to achieve this goal are many: from astounding the other in any way, to pretending to be like the person in front of them. The important thing will be to be the center of attention and be flattered. When people are no longer willing to gratify it, it will disappear from the scene. The peculiarity of this characteristic is that the narcissist does this only for his own gratification, to reinforce his self-esteem.
- ✓ Feeling that they are not sufficiently appreciated and recognized in value.
- ✓ Feeling of emptiness and apathy despite any successes.
- ✓ Excessive demand for admiration for their special qualities and belief in being unique narcissists consider themselves unique, irreplaceable, and unmatched. They believe that there are no people capable of understanding them and with interests and qualities in common with them, so they avoid establishing relationships with other people who prove to be special.
- ✓ Feeling entitled to special treatment narcissists love to be treated special. They demand privileges and feel they should be treated in the best possible way. All this because they are special and must be treated as such. For this same reason, the narcissist does not allow anyone to blame or criticize him.
- ✓ Tendency to exploit others. In practice, we consider the partner an accessory. She or he doesn't empathize with her (or his) partner and is unable to fall in love. Narcissists often take advantage of others to achieve their own personal goals. To do this, they manipulate and deprive others of resources, ideas, time, and contact to benefit from them. Narcissists are therefore people who like to have

everything under control, manipulating any situation or person in their favor, regardless of the consequences.
- ✓ He has mood swings: often the partner will wonder why this fluctuating mood, feeling responsible for her bad mood. The truth is these swings are inherent attitudes that the people around them have no power over.
- ✓ He or she is envious: narcissists typically feel deep envy of people who are better than them in one or more ways. Their envy can be open or hidden. Also, they are convinced that others envy them for their skills and personal achievements. He or she feels envious of the successes of others, thinking that he (or she) is the only one capable of achieving different goals. If the partner tries to tell him about a goal achieved, in 90% of cases he will try to belittle him to talk about his feat and to demonstrate once again his greatness.
- ✓ Lack of empathy and therefore inability to recognize and identify with the feelings and needs of others. Generally, the narcissist is unable to identify with the feelings and needs of others. This leads him to feel unable to love and to feel no remorse or guilt for his wrong actions.
- ✓ Feelings of contempt, shame, or envy, and arrogant and conceited attitudes. Narcissists are arrogant and domineering people towards those around them. A narcissist believes they are right in everything they do or say, which must be accepted without room for doubt. This attitude leads to imposing one's ideas on others.

Diagnostic criteria

Narcissism becomes pathological when it is a real mental health disorder, or narcissistic personality disorder, that is, an extreme manifestation of the narcissistic trait that can be diagnosed by a specialist, which comes to compromise the stability in its affective dimension and in private and social relationships. To define the profile of the pathological narcissist, the Diagnostic and Statistical Manual of Mental Disorders (DSM-5), published by the American Psychiatric Association, focuses on the following elements:

- ✓ Has a grandiose sense of self-importance (eg: exaggerates achievements and talents, expects to be seen as superior without proper motivation, etc.).
- ✓ He or she is preoccupied with fantasies of unlimited success, power, charm, beauty, or ideal love.
- ✓ He or she believes he or is "special" and unique and that he or can only be understood by - or that he or has to associate with - other special or high-class people (or institutions).

- ✓ It requires excessive admiration.
- ✓ He or she gets a sense of entitlement, i.e., the unreasonable expectation of special favorable treatment.
- ✓ Take advantage of interpersonal relationships, that is, take advantage of other people for your own purposes.
- ✓ Total lack of empathy: a narcissist is really unable to recognize or identify with the feelings and needs of others (especially chosen victims).
- ✓ He or she Is almost always envious of others (or believes others envy him).
- ✓ Displays arrogant and conceited behavior or attitudes.

How to recognize a narcissist? 7 foolproof signs

Here is a mini guide that will surely help you recognize and then realize the fact that you are dealing with a narcissistic person. First and foremost, we have to say that the problematic nature of the narcissist is that he often hurts the people he deals with. The first few times you meet him you get very hurt, but once you get burned, you will immediately learn to recognize him. In love, work environment as in other life areas. As we have already said, not all people "in love with themselves" are narcissistic in the pathological sense. And in the complex framework of these not-very-immediate personalities, there is a more or less "manageable" scale of narcissism.

Here's how to recognize the narcissist's personality, traits, and behavior in 7 steps, suggested by psychologist Stephen Johnson, author of How to Successfully Handle Narcissists.

To better explain, we will give some examples of narcissistic behaviors and typical phrases of narcissists.

1. The conversation is like a soliloquy

The narcissist loves to talk about himself and does not give you the opportunity to have a dialogue, i.e., to have a two-way conversation. If between one story and another, you happen to struggle to have your say, it is very likely that you are talking to, or rather listening to, a person who is very focused on himself. And if you do finally get an audience, know that your opinions may be corrected, rejected, or even ignored.

So, having a healthy discussion with a narcissist is quite a feat! He almost always talks about himself and in most cases does not listen to others. When your partner tries to converse with you, your partner will show interest, but only for a short time.

Further proof that you are witnessing a narcissistic soliloquy is the continuous interruption by your interlocutor who, struggling to tolerate that attention is not on himself, tries to (re)shift it continuously. In short, the narcissist shows very little interest in others.

2. Show open contempt for others

Often the narcissist has one for everyone, without bothering to hide their criticisms - often exaggerated - of others.
Listening to his speeches, he is a model of intelligence and knows how to face life better than others. He loves to tell his successes about himself, and it is precisely this skill in his life that authorizes him to judge others.
Related to this sense of superiority is the behavior of stepping all over others, ignoring concepts such as respect and sensitivity.

3. Aim to be admired

Many narcissists find pleasure in doing grandiose deeds that impress others. The purpose of these exhibitions is to be admired, from every point of view: physical, romantic, sexual, social, religious, professional, cultural, etc. In these situations, the narcissist uses people or more generally the context in which he lives to get gratification. The message they send is actually: "I'm better than you!" or "Look how special I am - worthy of the whole world's admiration!"
For these reasons, narcissists expect exclusive treatment from others. Often their implicit thought is that others are there ready to satisfy their needs, possibly immediately and without giving anything in return. In narcissists' minds, the world only revolves around them.

4. Shows a fleeting interest in people

Narcissists can be very charismatic and attractive. When they are interested in you (for their own gratification), they make you feel very special and go out of their way to win you over.
However, once they lose interest in you, they manage to get you off the pedestal on which they have placed you, with the speed of a nanosecond and without many scruples. Their interest in people is ephemeral and is often fueled by the attention they receive in return: they are all reinforcements for their fragile self-esteem.
Once he is sure he has conquered the other, he gets bored and needs other conquests to confirm that he is pleasant. And in fact, one of the classic behaviors of these people is the so-called orbiting: that is, disappearing without explanation and then reappearing randomly via social media with comments or simple likes.

5. Seeks attention through negative emotions

Many narcissists enjoy arousing negative emotions, such as guilt and sadness, in the other, all feelings that are means of attracting attention to themselves. Being very sensitive to criticism from others, they exploit their reactions to contrary opinions to increase the sense of omnipotence and control over others.

It's like: "I will show you that I feel so bad because of you: you have criticized me, so you will feel a great deal of guilt towards me (and thanks to this mechanism I will have you under control)."

Negative criticism may not necessarily arouse a bitter discussion, but it can also induce a reaction of silence. Certainly, the way to react is destructive, certainly not constructive toward an authentic confrontation.

6. He perceives himself as having a great personality

Narcissists perceive themselves as special people, with unique and admirable characteristics. Some truly believe that they are very important and irreplaceable, assuming that others cannot live without their wonderful help.

"Once again I have saved humanity from problems: without me, nobody can do anything".

7. Tends to manipulate others

Narcissists use others as an extension of themselves (of the self, as we would say in psychoanalysis). This personality trait manifests itself in two ways:

- ✓ Projection of one's unfulfilled desires onto others. "If my son or daughter won't grow up to be a professional soccer player, I disown him." "You are becoming as beautiful as me, fortunately!" Being very charismatic and charming it will be very easy to fall into his trap and be manipulated. He often manages to make his woman, or his man does what he wants. Usually, this arouses strong anger in the partner, an emotion which, however, the latter will not be able to understand where it comes from. Manipulative techniques could also be aggressive reactions to instill feelings of guilt, or absolute silence, which could even last several days.
- ✓ The instrumentalization of the guilt of others: "I have given you so much, and you are so ungrateful." Everything that happens is always the "fault" of the people around him. In fact, the narcissist has the tendency to put the responsibility for everything on the other. The repressed (and often unconscious) anger at the emotional void he had in his childhood leads him to unload his frustration on the people closest to him. He (or she) lacks empathy, but he/she knows his partner's weaknesses very well. Precisely for this reason the narcissist

knows very well where to strike. He finds satisfaction in seeing his partner sad and lacking in energy and will give the responsibility to her/him.

These seven signs indicated are important to recognize a narcissist will help you avoid, or at least limit, any relationship with such a person.
It is extremely important to know how to recognize this pathology, in order to avoid falling into their relational trap. Avoiding these relationships will save you from being manipulated or even psychologically abused. These people, in fact, derive satisfaction and strength from the abuse of others.

How to recognize the covert narcissist?

Since ours is a practical guide covering all aspects of narcissism, we will also show you all the possible signs of a "covert" narcissist. We have already talked about the covert narcissist in the last chapter. In fact, we have already been able to ascertain that the profile of the hidden narcissist has other traits, which we can define as passive-aggressive.
Although he is not arrogant or eccentric, he discounts the sense of superiority by simply ignoring others, in his feelings and/or needs.
The profile of the apparently covert narcissist presents traits that can identify him as a particular person, if not even special:

- ✓ Is reserved (to later become shy and elusive)
- ✓ Demonstrates a high degree of sensitivity and vulnerability (to become easily susceptible and react badly to any criticism, even constructive)
- ✓ Seeks reassurance by also minimizing one's own skills, talents, or results (up to using the sense of guilt and veiled accusation to make the other feel difficulty)
- ✓ May be excessive in generosity (but only to attract attention, being lacking in self-esteem and with great inner insecurity, or to get something in return).

Therefore, we are dealing with a person who does not feel all that special, on the contrary, he experiences his person as an ugly duckling or as the genie in the lamp that no one wants to rub.
If overt narcissists crave attention with arrogance and aggression, sarcasm, and criticism, activating direct and brazen behaviors, covert narcissists use more veiled means to receive attention and succumb to any inattention or criticism by falling into a deep sadness and a sense of bewilderment.

Generally, the introverted (or covert) narcissist has these characteristics:

- ✓ Manipulate the other by instilling doubts and leaving the answer open
- ✓ Use guilt, victimhood, shame, extreme sensitivity
- ✓ Shows disinterest in other people's time, inattentiveness, and vagueness (may miss appointments, not respond to phone calls or texts, and then reappear out of nowhere)
- ✓ Does not recognize the merits, talents, and merits of others.

Both overt and covert narcissists, however, suffer from low self-esteem and a deep sense of instability of self and identity.

Consequences of Narcissistic Personality Disorder

Let's see for a moment, to conclude this first part of the guide, what the possible consequences could be for a narcissistic person. Not always, but it becomes easy for them to accept this reality. But if you don't do it, you will face often very serious consequences.

Narcissistic personality disorder, in fact, can compromise the professional, social, and emotional life of the people who suffer from it. Furthermore, given that social status plays a fundamental role in his image, he often associates with famous or special people who provide him with reflex importance, developing opportunistic and superficial relationships.

The profile of the narcissist becomes clearer even in the face of disappointments, or the most common setbacks. It can be the loss of a job, a divorce, or a shipwrecked project.

Each of these situations affects the carefully polished self-image, putting the narcissistic person in crisis. Of course, all of us, faced with an unexpected, painful change, react with tension, sadness, and despair (sometimes).

The narcissistic personality, on the other hand, experiences loss as a drama of enormous significance, because it puts its finger on the wound, increasing the sense of vulnerability and weakness.

When in this emotional condition, the narcissist could also assume aggressive, and angry attitudes. The sense of shame is so high as to trigger a violent reaction.

When they do not receive answers to their constant requests for admiration, favorable treatment, and immediate satisfaction of their needs at the expense of the other, narcissists can become furious or show contempt and detachment and, lacking empathy, resort to manipulation to achieve their goals. their own ends up in the implementation of abusive behaviors to obtain the power they think they have lost.

Others could decide to push them away, feeling exploited, manipulated, and not respected in their needs, resulting in periods characterized by severe anxiety and depression, often the only motivation that drives them to seek help from a professional.

If left untreated, a narcissistic personality disorder can predispose you to various complications, including:

- ✓ Problems in interpersonal relationships
- ✓ Difficulty in daily activities (work or school)
- ✓ Depression
- ✓ Addictions (alcohol, smoking, or drugs)
- ✓ Suicidal thoughts or behaviors.

However, not all narcissists manifest their disorder in the same way. Some of them are less recognizable, but no less compromising.

With the consequences concludes the first part of our guide. In the second part, we will talk, in more detail, about the codependent relationship that develops the narcissist, both for himself and his victim.

SECOND PART- NARCISSISTS AND RELATIONSHIPS

Chapter 3: The relationship between codependency and narcissism

In this second part of the text, we're going to set up what kind of relationship the narcissist establishes with his victim and how the perpetrator, in this case, can see a feeling like love. We will start by talking about the relationship between codependency and narcissism

What is codependency?

In this book, we usually start with definitions. So, let's start by outlining the meaning of codependency. Codependency is a behavioral psychological condition inherent in any relationship in which an adult person is dependent on another person. In 1941, the German psychoanalyst Karen Horney spoke of "Moving Toward" personalities, describing people with little sense of autonomy who needed others to pursue their fulfillment. Among psychologists, this condition appears controversial, and therefore there are various definitions of codependency. In the 1980s, psychologists observed that codependence occurs not only among the families of alcoholics, but also among the families of drug addicts, and more generally of those with substance addiction problems. More recently, some specialists speak of 'codependency' to refer to the empathic partner of a narcissistic person. Indeed, the term codependency has been employed to describe a loving relationship in which the person remains in the bond solely because the partner needs him/her. The codependent who has adapted to living with a narcissistic partner is called a co-narcissist. In general, codependency can be said to be a pattern of dysfunctional behavior in which there is an extreme focus on another person and a lack of awareness of one's own needs.
Codependency is also considered a type of love addiction. We talk about love addiction because the co-dependent organizes his thoughts and behaviors not around a substance but around a person: the relationship with this person becomes a sort of "drug", with a dynamic very similar to drug addiction.

Difference between codependency and love addiction

We point out, at this point, a small difference. The difference between emotional dependence and codependency consists of the fact that in the first condition, one can choose a partner who has no particular problems. In the second case, however, the object of addiction is a person who in turn has pathological addiction problems (e.g., alcohol addiction). Love addiction is also a personality structure characterized by experiencing couple relationships in a dysfunctional way. It is defined as a pathological state where the affective relationship is experienced as necessary for one's existence, like an obsession. Let's see how the two elements of the couple experience this dysfunctional relationship.

As far as emotional dependence in the couple is concerned, it is due to a lack of experience in feeling lovable and, consequently, capable of loving. This lack is perceived as an infallible void. The impossibility of coping with such a condition causes couples who share this experience to experience precarious, dysfunctional, and very painful affectivity.

For this type of couple, the purpose of the relationship is not reciprocity. On the contrary, the two continuously "demand" an individual centrality, denying their own dependence and at the same time seeking the total dependence of the other.

It is a tug of war, where the rope often breaks causing both to fall into delirium for two. Indifferently, the two actors may belong to one genre rather than another.

Features and signs of codependency

Among the fundamental characteristics of codependency are low self-esteem, a demeaning submission or the presence of dysfunctional control mechanisms, mechanisms of denial, and an inordinate need for approval.

Typically, a codependent person:

- ✓ Finds it difficult to identify and express their emotions and feelings (insight)
- ✓ His (or her) need for attention and love is such that, blinded by these needs, he often clings to the "first thing that happens", contenting himself with having been noticed by the other
- ✓ He (or she) will remain anchored to the experiences of total dedication experienced in the first months of the relationship, continuing to seek them
- ✓ He (or she) fails to tell the difference between a loving partner and a possessive partner who tries to insinuate himself into every area of his life
- ✓ He (or she) tends to minimize or deny their emotions and feelings

- ✓ He (or she) feels responsible for what others feel (e.g., "if he's angry it's because of me")
- ✓ He (or she) thinks he is worthwhile only if he receives a positive judgment from others
- ✓ He (or she) relies on the approval of others to decide what to do and what to say
- ✓ He (or she) fears the reaction of others if they learn how they really feel
- ✓ He (or she) lets himself be influenced by the feelings of others, to the point of making them his own
- ✓ He (or she) gives up interests and hobbies in order not to irritate others
- ✓ He (or she) accepts compromises with his values and principles, in order not to irritate others
- ✓ He (or she) may resent that others do not recognize the "sacrifices" he has made so as not to irritate them
- ✓ He (or she) imagines that no one can really get by on their own
- ✓ He (or she) may willingly offer unsolicited advice and help
- ✓ He (or she) may resent it if others do not accept his advice and help.

To calm his distress, the codependent often tries to make himself (or herself) needed by others: another person's problems become his problems. He may become very controlling, offering unsolicited guidance and advice, or trying to convince others of the true feelings they should have. It can come to use sex as a tool to secure approval and acceptance.

Partners of codependents do not always report being in love, it is possible to detect the presence of ambivalent feelings. On the one hand, they appreciate what their partner does for them, but on the other they perceive attempts to control. In these cases, the relationship may not be balanced, but oscillate between submission and the desire to free oneself (Lyon & Greenberg, 1991).

An Important sign of codependent behavior Is when the person accepts aggressive, manipulative, and abusive behavior from the partner in order to keep the relationship going. The codependent may also feel anger or sadness about these behaviors yet does not break off the relationship and becomes colluded with the abusive partner. In the most serious cases, it can endanger his safety and her life. It is important to underline that the term "codependence", to date, cannot be used in a diagnostic sense, but in a descriptive sense: it is a subclinical condition that can be episodic or situational. If one partner behaves as a codependent in a relationship, it does not mean that you are using the same behavior pattern with other partners.

Further typical characteristics of the victims of when the codependency relationship will be established are:

- ✓ The moment the manipulation produces its effects, he (or she) doesn't realize the psychological abuse he's undergoing
- ✓ Due to the manipulation suffered, he (or she) is led to doubt his ability to perceive reality
- ✓ He (or she) doesn't listen to the inner voice, deluding himself that things will change. He sends the negative situations into the background of the relationship, continuing to keep the few positive moments in the foreground, even if they are now past, the first period
- ✓ In the course of his life, he has "learned" that to be loved one must satisfy the needs of others
- ✓ He (or she) has the idea that love is something that must be earned by being "good", or that it is necessary to adapt to the needs of the partner and avoid "disturbing" one's own needs
- ✓ It is usually family members and closest friends who notice the sudden change in the personality of the family member, abused by the perverse narcissist
- ✓ When the malaise becomes unbearable, he feels at a dead end, because he can't think about detachment, he doesn't feel capable of facing it.

Origins of codependency

The tendency to take charge of another person is most likely established in childhood, to combat the fear of abandonment: over time, the person has learned to think they have no value for themselves and to put forward the needs of others instead of their own. It thus becomes easy prey for emotional manipulation.

Psychologists have observed that there are co-dependent personalities, who without realizing it chooses partners who have substance addiction problems (drugs, alcohol, or drugs) or addiction to actions (such as gambling or sex).

This frequently happens to those who had a parent who also had an addiction. Those who are given a lot of responsibility as a child, in some cases end up almost "mothering" or "fathering" their parents, putting their needs aside (parenting). It has been observed that children with this experience can develop a co-dependent personality and have the tendency, as adults, to look for a partner with the same characteristics as the problematic parent. In this relationship, the codependent typically dream of changing their partner and saving them from self-destruction.

A similar dynamic occurs when a child is raised by narcissistic parents: also in this case, the narcissistic parent causes a reversal of roles, whereby the child is "parented". Children thus learn to put the parent's needs ahead of their own and get used to considering any attempt at autonomy as "selfishness". This adult person may tend to choose partners with a narcissistic personality.

The narcissist and his relationship of codependency with his partner

At first glance, it could be said that narcissists and victims look a bit alike. Attention is not a question of having common characteristics, but the origin of the causes of their problems leads them to have a trait in common, that is to establish a relationship of codependence. If you think about the causes just mentioned above, complacent people are characterized by common traits that reflect their insane self-defeating beliefs about themselves and interpersonal relationships. Things that may have helped them to cope in their families of origin stand in the way of later life and lead to further trauma. Just like the narcissist, the compliant person struggles with guilt and alienation from their authentic identity, they have low self-esteem and a strong negativity mechanism. He also resembles narcissists in his tendency to tie his worth to others, to take what happens personally as an injustice, and to feel victimized. However, they differ fundamentally from narcissists by having a greater potential to be able to overcome their self-destructive patterns and achieve well-being and more fulfilling and healthy relationships. Complacent adults have learned to let go of their own feelings and to overestimate those of others. Likely, they learned this behavior from a codependent parent or other family members who modeled it.

The compliant person compensates for the selfishness of the narcissist with exaggerated altruism, implementing the following behaviors:

- ✓ He (or she) dissociates himself from his own feelings
- ✓ Neglect his or her own needs
- ✓ Develop an exaggerated sense of responsibility
- ✓ Submits one's worth and happiness to others
- ✓ Fears loneliness
- ✓ It makes one's self-esteem dependent on being useful to others
- ✓ Provides unsolicited advice and help
- ✓ Help until you are completely exhausted
- ✓ Believes he can control events beyond his own will
- ✓ He (or she) has a lot of difficulty asking for help
- ✓ He (or she) has trouble understanding what he wants
- ✓ Accepts being reprimanded for things he (or she) didn't do
- ✓ He (or she) confuses addiction and pity for love
- ✓ He (or she) feels guilty about things that are not his responsibility
- ✓ Lies to himself (or herself) about your partner's behavior

- ✓ He (or she) believes he can save or improve it
- ✓ He (or she) believes his partner can't do it without him

Although our society glorifies excessive altruism, it is not a healthy and sustainable way of being. The codependent personality's compulsion to self-nullify in service to others, particularly to a dominant narcissist, is the prerequisite for victimization, emptiness, and nullification. Children raised by parents who enact these dynamics experience severe trauma and carry some sort of marker for further dysfunction in their adult relationships. Parents who model self-alienation and self-denial whether they are narcissistic, or codependent teach their children to distrust their instincts, fear their emotions and fight against their best interests. As long as people facilitate narcissistic behavior and values, the norm will always be injustice, despair, and suffering. You may have heard it before, but it bears repeating: it is not possible to help others without putting on an oxygen mask first.

Narcissistic and codependent

On the one hand, we have the perverse manipulator, who artfully and fictitiously builds relationships of esteem, friendship, and love, for personal and opportunistic purposes. On the other hand, the victim, on the contrary, seeks those feelings of esteem, affection, and love at the cost of anything. In reality, the two are victims of themselves and of each other.

In childhood, the narcissist learned to hide his weaknesses and insecurities. Over time he has built, with the complicity of the family affective model, a grandiose "I" behind which he hides that constantly commits him to be perfect. Brilliant, charming, charismatic, successful, having to live up to every situation. He is constantly looking for confirmation. He is pathologically self-centered and unable to love. For this reason, the narcissist looks for a partner in an emotional relationship who is willing to put himself aside to devote himself entirely to him. The narcissist knows how to touch the weak points of the co-dependent, activating the mechanisms of submission in her/him.

So, they represent a particularly common profile, that of those who are insecure and desperate for validation and acceptance, but other typical characteristics can unite the narcissist and his victim such as:

- ✓ They generally suffer from low self-esteem and have a rather linear and accommodating way of thinking, feeling, and behaving. This means that due to their condition of deep self-distrust, they desperately try to stay attached to the person they are dependent on, exhibiting codependent behavior.
- ✓ Codependent behavior includes dysfunctional attitudes such as: being permissive to the partner's shortcomings, unconditionally accepting any vices, helping the

partner, and replacing his duties. Generally, the emotional codependent binds to problematic and difficult partners because this is where these people can find ground fertile.
- ✓ Codependent love partners can come to accept cyclical estrangements and abuse. In general, these people will go out of their way to "take care of their partners" in the hope of not being abandoned or being reciprocated one day.

Building a codependency relationship

Once the lost victim has been identified, narcissists use to manipulate a codependent partner by alternating abuse with special treatments that are often a reflection of the narcissist's fluctuating thought between idealization and devaluation (we will see this better in the next chapters).

The narcissist is in fact very skilled in the so-called "honeymoon phase" in simulating genuine interest and esteem for his victim, thus creating a sort of addiction to such gratification which when it is lacking throws the person into a deep sense of isolation and abandonment.

A codependent person tends to avoid attacks while simultaneously seeking rewards such as affection, praise, sex, or money. In this dynamic the victim experiences the construction of trauma with the narcissist who commits the abuse, becoming emotionally and physically dependent or accustomed to the "roller coaster" of positive or negative validation. As adults, these people are subconsciously predisposed to seek out and engage in patterns of abuse, with women often playing the role of victim and men the abuser. Our cultural emphasis on authority, the privilege of being male, and women always seen as self-sacrificing, both reflect and perpetuate toxic masculinity and destructive power manifest at all levels of society. Whether you are in the role of the selfish doer or the excessively altruistic, alienation is the norm and self-realization is impossible.

The narcissist's partner often has a strong abandonment theme and is a personality with dependent traits. Although with a rich emotional world, these people are themselves very fragile and have traumatic childhood experiences. The joint of the victim-perpetrator, narcissist-affective addicted couple, therefore, becomes very solid since the dependent partner deeply fears abandonment and continues to seek the gratification of the first period of the relationship without being able to admit and understand that he has been deceived or that he has been deceived. Emotional dependence, as it occurs in victim-perpetrator relationships, is reciprocal and one can actually speak of co-dependence.

The relationship consolidates because, as happens in all relationships, but more specifically in those characterized by the narcissistic-dependent dynamic, the empathic partner projects onto the narcissist some unconscious contents of his own childhood experiences. The devaluing and abandoning relationship reproduces some of his traumatic experiences that bind the relationship together. These so-called victims in turn have very deep narcissistic wounds that declined on less pathological aspects than the partner but are still unresolved. The narcissistic partner can then represent, above all at the beginning of the relationship, a person on whom to project one's need for affection and one's ideal beyond the real characteristics of the narcissist who, precisely by his nature, cannot know himself and make himself known for what he and.

In this picture just examined paradoxically, the narcissistic love addict, just like the codependent, is in the incessant and ravenous search for widespread confirmations. The narcissistic emotional employee is bound to always miss his confirmations because, even if they reveal themselves in front of him, he would not be able to see them.

The narcissistic love addict uses the love codependent to obtain gratification and "narcissistic nourishment". His feeling "special" guarantees him a sort of right to control over others who, if affected by a trait of addiction (as in the case of the effective codependent), will end up pleasing him and indulging him in all respects.

The task of the codependent is to facilitate the life of the narcissistic emotional employee, among his duties, there is also that of carrying out the decision-making processes. Yeah, narcissistic emotional employees don't know how to choose and for this reason, they use others to validate every choice.

Often the codependent partners of narcissists stay in their relationships even when they realize they are being abused because they feel they deserve that treatment and/or see no way out.

Despite the ingrained pitfalls of codependency, there is a possible way out, and by continuing to leaf through this book, it will be possible for you to find it too. Only with deep self-work can the victim of the narcissist withdraw this projection and understand the manipulative reality of the partner. In both cases, these tendencies are aimed, more or less unconsciously, at vicariously nourishing self-esteem, i.e., through the control of the partner. The attempt to change the other "serves" therefore to fuel one's self-esteem.

A summary outlines

To complete this chapter, we offer you mini schemes summarizing what we have said so far.

Codependents typically:
- ✓ They are unaware of what they are feeling.
- ✓ They have difficulty identifying their feelings.
- ✓ They have difficulty expressing their feelings.
- ✓ They tend to minimize, modify, or even deny the reality of what they are feeling.
- ✓ They tend to worry and/or fear how others might respond to how they feel.
- ✓ They give power over their feelings to others.

Codependents often:
- ✓ They are an aware way of what others are feeling.
- ✓ They take responsibility for what others feel.
- ✓ They allow their serenity to be conditioned by external influences.
- ✓ They allow their serenity to be conditioned by the other person's difficulties.
- ✓ They allow their serenity to be conditioned by what others feel.
- ✓ They allow their serenity to be conditioned by how others behave.
- ✓ They condition feeling good about themselves on being liked by others.
- ✓ They condition feeling good about receiving approval from others.
- ✓ They strengthen their self-esteem by trying to solve other people's problems.
- ✓ They strengthen their self-esteem by trying to ease the pain of others.
- ✓ They rely on the feelings of others to determine what to do or say.

In addition, codependents generally:
- ✓ They are not aware of what they want.
- ✓ They have difficulty asking for what they want.
- ✓ They are more interested in what other people want.
- ✓ They find it easier to ask what other people want.
- ✓ They tend to put the needs and wants of others ahead of their own.
- ✓ They rely on the wants and needs of others to determine what to do and speak.

As such, codependents tend to:
- ✓ Pay attention to pleasing the other person.
- ✓ Pay attention to protecting the other person.
- ✓ Focusing their attention on solving the other person's problems (like narcissists).
- ✓ Pay their total attention to relieving the other person's pain.

In addition, codependents generally:

- ✓ They have difficulty making decisions.
- ✓ They have difficulty recognizing the good things in themselves.
- ✓ They are perfectionists and tend to have too many expectations of themselves and others.
- ✓ They tend to harshly judge everything they say or do by someone else's standards.
- ✓ They tend to feel that nothing they think, say, or do is 'good enough'.
- ✓ They tend to value other people's opinions more than their own.

As far as relationships are concerned, codependents typically:

- ✓ They have difficulty forming and/or maintaining close relationships with others.
- ✓ They need to feel needed to be in a relationship with another.
- ✓ They don't know or don't believe that being vulnerable is a means to greater intimacy.
- ✓ They don't know or don't believe that asking for help is okay and normal.
- ✓ They don't know that it's okay to talk about problems outside the family.
- ✓ They don't know or don't believe that it's okay to share your feelings instead of denying, minimizing, or trying to justify them.

In relationships, codependents tend to:

- ✓ Reduce their social circle when they get involved with another person.
- ✓ Connect their dreams for the future to the other person.
- ✓ Link their quality of life to that of the other person.
- ✓ Value the other person's ideas and ways of doing things over your own.
- ✓ Trying to control the other person's appearance, dress, and behavior by feeling that these things reflect on them.
- ✓ Feeling overly responsible for the other person's behavior.
- ✓ Fearing the other person's anger, fearing being hurt or rejected by the other person.
- ✓ Letting these fears dictate what they should say or how they should behave.
- ✓ Using giving as a means of feeling secure in the relationship.
- ✓ Set aside their hobbies and interests and spend time sharing each other's hobbies and interests.
- ✓ Questioning or ignoring your values to connect to the other person.
- ✓ Let the other's actions and attitudes determine how they should respond or react.

- ✓ Remain doggedly faithful even when such faithfulness is unwarranted and personally harmful.

With these patterns, we conclude our chapter on the codependent relationship between the narcissist and his victim. In the next chapter, we will look at a narcissistic person's perspective on love.

Chapter 4: How a narcissist sees love

In this short chapter, we will try to understand the narcissist's point of view regarding love.

Narcissism and love: are a possible duo?

Based on what we have analyzed so far, the possible coexistence of love and narcissism is practically impossible. The pathological narcissist's lack of empathy becomes central to relationships, especially sentimental ones. From the outside, the person with high levels of narcissism seems "the ideal person", the one that everyone dreams of, very well integrated socially and professionally.
He is usually skilled in appearing for what it is not, the first form of manipulation that he implements. He is often very intellectually gifted and appears very confident, although he needs to constantly nurture his self-confidence. In reality, the inner world of the narcissist is characterized by a great emptiness, he has often lacked gratification from his mother.
Those suffering from pathological narcissism have suffered traumas in attachment relationships, have not been protected, nor have they been provided with rules (they have often been a child who must become an adult so fast, at least in the family context).

Once he becomes an adult, he has to keep others under control, the world around him and for this reason, love is something impossible for him. When pathological narcissism predominates, the other does not exist, and all the attempts that the partner will make to try to change the person will be useless. The narcissist is insensitive to the suffering of others, is not empathetic, and does not know how to feel, even if he does everything to appear a sensitive and empathetic person. But beyond that, he is incapable of feeling love, the pure and disinterested one. If anything, he acts like that! The inability to confront others for who they are, including their limitations, is connected to the grandiosity referred to in the DSM. The narcissist is always looking for the "best of the best", he does it with himself and with others as well. This is why he is unable to pass from the state of falling in love, of novelty, of adrenaline to that of love. Loving the other deeply, having true intimacy with him, is only possible when you want him and you want him next to you for what he is, a complete package.

What is love for a narcissist?

The narcissist sees love practically as a means to achieve his goals and always exploits this noble feeling in his favor. We reiterate that the narcissist considers himself special, important, unique, and superior to others. A pathological identity that has distant roots and that the child matures in childhood when parents are unable to respond adequately to the child's requests and prefer instead to satisfy their own needs. According to psychology manuals, two characteristics distinguish a narcissist that is recognizable even when the latter falls in love: grandiosity and lack of empathy. Even in love, after an initial "normal" phase like all lovers, once she has secured the love of her partner, she imposes his superiority by demonstrating and behaving for what she is, that is, a person who prefers detachment and superiority.

Narcissists have a strong fear of abandonment and for this reason, they will implement a series of strategies within a relationship to keep their partner close to them and exercise control over their partner. One such strategy is the silence they can maintain following an argument.

The narcissist does not see a partner as a person to be loved but chooses "preys" with particular characteristics: they are empathetic, sensitive people who have a propensity for self-sacrifice, and who are therefore used to putting the needs of the other at the center. neglecting their own. They are people who at that moment are fragile, vulnerable, and have low self-esteem. The narcissist senses this vulnerability from afar, as well as availability, human warmth, empathy, elements that constitute his emotional nourishment, prey characteristics that feed the narcissist's ego, because they make him feel important, the "navel of the world" of the partner, and therefore a god who has the right to be worshiped and magnified. Oh yes, there is no reciprocity in these relationships, which is the basis of healthy relationships between adults: for narcissists, the rules are different than for ordinary mortals, they feel endowed with greater rights, and they are not part of the "rabble" for which laws and social conventions were made, are above. Therefore they find it normal for themselves to disregard agreements, arrive late, and use double standards.

So, having a relationship with a narcissist can be difficult - this applies to both friendships and sentimental relationships - but it is obvious that in a love relationship, narcissistic behavior is much more difficult for the partner to manage. Precisely because of this obvious problem, many people wonder how to manage a relationship with a narcissist, and in general how to behave with a narcissist. To answer these questions, we must bear in mind that it is difficult to relate to a narcissist authentically, precisely because of the typical narcissistic behavior.

Origins of the narcissist's inability to love

Why can't the narcissist love? Where does this drive for grandeur come from? Often, he was a loved, spoiled, idealized child. So yes, his parents loved him, but not for what he was of him, including his natural and legitimate limits. He was loved for what they wanted him to be as if they were looking in him for a sort of redemption from their frustrated ambitions. He, therefore, had to be the best, the most intelligent, the "most" to have a sense of worth in the eyes of the Other. Therefore loving the other for who he is is an impossible task for him. And this is also why, although he seems to have good self-esteem, deep down he is never convinced that he is lovable and therefore he constantly needs to receive input of approval from others.

Another reason why the narcissist runs away from intimacy, in addition to his superhomic dislike of the other's limit and defect, is linked to his difficulty in empathizing with his needs and feelings (the second characteristic highlighted in the DSM).

When confronted with the partner's request for love, this type of man becomes anxious. As if the partner's request for love, understanding, and sharing constituted a danger, a threat, a crack in her identity, based on an idea of compactness and self-sufficiency.

Responding to the desire of the other and deeply desiring the other could bring to light ancient needs of dependence chased away from the conscience, it could in a word make one feel lost, and disoriented, like a traveler who finds himself in a foreign country without knowing the language.

But does the narcissist fall in love?

To conclude this chapter, let's try to answer a very popular question: does the narcissist fall in love? Difficult to give a single answer, let's remember that we are not talking about criminals or mentally ill people. Narcissists are among us, and whether we like it or not, they are people who fit perfectly on the spectrum of normality. This means that they can find compatibility, and even a solid relationship with certain types of people and fail to bond with others at all.

In the couple relationship, the partner is treated as an object that reassures and strengthens the grandiose idea of oneself, a sort of distributor of self-esteem: to emerge, they tend to belittle the other. These are extremely childish personality aspects and as such, they stamp their feet when they are not satisfied when they feel they do not have enough attention.

Of course, it is true that in some circumstances the narcissist tends to mix his feelings (perhaps even sincere ones) with exercising power over another person, perhaps doing everything to make him fall in love because falling in love is very important for his ego.

In these cases, on-off relationships may be started which psychologically torture the victim. The put-it-and-leave game can go on for a long time, but at some point, the narcissist quits for good. It generally happens when another person is involved, or when the partner opposes a firm refusal, closes every window, and stops providing "nourishment" to narcissism.

To give a more scientific answer to this question, according to the Diagnostic Manual of Mental Disorders and the diagnostic criteria, which we saw in the second chapter, it is difficult for a narcissist to love precisely because of this natural inclination to love himself first and then, second bar, the others. Narcissists are very good at entering people's lives, they are very attentive and caring in the initial stages and one would think that, in the first place, they are the perfect men that every woman wants. The narcissist, however, then runs away from intimacy, because it is linked to his difficulty in empathizing with the other, with his needs and feelings. We can therefore say that the narcissist falls in love but does not love. The goal of the narcissist in a stable couple is therefore to deprive the other, according to the Diagnostic Manual, of feeding on his energy and confirming the sacred image of an idealized mother. When the narcissist's bucket is "empty", which is a perpetual problem for them, their experience of "love" mysteriously disappears.

Therefore, we can conclude this chapter by saying that the daffodil falls exclusively and unconditionally in love with itself. Insensitive to the suffering of others, the narcissus falls in love but is unable to have true feelings for others. There is a fine line between narcissistic personality and self-centeredness, instead, empathy and narcissism are opposites.

Being a self-centered narcissist, he focuses completely on himself and has no empathy for others.

Once this part is over, in the next chapter we will show you in detail how the narcissist subdues his codependent in a relationship to be able to achieve his (or her) goals.

Chapter 5: How a narcissist submits in relationships and what their goal is?

In this chapter, of fundamental importance for understanding the mechanisms by which the narcissist acts within the relational context, we will show you how he (or she) subdues his victim. We will show you how all the strategies implemented serve the purpose of realizing one's "profit" goals and making the narcissist's life easier. Therefore, our invitation is to pay a lot of attention to this part, perhaps to understand if you are inside this unhealthy mechanism.

The goal of the narcissist: the so-called narcissistic supply
The narcissist always seeks to take advantage of interpersonal relationships, which means that they exploit others for their purposes and regardless of what people may feel. The main focus of his is his well-being. The others, therefore, are nothing more than mere tools.
The narcissist doesn't care at all if his victim is going through a bad time or needs his space, the narcissistic person only thinks about satisfying his own needs, at the cost of totally ignoring those of others.
Well-being coincides only with the narcissistic supply. But what is meant by narcissistic supply? Narcissistic supply is a concept introduced into psychoanalytic theory by Otto Fenichel, an Austrian psychoanalyst. It describes a certain type of admiration, interpersonal support, and support that an individual extracts from his family and social context and which becomes an essential element of his self-esteem.
According to the author's definition, the narcissist needs someone to become his source of supply (to supply him with what he needs). This source of supply eventually becomes an extension of himself, as if it were part of him.
For this reason, there is no boundary between the narcissist's ego and the victim's ego. In other words, the narcissist expects his victim to feel, think and act like him, as the source of the narcissistic supply has no identity of its own, but is there to always please him.
"The narcissist is always looking for a source of nourishment: this, to regulate his low self-esteem and strongly support his ego. He always needs to reaffirm the mask he has created: his greatness, his superiority, and his unique and special character. In reality, under this mask lurks an insecure individual, with low self-esteem, who needs someone else for his own livelihood".
The source of the narcissistic supply is often unaware of what is happening to them and has no idea that they are a source of nourishment.

In conclusion, we can say that the narcissist assumes that his victim must feel, think, and act like him because his source of nourishment has no identity of its own, it must please him at all times.

The narcissist has his own well-being as his primary goal.

How does the narcissistic supply work?

To understand how supply actually works for the narcissist, it is really important to distinguish between the various components of the narcissistic supply process:
1. The Supply Trigger: It is the person or object that causes the source to relinquish the narcissistic supply by confronting the source with information about the narcissist's False Self (a grandiose statement of any kind or information that glorifies the narcissist.)
2. The source of the narcissistic supply is the person providing the narcissistic supply.
3. The narcissistic offer is the reaction of the source to the trigger.

Let's take a practical example: publicity (celebrity or notoriety, being famous or infamous) is a narcissistic supply trigger because it causes people to pay attention to the narcissist (in other words, it moves sources to supply the narcissist with a narcissistic offer). Publicity can be achieved by exposing yourself, creating something, or causing attention. The narcissist resorts to all three repeatedly (as addicts do to ensure their daily fix). The partner or a child is part of these narcissistic sources of supply.

Let us try to explain this concept in more detail. The primary source of supply is attention, both in its public forms (fame, notoriety, infamy, celebrity) and in its private, interpersonal forms (adoration, flattery, applause, fear, revulsion). It is important to understand that attention of any kind – positive or negative – constitutes the primary narcissistic supply. Hate is as sought after as fame, yet it is a way to get attention oneself.

For the narcissist, his "conquests" can be imaginary, fictitious, or only apparent, as long as others believe in them. Appearances matter more than substance, what matters is not the truth, but its perception.

The narcissistic supply comes in two forms: animate (direct) and inanimate (indirect). Inanimate bidding consists of all expressions of attention that are communicated impersonally (in written form or via third parties, for example) as well as aggregate measures of popularity and fame (number of Facebook friends, YouTube views, readership of your blogs, etc.). The animation supply requires interpersonal interaction with an "in vivo" narcissistic supply source. To sustain his sense of self-worth, the narcissist requires both types of supply, but especially the 'animated' variety. He needs to witness firsthand the impact his False Self has on living, breathing, flesh-and-blood human sources and his immediate environment.

Primary source triggers include, in addition to being famous (celebrity, notoriety, fame, infamy), having an air of mystique (when the narcissist is considered mysterious), having sex and gaining a sense of masculinity/manliness as a result/femininity, being close to or connected to political, financial, military, or spiritual power.

The primary sources of supply are all those who provide the narcissist with a narcissistic supply on a random and random basis.

Sources of secondary provision include leading a normal life (a source of great pride for the narcissist), having a secure existence (economic security, social acceptability, upward mobility), and companionship. Thus, having a mate, possessing substantial wealth, being creative, running a business (transformed into a Pathological Narcissistic Space), possessing a sense of anarchic freedom, being a member of a group or collective, having a professional reputation or otherwise, being successful, owning property, and flaunting one's status symbols – all also constitute a secondary narcissistic supply.

Secondary supply sources are all those people who supply the narcissist with narcissistic supply on a regular basis: spouse, friends, colleagues, business partners, teachers, neighbors, and so on.

This input, the primary and secondary, triggers and sources are embedded in a narcissistic pathological space.

The narcissistic supply could be also static or dynamic. The dynamic offering supports, enhances, strengthens, and envelops the narcissist's grandiose and fantastical False Self. The content of the dynamic narcissistic offering and the identity of its sources conform to the narcissist's image of himself, of his "destiny", of the evolution of his life, and of his place in the Cosmos. Static supply fails to do this even though it is largely positive, reliable, and plentiful. The static supply is like "hospital rations" or "junk food": it keeps the narcissist for a while, but, as an exclusive diet, results in malnutrition (deficient narcissistic supply). The static power supply is repetitive, and "boring" because it is predictable and banal. It does not push the narcissist to new "levels", nor will it fuel him when he is down.

We should say that there are hundreds of forms of narcissistic supply – and, consequently, hundreds of types of providers with specific functions (called "outside roles"). The narcissist trains family and acquaintances to act in these roles. He assigns these "scripts" and "narratives" to his spouse, children, subordinates, and dependents according to their strengths and weaknesses: it is the personality of the source of supply that determines what type of supply he must provide. For example, a shy, insecure, reticent child may be used to admire and serve the narcissist; intelligent, outgoing, and independent offspring can be used to perform impressive feats, improving the narcissist's standing in the community.

What are the functions of narcissistic supply in narcissistic pathology?

Let's briefly see what the narcissistic supply functions for this kind of disease are. So, the narcissist internalizes a "bad" object (typically his mother) in his childhood. It harbors socially forbidden emotions towards this object: hatred, envy, and other forms of aggression. These feelings reinforce the self-image as bad and corrupt. She gradually develops a dysfunctional sense of self-worth. Self-confidence and self-image become unrealistically low and distorted.

In an attempt to repress these "bad" feelings, the narcissist also suppresses all emotions. His or her aggression is channeled into fantasies or socially legitimate outlets (dangerous sports, gambling, reckless driving, compulsive shopping). The narcissist sees the world as a hostile, unstable, rebellious, unfair, and unpredictable place.

He defends himself by loving a completely controllable object (himself), by projecting an omnipotent and omniscient False Self into the world, and by turning others into functions or objects in a way that poses no emotional risk. And it's properly this reactive pattern that what we call "pathological narcissism".

To counter his demons the narcissist needs the world: his admiration, his flattery, his attention, his applause, and even his sanctions. The lack of a functioning personality within is balanced by the importation of Ego functions and boundaries from without.

Primary Narcissistic Offering reaffirms the narcissist's grandiose fantasies, reinforces his False Self, and, therefore, allows him to regulate his fluctuating sense of self-worth. Narcissistic Supply contains information regarding how the False Self is perceived by others and allows the narcissist to "calibrate" and "tune" it. Narcissistic Supply is also used to define the boundaries of the False Self, regulate its content, and replace some of the functions normally reserved for a functioning True Self.

While it is easy to understand the function of primary sourcing, secondary sourcing is a more complicated affair. Interacting with the opposite sex and "doing business" are the two main triggers of secondary supply. The narcissist misinterprets his narcissistic needs as emotions. For him, the search for a woman, for example, is what others call "love" or "passion".

Narcissistic supply, both primary and secondary, is a perishable commodity. The narcissist consumes it and must replenish it. As in the case of drug addicts, to produce the same effect, he is forced to increase the dosage more and more. While the narcissist uses his supply, his partner serves as a silent (and awed) witness to the narcissist's "great moments" and "achievements". Thus, the narcissist's friend "accumulates" the narcissist's great and "illustrious past". When the primary narcissistic supply is low, she "releases" the supply that she had accumulated. She does this by reminding the narcissist of those moments of glory she had witnessed. She helps the narcissist regulate his sense of self-worth.

This function – of accumulation and release of narcissistic supply – is performed by all sources, male or female, inanimate or institutional. The narcissist's colleagues, bosses, colleagues, neighbors, partners, and friends are all potential sources. All witnesses the narcissist's past successes and can remind him of them when new supplies dry up.

The other side: narcissistic extension

If on the one hand, there is a narcissist who needs continuous supply, on the other hand, there must be someone who must always offer this supply. This other part is called the narcissistic extension (or narcissistic supply), i.e., a person who provides the narcissist with unlimited admiration and the support he (or she) needs. The narcissist sees her as a personal extension of him and therefore seeks to dominate her. Indeed, the narcissist expects his extension to offer him everything he expects or desires. He (or she) assumes that your needs and wants are the same as his and therefore demands your attention. For example, if you are in a relationship with a narcissist, he may expect you to stay in or out at night depending on his needs. He gets angry and even hostile if you express a need to be alone or cultivate other interpersonal relationships independently of him. He is unable to understand that you could have an independent life. Furthermore, the narcissist sees his extension as an extension of himself. Therefore, he does not think that there are any limits to the relationship. He (or she) never notices when you're nervous or uncomfortable, and he continually crosses the lines you've set in order to satisfy his needs. Another typical feature of the narcissist/extension relationship is that the narcissist sees his extension as a reflection of who he is. Therefore, he takes credit for the accomplishments his partner manages to achieve. That said, we can say that the narcissist does not view as an independent individual, with personal opinions and ideas. But he only sees her as a reflection of himself and his beliefs. Therefore, the chosen victim will not have much energy left to devote to people or things other than those of his tormentor.

Often the "victims" of the narcissist have talents, particular skills, or beauty because the narcissist must have the feeling of being connected to special people, of whom he can boast and to whom he can say: "I am enviable" or "I get everything that I want". The partner for the narcissist is not seen as a person, with needs and rights equal to hers, but is an extension of himself, represents him". The partner's qualities and successes become part of his person, reinforcing the idea/illusion of being better, superior to others. What binds the "victim" in a double thread is his own extreme need for guidance, support, confirmations, because he does not trust in her value, he always feels incomplete, empty, incapable, if alone.

Indeed, in the eyes of the narcissist, the feelings perceived by his extension represent an obstacle to overcome. Therefore, his (or her) emotion must be approved by the narcissist.

How the narcissist seeks to achieve their goals through relationships?

To understand the mechanism by which the narcissist tries to provoke a reaction in others and build functional relationships for him, an article explains it to us. This article in the Journal of Personality and Social Psychology (Mitja Back, lead author) states: "What attracts us, at first sight, does not necessarily make us happy in long-term relationships. While narcissists exhibit bright and charming personalities, it's often only a matter of time before the clouds appear. Basically, there are two sides to the narcissist: the charming and the unpleasant."

We have already seen that the narcissist focuses his entire behavior, indeed his life, on getting nice morsels of attention. He incorporates them into a coherent, completely partial image of himself. He uses them to regulate his labile sense of worth and self-worth.

In other words, the narcissist will most likely show the kinder side of himself to achieve his goal and if the person in front of him does not act as expected, he will show the worst side of themselves; it's likely that once you get what he wants, he'll be cold, uninterested, elusive, and even angry.

The new attitude is aimed at provoking a reaction that produces the desired behavior. For example, he proposes to see us on a specific day when it's just not possible for us, and for this, he appears distant because we haven't met his needs for him. Remember, however, that your needs always come first. To put it in simpler terms, the narcissist is mentally the equivalent of an alcoholic. It's insatiable. She compulsively directs all of his behavior, actually his life, to get attention. He incorporates it into a coherent, thoroughly biased, even fantastical image of himself. He uses it to regulate his labile sense of self-worth. He needs narcissistic supplies to perform basic mental (ego) functions. Without them, he crumbles and becomes dysfunctional. To arouse continued interest, he projects to others a fictitious version of himself, known as the False Self. The False Self is everything the narcissist is not:

omniscient, omnipotent, charming, intelligent, wealthy, or well-connected. The narcissist then proceeds to gather reactions to this projected image from family, friends, colleagues, neighbors, business partners, and colleagues. If these – flattery, admiration, attention, fear, respect, applause, affirmation – are not forthcoming, the narcissist demands or extorts them. Money, compliments, a favorable critique, a media appearance, and a sexual breakthrough, are all converted into the same currency in the mind of the narcissist.

Narcissists relationships: a way to achieve their goal

The narcissist's inner lived experience is one of emptiness and worthlessness that constantly requires to be filled by external confirmations.
Its goal is to completely erode the identity, integrity, and self-esteem of the victim with the aim of creating a narcissistic supply, which narcissists need as oxygen. Forcibly abuse and draw supply: this is a key issue; it is often believed that the narcissist wants fame and control but this is not the case. A similar term of supply is fuel, and it is everything that moves a narcissistic person. This doesn't abuse the other just because it likes it but to draw fuel, and energy, which it needs to stay alive.
When these people get affirmations through money, success, or an increase in social status, they begin to behave in a grandiose and arrogant way, they devalue and look down on others, especially those they consider inferior.
The narcissist associates with people for a utilitarian purpose: to obtain a narcissistic supply and to maintain a grandiose self-image. By lowering her partner's self-esteem, he feeds his own.
In the case of codependency, the toxic bond can go on for years. The narcissist practices what is called "hoovering", i.e., the possibility of sucking in the victim, like a vacuum cleaner, even after several months or years. If, on the other hand, the attendance begins to bore or is no longer needed, he will disappear leaving the person in pieces ("ghosting").
As we have seen before, a narcissist is a person unable to establish a true relationship of intimacy in interpersonal relationships both in the couple and in friendships.
For the narcissist, it is as if the other did not exist except to be used for his own purposes of fueling self-esteem (what in psychology is defined as self-object). Others are not people but self-objects.
The self-object is someone who functions as both an external object and an internal part to fuel their self-esteem. A painful feature of narcissists, as we have seen in the last chapter, is their inability to love.

He doesn't really love others but he needs them and uses them to support that part of himself that is missing or lacking. In the deepest forms, it can get to the point that people are interchangeable for him as long as they provide him with what he needs. It is understood from this how seriously destructive these people can be toxic to others who are unaware of all this approach them and who unfortunately find themselves trying to build a relationship with them.

Narcissists don't really feel guilt or gratitude like most. However, some humans can simulate them, but only to always achieve their goals.

The narcissist and the victim role: another way to achieve the goal

Another way to achieve his goal of forgiving satisfaction, the narcissist can also set up the relationship by playing the victim.

In conflicting relationships, both as a couple and in general, the narcissist tends to identify with the role of the victim and for this reason, he is defined as an affective manipulator. He often describes himself as hindered by others in achieving results or recounts painful past experiences. In the sentimental sphere, he can distort his memories of previous relationships after a love disappointment.

Here are some of the reasons why this happens:

- ✓ Describing himself as the victim in a relationship can preserve his social image: for example, in a marriage, the narcissist can deny a betrayal and pass off the partner as excessively jealous to preserve his image as a "good family man"
- ✓ The expectation and claim to receive admiration and attention from others, when it is not satisfied, leads to experiencing interpersonal situations with disappointment. Narcissists are particularly sensitive to negative interpersonal situations, becoming more suspicious and inclined to read the world as hostile
- ✓ On some occasions he can actually be the victim of hostile actions: it is probable that his behavior, inclined to neglect emotional ties and to manipulate to get what he wants, leads others to react in an actually adverse way towards him.

Rhodewalt and Morf's self-regulation model (Morf & Rhodewalt, 2001; Rhodewalt, 2001) explains how the narcissist approaches intimate relationships, stating that one of the narcissist's primary needs is to display a grandiose self-image and positivity thus influencing his way of approaching social relationships. The narcissist also has a tendency to describe himself as a "victim", thus managing to manipulate others and exploiting this whole situation to his own advantage. As can be seen in reality, the real "victim" is not him but the person with whom he approaches.

Precisely because of this lack of empathy, the narcissist can very easily exploit and manipulate people if they do not correspond to his ideal. This tendency to keep one's self-esteem high also has consequences in intimate relationships and is linked to the psychological characteristics of the other partner: it can lead to rupture when the partner also expresses his need to be recognized and appreciated and when presents requests that overshadow the needs of the narcissistic subject or it can lead to a pathological relationship that is difficult to interrupt and which can also lead to tragic events as it is fueled in the couple by an unconscious victim/aggressor role-playing game.

The stages of the relationship with narcissists

As we have already mentioned in this guide, the narcissist chooses "prey" with particular characteristics, characteristics that make him a candidate to be the extension of the narcissistic supply. These are empathetic, sensitive people who have a propensity for self-sacrifice, and are therefore used to putting each other's needs at the center, neglecting their own. And with these, obviously, he will be much more inclined to establish a relationship. Relationships will take place in a phased system.
In particular, three phases can be identified in the relationship with the partner in order to obtain total submission and satisfaction of one's needs. We should say that couple relationships with a narcissist usually follow the cliché of these three phases, it should be pointed out that none of them has a precise duration, they can be cyclical and even cross over into each other. So, let's see what the fundamental phases are in which narcissists achieve the objectives indicated above.

Stage 1 – Seduction, Love bombing, or the golden age

The expression love bombing was coined in the 1970s by members of the Unification Church in the United States. It describes the mechanism by which the leaders of some religious sects lured their followers and exercised control over their followers. We were therefore referring to those indoctrination strategies aimed at encouraging new recruits to join.
Only later did the psychological community, in the figure of the psychologist Margaret Singer (1996), decline it to romantic relationships. It is one way to describe a toxic and manipulative type of effect. In fact, love bombing can be described as a manipulation strategy in which the partner literally bombs, and floods with love, admiration, and attention.
This is in order to gain power and control over her life. The love bombing, as the expression goes, is a real bombing. It's something excessive, intense, and constant

that can generate discomfort in the partner feeling that it's not commensurate with the knowledge phase. It all seems too much, too soon. Love bombing can fit into phases that tend to repeat themselves cyclically and which represent a sort of script in the relationship with the partner. We speak of the cycle of abuse, and this includes 3 phases: idealization, devaluation, discard, and then recovery.

Love bombing typically takes place during the initial courtship phase and may continue until the person feels they have established the necessary level of control over their partner to ensure their trust and loyalty. After all, however, love bombing could be reactivated if you want to recover the relationship with the other.
It is the phase of hooking up, of falling in love, of positive sensations. It is a phase in which the narcissist wears a mask and shows himself wonderful, the ideal partner, everything the other could wish for those with high levels of narcissism to show their best self. Right now, he pays close attention to showing a false self, lying, and playing some kind of role. The goal is for the other to fall in love with him and take care of him.

In the beginning, therefore, he shows a vulnerable side of himself, trying to activate the sense of nurturing in the partner. Often recounting an unhappy childhood, he evokes in the other the desire to make himself happy at all costs, changing, and modifying himself to meet his expectations of him, thus entering the challenge circuit.
The first stage is that of idealization. It is the initial stage where the relationship feels like the most beautiful in life. There are compliments, gifts, and lots of attention.
The person communicates constantly, flooding with messages as if they want to be in contact with each other all the time. It seems almost impossible that the other can fully correspond to expectations, after all this overabundance of love can be initially very rewarding.

Everything seems perfect, perhaps even too perfect.
The partner is convinced that he can satisfy him and that he can change him. It can include grandiose acts of love, for example, gifts, compliments, promises, attention, and grand gestures. A healthy person, who has solid self-esteem, in this phase realizes that there is something inauthentic in these attitudes, the partner is playing a part. But since the "victim" has an enormous need for recognition, for value, she is easily deceived. During this phase, the narcissist forges ahead and can get to talking about cohabitation, marriage, and children, and this has a twofold purpose:

- ✓ Try to hook the victim, satisfying his need to feel valuable, and important, and reassuring him about the depth of the bond
- ✓ Shorten the love bombing phase, which for the narcissist requires a strong commitment, and expenditure of resources, and thus get to the second phase in less time.

Phase 2 – Intrusion

In this phase, the narcissist can relax because he feels he has established a solid relationship and has power over the other, who is placed in a secondary, servile role. The two partners form a couple, and their lives intersect at various levels: sentimental, economic, and social.

The subject with pathological narcissism acts to isolate the other from his family, his friends, and from work. On an individual level, he acts by making himself feel increasingly fragile using criticism, which he uses at first subtly, then increasingly heavily. Socially the narcissist is highly appreciated, therefore if the partner complains to his family or to the people he has as a point of reference, they will tend to diminish her observations.

The second stage is devaluation. At some point in the relationship, there is a sudden change in mood and attitude. That person who was so present at the beginning now appears distant and dull.

All this without any quarrels taking place within the relationship. The vision of the perfect partner deteriorates. Romantic gestures, compliments, and proclamations of love can quickly turn into coldness or even malice.

Although it usually starts subtly, this is the stage where emotional abuse emerges: the partner becomes frankly devaluing, and critical of the other, and the relationship.

There is an abrupt change in the type of attention: from warm and loving to controlling and angry. The dream collapses and leaves room for rejection.

At this point narcissist shows himself for what he is: inconsistent, unavailable, not empathetic, doesn't keep promises, lies, demands, and can have incorrect behavior. The partner rebels against this, because he does not correspond to the idyllic image shown in the love bombing phase, expresses disagreement, express criticism, and makes requests. In a healthy relationship, the argument leads to questioning and finally reaching common ground, while with the narcissist the arguments lead nowhere, because the narcissistic person does not admit his mistakes and has no interest in seeing the point of view of the other, nor to satisfy their needs: for this reason, they can go so far as to distort and deny the evidence because they cannot afford to dent their perfect image. The fault is always outside, there is no assumption of responsibility. Indeed, criticisms are experienced with extreme anger, the narcissist will not think of treasuring the observations made to him, using them to evolve, he will rather try with devaluations or manipulations to demonstrate how wrong the other is. At this point, a person with good self-esteem would run away.

For an addicted person, on the other hand, it's too difficult to close, it seems impossible to do without him/her. The victim does not run away because he clings to the first image, the one seen during the love bombing, and then, unable to give it up, he falls into the trap of manipulation: he justifies, forgives, "gets over it", he tells himself that it is also his fault, or that it is a particular period then maybe things will change. Instead, there can be no hope for this: the narcissist does not change because the perfect image of himself that he has created is vital, he cannot survive the unmasking that reveals his limits and defects, because it is too painful.

If the manipulations don't work, he will react with aggression, in some cases even with violence, and fury. Alternatively, or in addition, he can portray himself as a victim, and have explosions of depression and desperation that serve to restore the initial order, because an empathic person, faced with so much pain exhibited, will easily give in to the temptation to rush, welcome, look after. However, if this does not happen, the narcissist will only have one card left to play, namely the discard.

Stage 3 – Discard or Destruction of the other

At this point in the relationship, the narcissist has already managed to make the other feel worthless, insecure, and often inadequate. It is quite usual for the narcissist, in this phase, to use verbal and/or physical violence. On a verbal level, he alternates moments of sweetness with moments of aggression, and it is precisely these oscillations that make the partner even more dependent, who becomes destabilized and no longer knows how to behave. She or he hesitates to forgive him (or her) and then forgives him thinking he will change. Through mistreatment (psychological, emotional, and much more rarely physical) the partner is paralyzed, thus losing their abilities. So, now pathological narcissism emerges with all its force and the subject becomes more demanding, violent, jealous, and distant. It's a discard phase.

In the discard phase, the partner could abruptly leave the relationship, literally disappear (ghosting), or it happens that the closure takes place in person or by other means (messages, mail, or a phone call). What is surprising is the cynicism and coldness of the narcissist who until recently had expressed love and promised a fantastic future together. It is disorienting and can be hard to give up because many memories are happy and wonderful.

So, the discard consists of a drastic break, made contemptuously, from one moment to the next, without warnings. Annihilating the victim is the last weapon available to the narcissist, so he chooses the date and moment carefully, selecting situations in which the partner is particularly fragile (for example after an illness, or a death), or a day that should be happy (e.g., birthday), to have the greatest possible impact because the other is unprepared, helpless. The intent is to destroy in a cruel way when the other has fewer resources to react, because of shock.

The rejection is often carefully prepared in advance, just as it is possible for some time that the narcissist has been talking behind the partner's back with friends and relatives, portraying him/her as a negative, unstable, problematic person, etc... and thus convincing others that he/she is he the victim. While the others (perhaps even future preys) are intent on consoling him and advising him to end the relationship, he prepares the final attack, the discard, which has two purposes:

- ✓ Restore the grandiose image because the other, annihilated, despised is no longer a threat to one's self-esteem. The weak condition of the victim prevents her from rebelling and therefore the narcissist can break off the relationship without addressing his responsibility, his faults, and shortcomings.
- ✓ Weaken the other in order to keep him available, because it is possible that in the future there will be a new attempt to hook up.

There is also a possible sub-phase of recovery, also called recapture. In this phase, the partner could behave to recover the relationship with the other by preventing him from leaving. It is in this phase that love bombing could emerge again to be forgiven and win back one's loved one. It may happen that the injured partner feels confused in the face of new demonstrations of love and therefore legitimately needs time to process his feelings and learn to trust again.

After all, a part of the person can feel flattered and loved by the actions that the partner is carrying out at that moment and would like to believe in the genuineness of those actions, confirming that even that initial idyll was something true and authentic. At the same time, the partner fears that they could be behaviors contingent on the phase in which the other feels the risk of abandonment and that they could then lead to reliving again the phases of idealization, devaluation and discard in a continuous cycle.

In the next chapters, you will be shown how to break this unhealthy cycle. But not before warning you about the possible consequences for your mental health. Because, as we will show you in the next part of the guide, you will risk a lot on a psychic level from a toxic relationship with a narcissist.

THIRD PART- SOME WARNING FOR THE POTENTIAL VICTIM

Chapter 6: Long-term effects on your psyche

Let's move on to another important part of our guide: the one that really puts you on guard, and draws your attention to all the possible negative consequences that can arise from a relationship with a narcissist. By now, you will either have mirrored yourself in the relational stages described in the previous chapter or have recognized the signs of a possible narcissistic partner. Now it's our turn to make you understand what could happen to you, both in the short and long term due to the continuation of a relationship like this.

The immediate consequences for the narcissist's victim

We have been able to ascertain up to know that narcissistic personality disorder presents subjects who feel superior, demand admiration and are poorly empathetic; they believe that their value is very high, and grandiose, that their needs are prior to those of others and, therefore, authorized to claim, exploit, offend, trample on others, who on the other hand they consider of little value, of second order. Narcissistic subjects are generally self-centered, arrogant, selfish, and feel superior and envied. Indeed, a relationship with a narcissist can lead to devastating consequences.
But what immediate consequences does anyone who comes into contact with this subject face? What can it mean to enter a relationship with a person suffering from an important clinical picture such as that of a personality disorder?

The narcissist's partner can in fact completely cancel himself for him, going so far as to put all his needs into the background, he can manifest feelings of internal emptiness, confusion and anger for the unfair behavior of the partner that the victim is unable to explain. According to Ponzio (2004), the requests for help from the victims are often underestimated by friends and relatives. This aspect is very important as the situation can lead to psychic isolation of the victim who may feel alone and misunderstood, sometimes thinking that she herself is the problem in the couple and shouldering guilt that she doesn't actually have. In fact, the victim begins a psychic process in which she feels wrong, she thinks she has exaggerated attitudes due to her partner's behaviors that make her suffer. There may also be somatizations in which mental illnesses are poured into the body, for example, it can happen that the victim manifests a lack of appetite and lack of sexual desire, or headaches and migraines.

To also explain the possible consequences of a relationship with a narcissist, a new disorder has been introduced in America, Narcissistic Abuse Syndrome, although not yet officially recognized, which in the opinion of professionals in the Mental Health sector aims to give dignity and understanding to a symptomatological framework detectable in subjects who are victims of narcissists, and which are not attributable to the personality characteristics of the subject himself.

It may happen that people with a healthy relational life establish romantic relationships with people who lie, manipulate, and abuse them to the point of causing such a high level of stress that it activates a whole series of consequences:

- ✓ Feelings of sadness to despair
- ✓ State of hypervigilance resulting in anxiety and fear
- ✓ Sudden mood changes, with a predisposition to irritability, anger, shame, guilt, self-blame
- ✓ Mental states of perceptual doubt, denial, disbelief
- ✓ Difficulty concentrating, resulting in derealization
- ✓ Social isolation
- ✓ Loss of control in different areas (personal, family, work).

The symptomatology described appears like that found in Post Traumatic Stress Disorder (which can start from living strong and upsetting experiences, such as earthquakes, fatal accidents, wars, and physical and sexual violence), what varies is the cause activating the disorder.

In Narcissistic Abuse Syndrome it is the abusive relationship that initiates the symptomatological picture (it does not derive from pre-existing psychological characteristics in the victim), it is always characterized by a form of dependence induced by the abuser, above all with narcissistic or psychopathic personality characteristics.

Long term effects
We are now fully aware that being in a relationship with a narcissist is debilitating and the consequences of ending this relationship could even be protracted over time.

It's normal to feel pain after a breakup. Even ending a toxic relationship comes with a period of mourning.

An experience of this type can leave you very tried, psychologically and physically: self-esteem is on the ground, and you can lose part of your identity and your Self. You lose lucidity, you no longer recognize each other, and you feel guilty for not having been able to separate in time. You may experience severe anxiety and depressive feelings. One doubts one's version of the facts and one's own thoughts, since these have been called into question by a contradictory and ambivalent communication, and the truth has also been denied in the face of the evidence: one finds oneself in a state of profound confusion, one he fears that he has lost touch with reality, and he doubts himself and his own reliability ("gaslighting ").

At the same time, you will be afraid of being alone, of no longer being able to experience such intense emotions and feelings. You may feel drained and even more vulnerable, with feelings of anxiety and deep sadness. This really could be a very painful phase.

He often develops a real emotional dependence: a vicious circle in which separating is impossible but remaining in the bond is even more painful.

Also in America, long-term studies have also been carried out on the brain modifications determined by narcissistic relationships as the primary source of stress, in order to validate what emerged in the clinic. On the other hand, regardless of the cause, stress causes significant negative changes to the body and mind, deteriorating them and affecting the quality of life and the future: chronic stress can change the size of the brain, its structures, and its functioning and can modify the genetic heritage. In particular, chronic stress affects the increase in brain connections of fear and the increase in cortisol release, with 2 important consequences: a decrease in electrical signals in the hippocampus (site of learning, memory, stress control) and a loss of connections synaptic reactions between neurons and contraction of the prefrontal cortex (area of the brain involved in concentration, decision making, judgment, social interaction).

However, one of the most important consequences to underline is that which concerns the repetition of the trauma, in fact, the person tends to seek situations like those already experienced in the past. Some studies show that children who are victims of abuse have a greater risk of suffering violence as adults (Williams, 2009), in fact, consistent with what has been stated, past experiences of abuse and neglect can lead the individual to seek ties with other people and of life situations that tend to confirm one's own image and what happened in the past, like a circle that repeats itself. Therefore, the relationship with an abusive subject, with a narcissistic personality disorder, can leave important signs on a person's psyche, signs that should not be hidden, understated, or denied, but listened to and evaluated by mental health specialists, in order to intervene promptly with effective psychotherapy courses that are able to give voice, acceptance, support, concrete help to the abuses suffered and new lifeblood.

It is important to reflect on these aspects and seek the advice of a psychologist if you recognize some of these characteristics in your partner or in yourself.

Post-trauma psyche effects

The relationship with a narcissist and its end is traumatic as they are characterized by a spiral of psychological violence such as devaluations, lies, double binding, "gaslighting", silent treatment, isolation, manipulations, and slander. Eventually, the mask falls off and the target is confused and desperate as he no longer knows what happened in the relationship, no longer knows who the narcissist is and has the feeling of dealing with the "good twin" and the "bad twin", cannot recognize what is real and what is not. They are consequences of the narcissist's mental manipulation. He will feel profoundly inadequate and wrong as a person, he will have the sense of no longer knowing who he is due to the devaluations and projections of narcissism or he will no longer feel recognized and seen as he really is by the person he loved, he will get angry at having been cheated and he feels he has suffered an injustice, struggles to close by developing an emotional dependence on the narcissist.

Why is it equally difficult to take control of one's life after a definitive estrangement? We see the long-term emotional repercussions of the narcissist's victims. Let's start with the victim's perception of himself.

Usually, for people who have dated a narcissist, the knowledge of themselves that they carry with them is always the same: "I am worth nothing", and "I am not enough". In essence, the victim of the narcissist thinks that there is something wrong with her and that everything she has suffered is somehow deserved.

She or he without realizing it slowly enters a process of devaluation, dissociation, and dehumanization: she feels useless, alone, and humiliated. She or he feels like there is no future for her (or him) anymore.

The most frequent symptoms are low self-esteem, anxiety, depression, suicidal wishes, somatization, and anger. Another characteristic that the victims have in common is the initial unawareness of who they have been dealing with all this time.

Some people feel a general malaise, while others may have come to know through other sources. But the common point is that when they were with this person everything seemed "normal".

At first, the victim ignores the relational dynamics in which she has been entangled (lies and manipulations) and she does not realize that she has been the victim of very deep psychological abuse. For many, the fact that a person is not violent in gestures but "only" in words is something that can be easily justified and forgiven (especially if the perpetrator seems repentant), but the wounds that words leave are much deeper and more difficult to be eradicated.

The difficulty in understanding the narcissistic person lies in the fact that the ideas we have about the narcissistic disorder are very vague, often erroneously promoted by cinema and literature: they are described as crazy and easily recognizable people. It's actually not like that. They blend in very well. Since these people are profoundly different from us due to their low empathy and low introspection capacity, the victim will have a compulsive need for information on everything related to the world of the narcissist.

Another painful feature of the victim's psyche is the sensation of having fallen in love with an illusion.

What hurts the most is realizing that you have loved a person who, in reality, never existed.

In fact, the narcissist does not give the victim the opportunity to make himself known. Apparently, kind, innocent, cheerful and seductive: this, unfortunately, is only a mask.

The victim will realize it (maybe!!!) when it's too late. Even all the beautiful moments spent together are just the result of an illusion.

I often hear phrases like "I loved a projection of myself". That's right: it's love toward who I imagined my partner to be.

This investing all of herself in another person means that the bond that will be created will be very deep: in reality, she is investing her energies in chasing an illusion, but unfortunately, she does not realize it. However, like the narcissist, the victim is also a very insecure person.

They are two people who react in completely opposite ways to a similar problem: one does it through manipulation and control, the other through compassion and caring for the other. And it is precisely here that the perpetrator will hook his victim: the latter will no longer be able to do without his approval, continuously experiencing the fear of abandonment and feeling an indescribable void whenever the narcissist tries to get away.

To recap: all the effects and consequences of the relationship with the narcissist

Let's briefly recap what the immediate and long-term effects of a relationship with a narcissist can be:

- Confusion about what is real and what is not due to gaslighting
- Affective dependence and difficulty in detaching from the narcissist
- Despair and anguish
- Depression and anxiety
- Fear
- Anger towards the narcissist and towards herself
- Suicidal thoughts
- Pain in waves and crying spells
- Impulsivity and loss of self-control
- Paranoia
- Social phobia
- Guilt and shame about having an affair with the narcissist
- Feeling of helplessness
- Sleep disturbance, nightmares, insomnia, interrupted sleep
- Altered appetite, nausea
- Lowering of the immune system and psychosomatic disorders
- Verbal and written logorrhea
- Want to tell everyone the truth
- The feeling of loneliness and emptiness
- Isolation or the need to always be in the company
- Sense of inadequacy, of being "wrong" or defective as a person
- Loss of identity

Conclusions regarding the psychic effects on the victims

To conclude this important chapter, we can say that the victim takes a long time to rebuild because, as I mentioned above, the emotional repercussions are very deep. They settle down slowly over time and it ends up that the person truly believes that they are worthless and that their life no longer has meaning.
The most dramatic aspect lies in realizing that she is dependent not on the attention of the narcissist, but on the attention that she has given to him: this is what made her

feel important, but at the same time a subject is missing and it is not possible to elaborate the lost.

We have seen that, among the consequences, both in the short and long term for the victim are the loss of self-esteem, confusion, a sense of guilt, and loss of energy. These are some of the consequences of the abuse of a narcissist. The person, therefore, feels like a rag and develops a distorted, belittled idea of himself. Violence can lead to the erosion of one's integrity, of one's values and one feels in total confusion, due to the inability to understand the nature of one's pain. Plus, the absence of answers weighs, the narcissist discards you and doesn't hear from you anymore but there's no closure, so those who suffer manipulation keep wondering if it's their fault if they've done something wrong.

So, the advice we can give to all people who have suffered psychological abuse is to ask for help, not to close in themselves and above all to stop justifying their perpetrator. Talking to other people, going out, asking for advice, getting to know people who suffer from the same problems and, why not, getting help from a psychotherapist? As painful as it is, you can get out of this state of malaise.

In the next section of the book, you will be shown a way out of this nightmare. In the next chapter, to help you more, we will provide you with a mini guide on how to recognize a narcissistic partner from some well-defined signals.

Chapter 7: 9 signs of a narcissistic partner

This chapter will briefly review the signs that indicate the presence of a narcissistic partner in one's life. We have already discussed this in the first part of the guide when we talked about recognizing the narcissist through his typical characteristics and signals. In this chapter, the question will be explored from your point of view, in the sense that these are signals that you will have to observe within your daily context.

How do we know if we are dealing with a pathological narcissist?

Charmers, seducers and trustworthy. This is the way narcissistic people show themselves at first sight. Their real intention, however, is to make others feel inferior and have a continuous self-fuel; for this reason, it is important to learn to recognize a narcissist as early as possible.
To protect ourselves in everyday life, it is better to learn to recognize a narcissist, so as to avoid him. Having a conversation with a narcissist can initially feel like a rewarding experience. However, he won't be slow to reveal his true intentions, which are to make others feel inferior and take advantage of those around him.
In the first part of the guide, a whole series of signs have been indicated that we can recognize in a pathologically narcissistic person. While some of us have been guilty of some of the following behaviors at least once in our lives, a pathological narcissist tends to habitually engage in them in day-to-day relationships, while remaining largely unaware and/or indifferent, as if his actions do not have consequences for others. In the next paragraph, we will see specifically what are the tangible signs that you can and will have to notice every day and increasingly assume the awareness that you are dealing with a narcissist. And fix it as soon as possible.

9 irrefutable signs of a narcissist partner

In the second chapter, we talked about 7 signs that show who the typical narcissist is. In this paragraph, we will go deeper into the matter, and we will show you well-defined signals that should set off the alarm in you. Let's see what these certain signals are (we will indicate nine of them):

1. **Talk about himself or herself**

The pathological narcissist loves to talk about himself and does not give the opportunity to make the other speak, transforming the conversation into one-way. You have to fight to get your point across, and even if you do succeed, if the narcissist disagrees with your point of view, he will reject or ignore you. Typical expressions will therefore be "...but", "actually...", and "it's not like you say".

It also interrupts the conversation. While a civil conversation sees the speaker interrupting himself when his interlocutor takes the floor, the pathological narcissist interrupts the others and quickly moves on to a conversation that concerns him. He will show little genuine interest in you.

2. **He or she knows no rules and limits...and respect!**

Have you noticed how often your partner breaks the rules? The pathological narcissist enjoys straying from the rules and violating social norms. In the most serious cases at a diagnostic level, a narcissistic subject could be confused with an antisocial disorder precisely because of this characteristic. The narcissist wants to be the best no matter what. Being second to someone, for him/her, means being invisible and irrelevant. For this reason, he often tends to select outsized goals (getting the greatest vote in all the exams in his course) and short-term hobbies (becoming a tennis champion in four lessons) in which to excel, and then abandon them when the commitment required it becomes too difficult to deal with. He doesn't accept half-measures, nor does he consider nuances interesting. And all this, even at the cost of breaking the law.

The narcissist is an upstart and does not care to pass over the commitments and promises made if this could bring advantages in terms of self-image (which, we remember, must always be ideal, perfect, and unshakeable), money or other immediate goods. The commitment to achieve something, as well as sacrifices, is not well seen by this type of person, who prefers to have everything immediately and is convinced that he is entitled to it.

Furthermore, he shows contempt for the ideas of others but also for the feelings, possessions and physical or character characteristics of others. He passes them without any sensitivity. He borrows other people's items or money without bothering to pay it back. He, therefore, shows little remorse or guilt, instead blaming the victim for his own disrespect. For example. "It's your fault I forgot; you should have reminded me." Does it look familiar to you?

3. **Apparent splendor**

A narcissist always shows his or her best. Many narcissists do things just to impress others. This first place on the podium is earned physically, economically, materially, professionally, and culturally. In these situations, the narcissist uses people and objects to postpone a highly positive self-image thus replacing the True Self that they believe is inadequate.

They look charming and friendly. Narcissists are very interested in appearing good and being looked down upon by everyone to improve and "perfect" their self-esteem.

The theatricality in displaying these trophies is perceived by the interlocutor as exaggerated, because the underlying message is "I'm better than you" or "Look how special I am and worthy of love and admiration from everyone". The pathological narcissist expects preferential treatment from others. He expects others to be there to meet his needs, without reciprocating. His idea is that the world revolves around him. Apparently, he is also charismatic. The pathological narcissist can be very charismatic and convincing. When he is interested in a person, he is able to make them feel special and wanted. However, once he loses interest in the person (probably after they get what they wanted) he dumps or pushes her away for no real reason. A narcissist can be very involved and sociable as long as he is getting what he wants by giving him all the attention he expects.

The pathological narcissist thinks of himself as a kind of king or queen having an exaggerated sense of his own power and importance and believing that others cannot live or survive without his magnificent contributions.

4. **You feel anger and humiliation in their presence**

Precisely because of their need to feel admired and special, narcissists tend to devalue anyone who could threaten their "status" or be considered a rival. The way they do this is often demeaning and derogatory. It is normal, in the face of these behaviors, to feel anger and humiliation. The best thing, however, would be to avoid showing them and run away, since the narcissist feeds on the reactions (even negative) of others, and what displaces him most is simply being ignored.

It is no coincidence that these people tend to mate with those with low self-esteem (even the narcissus has it, but flaunts a high one), dedicated to caring for others. In fact, with these individuals, it is easier to proclaim yourself the absolute winner of life and flaunt a strong and unshakeable self-image, in contrast to that of your partner. It is a natural consequence that, in a conflict, the "loser" will be driven to feel emotions of guilt and shame. This is because the narcissist, never taking responsibility for the mistakes he makes, unloads them on those in front of him, making him feel as if he has to "pay the bill twice".

The narcissist will always give a bad image of you. Many narcissists badmouth their exes, criticize them, and blame them for the end of the story. Expect this treatment too. If you have had a fight or have not done what your partner expected, rest assured that you have already fallen into the trap of your narcissist who will already be badmouthing you.

5. They change their minds; they deny and seem the same charming

Changing your mind is seen as an affront. "You said you would go to the cinema at 6. But now you are saying you will go at 8. How do you change plans like this?" the answer would be "because I enjoy free will!!!". Human beings have the right to change their minds at any time and for any reason. Changing a narcissist's mind instead has to do with the loss of control that he will try to regain through guilt, and something called gaslighting which you will read about later.

They also deny something he said or did by making you think he was wrong. The pathological narcissist may completely deny that he said or did anything making you think he was "crazy" or perhaps you just imagined. This aspect respects the charismatic and convincing characteristics of the narcissist. And even if you have proof that the narcissist said or did something, he will tell you that you misunderstood and that it never happened by making you out to be a liar. This phenomenon of denying or altering reality is called gaslighting, and it is a hallmark of the narcissist. It takes its name from a 1938 play Gas light, in which a husband manipulates elements of the environment by making his wife believe that she remembers incorrectly and that no change has taken place.

They are addicted to future faking too, i.e., they often talk about a future that they have no intention of realizing (moving in together, getting married, having children, etc.).

They manipulate through mystifications or will make you believe, with mastery, that what brings an advantage to them is what is best for you. So, you could, for example, end up quitting because he or she will convince you that you are wasted at work or you could quit the gym you go to because he/she will make you think it's a bad place where they don't respect you.

6. Control and fear of abandonment

Narcissists have a strong fear of abandonment and for this reason, within a relationship, they will implement a series of strategies to keep their partner close to them and exercise control over their partner. One such strategy is the silence they can maintain following an argument. In fact, silence allows you to obtain and re-establish control over the other, and if this calls, the dynamic narcissistic relationship will have been re-established: he has once again obtained attention. If you encounter these attitudes every day, well you have a narcissistic person next to you, intent only on harming your person. Never mistake this attitude for affection!

7. <u>They are envious of your relationships with others</u>

At first, narcissists will tell you that they admire the loving relationship you have with family and friends. But soon they'll start criticizing your acquaintances,
"It's a matter of control," the doctor tells us, adding that the reasons are often twofold: "He (or she) may be envious of your relationships with other people or may want more attention for himself. By nature, narcissists are demanding, they want to feel that they are in complete control over you. This is just another way to practice it. To do that, they have to isolate you from the rest of the world. Tell me, have you been feeling a little isolated lately?

8. <u>Superficiality...sounds familiar?</u>

Narcissists cannot really get to know a person. If you are lucky to receive a gift from a pathological narcissist, don't expect this to be meant for you! Most likely he will give you something that has little to do with your tastes. In fact, it is difficult for narcissists to be able to really get to know you because they have no interest in doing so. They can't dwell on what you tell them about yourself, they are so attentive only to themselves. But if you celebrate your birthday with friends, and therefore you have to open your gift in front of many people, expect a great expensive gift because it is important to leave a good impression on your audience.
Their superficiality, from another point of view, can be noted by the fact that the interests and activities of the narcissist are often focused on everything that nourishes the self-image, understood in its aesthetic sense. Beauty is very important, as well as success and fun (exposed, inauthentic): nowadays, this could translate into an intense activity of "self-advertising" on social networks. Instagram, Facebook, and others, in fact, allow you to show only what he (or she) wants to show about himself or yourself.

9. <u>And finally... love bombing: you must be more careful about this!</u>

As we have already seen, love bombing is the fundamental technique with which the narcissist hooks his victim. And that's probably what happened to you! 'Love bombing' is often a form of emotional abuse. That is, people use this tactic to establish control and power over the other person. The goal of this manipulation is to develop a false sense of bond and trust at the beginning of a relationship and then emotionally abuse the other person. Typically, these manipulation tactics are often used by people with a narcissistic personality disorder.

We want to dwell in particular on this last signal because it is important that you can recognize it in your relationship and can still save yourself. There are some behaviors or attitudes that can be due to this manipulative tactic in couples.

Even if you recognize these signs, it doesn't necessarily mean your partner is toxic, but when they repeat themselves too often and you feel uncomfortable, your alarm bells should go off:

- ✓ They give you too many gifts: Love bombing often involves exaggerated gestures, such as sending inappropriate gifts at work (such as bouquets) or constantly buying overpriced items. While these gestures may be harmless, they can sometimes disguise the intent to manipulate you into believing that you owe this person something.
- ✓ Continuous praise: We all love attention in a relationship, but continuous praise can be another sign of these coercive tactics. For example, if someone expresses words full of love in an exaggerated way, it is possible that these feelings are not authentic. Narcissists can use some expressions like: "I've never met anyone as perfect as you", "I love everything about you", etc.
- ✓ Too Many Calls or Texts: At the beginning of a romantic relationship, it's completely normal to be too present in the other person's thoughts. But when this continues over time, it can be a sign that this loving attention is not genuine. Especially when they continuously text or call you.
- ✓ They want your undivided attention: when you don't give them the same attention they do, they can end up getting angry with you. This need for constant attention can also be a sign of 'love bombing'.
- ✓ Seeking Immediate Commitment: Love bombing is also characterized by the constant attempt to pressure the other person to rush into committing to the relationship. These people may talk about marriage or moving in with you when they've only known you for a short time.
- ✓ They get angry when they set limits: One of the warning signs of these manifestations of love is when you try to set limits and these people get angry. You must know that one of the symptoms of true love is respecting your wishes and backing down if you specify it.
- ✓ It feels uncomfortable: When the attention in love is too strong, it is normal that you end up feeling some discomfort.

In the face of all these signs, it's important to pay attention to what your intuition is telling you. If you see that there is something not normal in your relationship, you could be a victim of this manipulation tactic. From these signs, you may very well have deduced, again, that you are dealing with a toxic person, a narcissist. If you are in love with a narcissist, your needs will always come second. They are too busy evaluating what they want from you to see you as an independent person, with your desires. But you just wondering, is it really worth living like this? This is why we are warning you, precisely to make your life better.

From the next chapter onwards, now that you've realized you're dealing with such a person, we'll guide you, step by step, to get rid of him... and go back to being happy!

FOURTH PART- COMING OUT OF A RELATIONSHIP WITH THE NARCISSIST

Chapter 8: First solutions on what to do once you realize you have a narcissistic partner

In this chapter, we will move on to a slightly more practical, and perhaps for you, the most painful part: coming out of a toxic situation with a narcissist. Let's see what the first steps are to take to return to being free from this burden.

A premise

If you have reached this part of the guide, you probably have the feeling, or perhaps by now almost the certainty, that you are dealing with a narcissistic partner and you expect to find confirmation of it. We want you to know and we repeat that, despite the signs indicated in the previous paragraph, it is not at all easy to trace a profile. Yes, we have a large number of world-renowned illustrious predecessors who have tried this with great success and, in doing so, have coined new terms to better describe the various types, but first really make sure you are dealing with a narcissist. With this premise, we're giving you a little reminder again to understand if the dynamics of your relationship have taken a turn in favor of the narcissist, to say the least. Evaluate if you are inside these spirals:

1. Every relationship with a narcissist has an identical sequence, although it is not always possible to recognize it in time. This sequence is divided into three phases: idealization or love bombing (you are the partner of my life, I will always love you!), devaluation (you are not that special, you won't let me live, you are like all the others [the others] even worse, by doing so I will be forced to leave you!), abandonment, experienced as inevitable, as if there was no other way to behave. It is likely that they will end the relationship by operating ghosting, also known as "the art of disappearing".
2. They cyclically have an inescapable need to cause separation. They do it in an attempt, dysfunctional and desperate, to manage the abandonment anguish that would ensue and that they would absolutely not be able to tolerate. To do it without feeling guilty they will paint you as inadequate and will start to consider

you as an enemy, they will look for excuses to quarrel, they will probably betray you. So it will be easier to part with you.

3.

If you can identify with this dynamic, then you are dealing with a narcissist! let's see some preliminary solutions that can really save you from this daily nightmare.

Maybe you've realized it now, but know that with you there are also conscious victims. Let's see a typical situation: when you were still together you did everything to meet his way of being. You researched and read every article on the subject. You had an assumption that the narcissist could change. You wanted to know better the characteristics of the narcissist to enter the world of him. You were hoping you could make the narcissist fall in love with you. You were hoping the relationship would get serious. It ended with the narcissist because despite all your efforts his nature prevailed.

And now you realize you are the victim of a narcissist. The same thing happens to those who were unaware of it, only that maybe you could have anticipated the times. Obviously, we don't want to blame anyone, but we tell you that you always have time to run away from the narcissist.

What can I do?

Well, we're pretty sure that, by this point in the guide, you will have realized that you are dealing with a narcissist. It will be rather tragic, painful, and a real shock: how did I have some deep feelings for such a person?

You understood that you were in a codependent relationship with a toxic and destructive person, that you participated in his complacency, and that you fueled his mental disorder even more. You will probably be disappointed, you will feel so much anger, frustration, and sadness. Not to mention the emptiness you will feel right now. The reason is simple to understand: the narcissist often creates problematic relationships that create suffering and discomfort in the partner. What can I do now? The signals indicated in the previous chapter, we understand, can really scare. Pathological narcissism is a serious and, in some cases, very serious disorder. It is important first of all to help the person in whom you observe these signs, by contacting a private or public mental health facility together, convincing the person to get help. This could be a first step, but most of the time it is really impossible to do. Think about it: a person so convinced that he is the best, that the whole world must stand at his feet, how could he ever accept the idea that he needs help? For this reason, this road is really impracticable.

When the victim of a narcissist realizes the manipulation, he has undergone and tries to point it out to his or her tormentor, in fact, it happens that this victim feels a very strong sense of guilt for blaming him, but not only. In fact, among the psychological consequences, there can be outbursts of anger, attacks of depression, fear, anguish, anxiety, etc.

And often, once the narcissist has been blamed for his manipulation, this tends to turn the omelet around, making the victim feel like a false person, who has invented everything, is almost crazy in what he says and thinks, and who doubts his kind heart. Imagine the sense of frustration in this victim. The only thing you can do, as soon as you realize the dangerousness of this subject, is to walk away. As soon as possible!

Also given the fact that we have realized that this person has used us, humiliated us, and made us his puppet, the most instinctive reaction of most people is precisely revenge, the desire to repay the person who hurt us with the same coin. He has made victims of real psychological violence with his behavior.

For all these reasons planning "revenge" has no sense. Often the only effective response to a narcissist - who in our view has harmed us - is simply to shut down, and withhold any contact or attention. In a word, stop feeding each other's narcissism.

We should also say that, often, the codependent partners of narcissists stay in their relationships even when they realize they are being abused because they feel they deserve that treatment and/or see no way out. Despite the ingrained pitfalls of codependency, there is a possible way out. While narcissism is an intractable condition and extremely difficult to recognize and change, codependency is easier to treat. Unlike the narcissist, the codependent person usually possesses empathy, a strong sense of responsibility, a desire for intimacy, and a willingness to help and support others. Therefore, building self-awareness and self-esteem is within the codependent's reach and are both keys to a healthier way of being and building balanced relationships.

The codependent person can turn their vulnerabilities into strengths. In fact, he could use:

- ✓ Awareness of the needs of others to become more aware of your own.
- ✓ Empathy towards others to feel compassion towards oneself.
- ✓ The desire to help and heal others, to be able to help oneself

Basically, what we're telling you is to let go of feelings of recovery (I want to help him heal) or revenge. The best thing to do is to, in addition to walking away immediately, take responsibility for the "victim". Warning: we are absolutely not placing the blame on you! But we ask you to do some self-examination and not fall into the trap of placing all the blame on the "bad" partner. In fact, if the partner actually suffers from a narcissistic problem, it would still be a person who is in any case "suffering" internally as much as the victim.

A more useful and constructive awareness consists in taking responsibility:

- ✓ Why did I choose that person?
- ✓ Why do I choose to stay in a relationship that makes me suffer?
- ✓ Why can't I break this link?
- ✓ What ancient wounds is this relationship reactivating and what are my unconscious expectations?
- ✓ How did I become an accomplice to this perverted script?

You can start from these questions and, as we are about to advise you in the next paragraph, start all over again…by yourself!

The First Step to Healing: It Starts with You

Far from demonizing those with a narcissistic character, we also try to focus on the behavior of those dealing with a narcissist. Often the suffering and the creation of a dysfunctional relationship derive from the interlocking of the fragility and insecurities of both.

While it's true that the narcissist tends to be unempathetic, the other lacks self-awareness. Far be it from us to blame this thing: it can really happen to everyone, not to mention that falling in love can make us lose our lucidity. But it is necessary to trigger a process of self-valuation that will slowly lead us to admit that if a relationship is not satisfactory, we can close it. Leaving a narcissist isn't easy, because we are often overwhelmed by the fear of loss, and by the fear of being alone, which are very normal. This is exactly the crux we need to work on.

The greatest challenge in freeing yourself from destructive partners is giving up your primitive defense of reality denial. When parents are abusive and/or indifferent, children must deny themselves this situation to survive. However, as they grow up, they may be able to recognize the process of denial so that they can evolve and heal. Children who fail to recognize the denial of reality get stuck in this condition, continue to be hurt and hurt others.

One of the hardest forms of reality denial to get rid of is the belief that you can get the narcissist to love you. Narcissists are unable to reciprocate the other's love, respect, compassion, concern, or care. Narcissists demand all of this from their partners but are unable to give it back. To free yourself from the narcissist it is essential to replace your beliefs and behavioral patterns with more functional ones. This involves a lot of reflection, education, support, and a lot of practice. The more honest you become with yourself, the more you learn about healthy alternatives to the ones you grew up with. In one's relationships, one moves from codependency to interdependence, learning to:

- ✓ Respect yourself
- ✓ Listen to your needs
- ✓ Valuing your feelings
- ✓ Ask yourself what you want
- ✓ Refuse what you don't want
- ✓ Separate your own happiness from that of others
- ✓ Recognize imbalances in relationships
- ✓ Establish healthy boundaries
- ✓ Recognize your own power and limitations
- ✓ Give up the need to control others
- ✓ Let go of the guilt
- ✓ Self educates.

But, despite these very important strategies, the only step to save yourself is to learn to love yourself and take care of your needs by cutting off all contact with the narcissist. We'll talk more about breaking off contacts in the next few chapters.

Bottom line: it's about taking back your life

It takes the victim a long time to rebuild because it is hard to really realize the fact that one has had such a self-destructive relationship.
Anger and a desire for revenge are among the two most intense feelings on the part of a narcissist's victim. But these destructive forces won't help you recover and become serene.
When these feelings persist and are not reworked it means that the person is also affected by an emotional addiction.
Emotional addiction often arises when the person in his past has had previous bereavement or previous traumas. Such traumatic events do not allow the person to detach himself definitively from the source of suffering. The person then continues to think of the narcissist while remaining tied to these feelings. The suffering inflicted by pathological relationships is truly enormous and excruciating. The victim of a narcissist feels hurt and anguish. She or he is aware that has given all the love possible and that he or she has really given it her all. For this, she or he now cannot react. She can't let go of the shot. The victim does not accept to have been rejected

or disdained. She is angry. The victim also may not feel understood in her pain. She or he doesn't realize that if she feels too victimized, she is hindering the healing process. To takes the victim's life back into her hands, in fact, she must at some point understand why she was attracted to a narcissist. Of course, there are times for healing.

So, the main advice, as well as starting from oneself, is to ask for help, not to withdraw into oneself and above all to stop justifying one's perpetrator. Talking to other people, going out, asking for advice, getting to know people who suffer from the same problems and, why not, getting help from a psychotherapist? We will talk about this in the next chapters of the guide.

In dealing with a pathological narcissist there isn't much of a choice other than rejection and abandonment. In fact, those who are narcissists have many difficulties in understanding their true nature. You can't expect to change it, and women who have tried have often been very badly burned. Consider that people with narcissism find it very difficult even in therapy to free themselves and to get in touch with their narcissistic wounds.

As painful and difficult as it is, know that you are not alone, and you can get out of this state of malaise.

Chapter 9: Do's and Don'ts of a Toxic Relationship

In this chapter, we will try to meet those who are still living in a relationship with the now-identified and unmasked narcissist. A small guide of what to do and what not to do if you are in this type of relationship will be indicated.

Types of toxic relations

Even though the definition of toxicity belongs to the field of medicine, this term is widely used in the psychological field too, especially in the case of masculinity toxic behavior. With respect to relationships, however, this term is used to refer to when living in a relationship that can hurt.

A toxic relationship is in fact any type of relationship within one's private or professional sphere, in which dynamics are established that are harmful to the psychophysical health of one or both of the parties involved. The common denominator is the discomfort caused by manipulative, passive-aggressive, controlling, or violent attitudes, both verbally and physically. Severing this type of bond is somewhat complex, as often those who succumb do not fully understand or accept what is happening, while those who abuse do so even unconsciously. Even when one is aware of the state of suffering, it is difficult to get out of it because in the meantime a real emotional addiction has been created or one is terrified of loneliness.

Relationships evolve. They change and grow. Sometimes they wear out and become worn. A relationship is "toxic" when it becomes an element of one's life that one is "intoxicated" with and from which one deems it necessary to detox.

Wanting to give a definition of a toxic relationship we can say that it is toxic: "any relationship between people who do not support each other, where there is conflict and one tries to undermine the other, where there is competition, where there is lack respect and cohesion".

While every relationship goes through its ups and downs, sometimes resulting in a couple of crisis, a toxic relationship is constantly unpleasant and draining for the people involved, to the point that the negative moments outweigh the positive ones. Toxic relationships are mentally, emotionally, and possibly even physically damaging to one or both partners.

There are however different types of toxic relationships. Because the narcissist isn't just our partner: he could be within our family circle, in our job environment, or be someone we consider our friend.

Toxic love relationship

There is no perfect couple, just as it is not possible to be constantly happy and satisfied. Quarrels, jealousies, misunderstandings, tensions, and moments of the crisis must however be limited to short periods, and linked to specific, explainable and real circumstances. If the perception of unhappiness and discomfort goes on for too long or is even a permanent state, then surely something is wrong. Unfortunately, toxic relationships in love are the most frequent because in the name of this feeling we sacrifice ourselves until we find ourselves involved in abusive and harmful dynamics.

Toxic friendship relationships

As mentioned, toxic relationships can also arise in the field of friendships, in this case, bonds are created between individuals who simulate the role of ally or confidant. In this type of relationship, there is no listening and empathy but, rather, hidden envy. Through negativity, these people block or slow down the emotional growth of others, boycotting their progress and fueling frustration and inner tiredness. Unfortunately, the relationship often continues due to habit or lack of alternatives but carrying on a friendship in which the cornerstones of respect, loyalty and mutual support are missing.

Toxic family relationships

The family is perhaps one of the worst-case scenarios in which toxic relationships can develop because it is unlikely that one breaks up with one's family altogether. At the root, there are usually jealousies, unresolved conflicts, power plays, silly competitions, disagreement on specific issues or differences of thought due to generational separation. The best solution is almost always to try to put distance between yourself and the source of the discomfort. Another way is to face the situation by stating one's reasons firmly but always with respect, calm and tolerance.

Toxic relationships work

The professional environment is not a territory isolated from the rest of an individual's life, so inevitably each person brings a part of himself to work, including personal and emotional problems. A serene and collaborative environment would be ideal for ensuring productivity and well-being, but this habitat can often become hostile, causing anxiety and stress. Regardless of the job or the degree of satisfaction, the reason for the unease can be superiors or colleagues, guilty of adopting unpleasant and vexatious attitudes.

This situation affects both performance and privacy, generating a dangerous vicious circle. There are various solutions, such as: changing jobs (if possible), contacting the boss (assuming he's not the problem), defending oneself or ignoring him. Whatever path you intend to take, you need to act with clarity and evaluate the pros and cons of each action, avoiding getting caught up in impulsivity.

These are the types of relationships that unfortunately, more or less, have been able to experience in the course of life. In this chapter, in particular, we will talk about toxic relationships at the couple level, and therefore how to get rid of a narcissistic and therefore toxic partner.

Toxic relationship: the warning signs
Symptoms of a toxic relationship include any form of violence, abuse, or harassment, which should be addressed immediately. But in many cases, the signs that help us tell if a relationship is toxic are much more subtle.
The first, and simplest, is persistent unhappiness with the risk of becoming a depressed partner. If a relationship ceases to bring joy and instead leaves us feeling constantly sad, angry, anxious, or "withdrawn, like we're burnt out," it could be a toxic relationship. We may also feel envious of happy couples. Negative changes in our mental health are all red flags. Other signs of a toxic relationship are:

Lack of support

Healthy relationships are built on a mutual desire to see each other succeed in all areas of life. But when a relationship is toxic, every accomplishment becomes a competition. The partner is often absent or unreachable and one gets the impression of being satisfied with the crumbs.

Toxic communication

Instead of treating each other kindly, most of your conversations are filled with sarcasm, criticism, or open hostility. One of the two might even avoid raising issues so as not to cause tension, keeping all the issues to himself. In other cases, the communication becomes ambiguous, resulting in gaslighting, a real psychological manipulation.

Controlling behaviors

While it's normal to be jealous of time to time, it could really become a problem. Constantly asking where your partner is and getting excessively angry when she doesn't respond to texts immediately are both signs of a control freak, which can contribute to toxicity in a relationship. Control can also be expressed through affective manipulation when one of the two partners controls (more or less consciously) the other to achieve their goals. "If you love me, you must do it" is one of the phrases used by emotional manipulators to implement emotional blackmail.

Resentment

Resentment consists of holding on to grudges and letting them deteriorate intimacy, not fully understanding what anger is hiding. Over time, frustration or bitterness can build up and make a small chasm that much bigger.

Dishonesty

A relationship is toxic when you find yourself constantly making up lies about where you are or who you are dating to avoid spending time with your partner. And this also applies to long-distance relationships.

Constant stress

Every relationship goes through tense moments, but constantly finding yourself on edge is an indicator that something is wrong. This continuous stress, in a short time, can take a toll on your physical and emotional health. In abusive relationships like this, it can be possible to experience some true post-traumatic stress.

Ignore your needs

It's one thing for two people to be in synchronicity, it's quite another to indulge in whatever your partner wants to do, even when he or she goes against your wishes or comfort level. This is another sign of toxicity. For example, you might agree to a vacation that your partner has planned on dates that aren't convenient for you.

Lost relationships

You've stopped spending time with friends and family, both to avoid conflict with your partner and to walk around having to explain what's going on in your relationship. You may soon find that your free time is focused solely on your partner. These are the alarm bells that should really scare you. In the next paragraph, we will do some tests to further understand if you are in a toxic couple relationship.

What happens in toxic relation with a narcissist? A small verification questionnaire

Before we indicate dos and don'ts, let's take a moment to understand what's going on in your current relationship. Generally, people like you who meet those who suffer from a narcissist pathology begin to behave differently than usual and eventually realize that they have completely changed their personality to adapt it to the needs of the narcissist. This means you need to learn how to deal with a narcissist for your mental health! When you met him, you saw in him a handsome, attractive, charming, and funny man. That's probably why you fell in love with him. It is not strange at all: unfortunately, many narcissistic men are attractive.

If you are next to a narcissistic man, you perceive a lot of his sense of "if great", and his high self-esteem, but in reality, it is all bogus. Actually, the man (or the woman) you are dating (if he really is a narcissist), is a very insecure person.

Ask yourself these questions again, based on the signs indicated in the previous paragraph:

- ✓ Does he (or she) always "wait" for admiration from you and others?
- ✓ Does one overestimate one's own abilities by underestimating any help from others (that's why it's difficult to rely on a psychologist)
- ✓ Does he (or she) dream of getting hugely successful in whatever he does?
- ✓ Does he (or she) often relate to successful people because he feels understood only by them?
- ✓ Is he (or she) often unreasonably demanding?
- ✓ Does he (or she) contribute very little to the relationship?
- ✓ Has he (or she) little empathy?
- ✓ Does he (or she) want to talk about feelings?
- ✓ Does he (or she) say little about himself (or herself)?
- ✓ Does he (or she) appreciate your successes, your values and everything you do for him?

Evaluates and observe these behaviors: is this really what is happening within your relationship?

If you answered yes to most (if not all) questions, I feel sorry for you, but you are in a toxic relationship by all standards present.

Over time you've gotten to know him, and you've noticed how his life is built to revolve completely around him. It's all an "I".

One question you are surely asking yourself is what is wrong with my narcissistic partner?

Now that you have discovered that your partner is a narcissist you will wonder what is behind his personality so problematic of him.

The general picture is as follows:

- ✓ He (or she) is an extremely vulnerable person
- ✓ He (or she) has an unresolved conflict that he's unlikely to acknowledge
- ✓ He (or she) will never give you emotional satisfaction
- ✓ He (or she) will never confide in you the unpleasant memories he defends against in a narcissistic way

Before reaching a tipping point, you need to learn to pay attention to the warning signs that can reveal a toxic relationship:

- ✓ Progressive isolation
- ✓ Clear imbalance of roles
- ✓ Emotional addiction
- ✓ Loss of self-esteem
- ✓ Constant discomfort and tiredness both physical and mental

This little questionnaire was also done to make you understand the dangers of any toxic relationship. Treating a narcissist is a difficult challenge, but in the meantime let's see do and don'ts of a toxic relationship.

Dos in a toxic relationship

Well, you have come to realize that you are in a toxic relationship up to your neck. The advice we are about to give you, which relates purely to the love relationship, however, could also be useful if you have a toxic person in your circle of personal acquaintances (so, friendship or work).

<u>Cultivate self-esteem</u>

First of all, we highly recommend that you work more on yourself than on trying to save him. So, he tries to base your self-worth on you and not on your relationship.

At this point, you may think and say: "but how can I do such a thing if I'm a romantic person?"

It is the main difficulty that many women (but also men) encounter, but it is absolutely necessary to look at the relationship from another perspective beyond the romantic one.

Give up having his esteem

The second thing to do to defend yourself from the pathological narcissist is not to wait for the moment when you can please him. Because of his personality disorder, the narcissist sees you and will always see you as inferior to him. This means that often you will not feel worthy of him and that you will almost never feel that you are in his esteem.
This is the mechanism that will lead you to be dominated by your story. You will do everything to win his esteem and, when you manage to get it, you will have the feeling of walking 3 meters off the ground for happiness. In fact, in the long run, you will lose it again and find yourself having to work hard to get it again.

Indulge his narcissism

The third point of defense is to smile and nod if you want to continue this relationship and if you really care about him. Even if it goes against your person, treating a narcissist badly means reopening the narcissistic wound in him, and at that point he will make you pay in any way, taking the part of the offended narcissist.

If every strategy you've tried to implement fails to resolve the situation or make you happier in the relationship, then you should think about leaving him.

Now let's explain what are do for leaving a narcissist without any kind of dangerous (or tragic) consequences.

Try to mortify him

We have reached a crucial moment, where you can put your escape plan into action
To know how to mortify a narcissist and escape from this subject, you will have to take action toward him, especially now that you better understand how his psyche works.
Considering that a narcissist is a person who lives by the reflection of others, now, if you really want to hurt him, in this case, you should first of all, no longer respond to his needs.

So, think of yourself and make yourself desired

First, make yourself as beautiful as you can, like wearing some clothes you know he likes. Learn to make yourself desired: if you know him well you know how to do it. Now that you have increased your desire for him, all you have to do to take revenge on him is to refuse him, refuse his kiss, refuse a caress from him or an invitation from him.

Indifference

If you don't want to go directly to rejection, you need to know that treating a narcissist with indifference is one of the few ways to really make him suffer. Using the weapon of silence to deal with a narcissist is an extremely smart move: not responding to his provocations, not expressing interest in his speeches and his protests could literally tear him apart.

But the best do's is always the same: silence

Our duty, however, at this point is to warn you that the best way is not revenge, but if you really have to put him to the test or want to repay the suffering, he has caused you, rejection and silence are the best tactics.

And finally: ask for some help

Are you starting to realize that you are trapped inside a suffocating relationship? Do not hesitate to ask relatives, or friends for help. In some cases, the intervention of a psychotherapist could be useful to become aware of the dysfunctional dynamics that we are facing and to get out of them to find a personal balance. To leave a narcissist you must have considerable inner strength, the same that will allow you to destroy the narcissist who made you suffer. To build and maintain that inner strength you need to work on your self-confidence, hoping your relationship with him hasn't damaged it too much.

Can't find inner strength on your own? Do you need help? So, one of the ways to leave a pathological narcissist is to ask for psychological help. Unfortunately, many of the women stuck in a relationship with a narcissist find it very difficult to free themselves.

Even when they try to leave him, they then find themselves dealing with long-suffering and with a very low level of self-esteem, as they are convinced that the failure of the relationship is to be attributed exclusively to those who were not good enough to deal with the narcissist and heal him of his traumas.

With the help of a psychologist, all this emotional work will be much easier! The psychologist will focus on boosting your self-esteem and building useful and viable escape routes that will take you out of your relationship with the narcissist.

Don'ts in a toxic relationship

Now that we have explained what to do in a toxic relationship, now we will show you what is better not to do to protect your safety. We are still talking about a toxic relationship.

Don't let it get to the point where it sucks all your vital energies

The narcissist is an emotional vampire and feeds on the need for love, the fear of loneliness, the need for contact, and the crazy idea of being the only one who gives value to the life of his victim. He puts himself on the podium every time the victim shows him her abnegation and does everything to save him, not realizing that he is just a pawn in a perverse game from which he will always come out suffering. He or she will try in every way to approach the victim until the latter has undertaken the liberation process, definitively moving away from him/her.

Avoid becoming completely addicted

The key step to avoid becoming completely addicted and creating a virtually irreparable situation is to cut off all contact.
If you have already reached the point of understanding that you are dealing with a person who can only harm you, you have already taken a big step forward. You will have to do it, despite the inevitable initial difficulties because at the basis of the relationship, there is a strong emotional dependence that characterizes the victim and allows the narcissist to manipulate her. The healing journey goes through the understanding that we are the only ones who can define and give flight to our existence, and we have no need for this to happen through someone else. If you don't focus on your need for healing, if you imagine it can save a narcissist, if you believe that " deep down " he loves you, you will never get rid of him! The transition from emotional dependence to emotional autonomy takes place exclusively when you start to focus on yourself and no longer on the reactions of the narcissist.

Never think you can change him or her

The narcissist may come back but not change. He will never change, despite the thousand promises. As he has not kept them until now, he will not in the future. As

he has treated you badly until now, he will continue to do so. The situation will only get worse. The clichés of the genre "he needs to find the right one", and "maybe with a good girl he will change and settle his head" are unfounded and far from reality in the case of a narcissistic subject. It's done like this, and it won't change unless you want it and assiduously follow a long and profound psychotherapeutic journey. Then maybe it will change. Furthermore, a thorough investigation of the needs that brought you into the sick relationship is necessary. Often, in fact, due to a great lack of affection and closeness suffered in the past, they seek great outbursts of love.
Basically, love bombing. Art of which the narcissist is a master. All these elements are presuppositions of a sick love. So, it should be really essential to take them into consideration.

Never justify the narcissist

Understand and accept that the person you loved doesn't exist and stop deluding yourself that it will go back to the way it was before or that it will change.
Understanding that a narcissist is a person affected by serious psychopathology, who will not recover except with the help of professionals, who is an adults capable of understanding and therefore aware of the harm he brings to others. But he chooses to stay the way he is and live this way. He's fine with that. So, he shouldn't be justified.

Avoid blaming yourself

Reflecting on having been exploited and humiliated can be painful for someone who is a victim of a narcissist. When it comes to ending this relationship, many victims may also feel guilty. They are unable to accept that they somehow have a co-responsibility for what they have lived. But co-responsibility is upstream. It makes no sense for you to mourn over spilled milk and dwell too much on what has been done. It just happened! Don't blame yourself too much and just try to avoid it in the future. Here it is necessary to self-reflect instead on the choice of the partner itself. In the mechanisms that first attracted and then ensnared them. In dysfunctional attachment models. You need to approach these topics in stages and make sure they are well received.

No stalking

Avoid stalking in a desperate search for clarifications: the narcissist will continue to deny himself, lie and criticize, furthermore, you may risk being sued.

No anger

Avoid expressing anger consistent with the mistreatment through insults: they constitute narcissistic feed, and the narcissist will use them to ridicule you and manipulate others into believing that you are crazy.

If you have decided to leave him, avoid any contact

Having no contact (and the concept will be explored later in the book) means having no expectations of changing him, not believing that your love can make him different, and not reacting to his provocations and requests. Don't invest energy in any form and don't accept his proposals that have the sole purpose of manipulating you as he pleases. To stop him you have to change your phone number, email and any kind of reference that can put him in contact with you. If it can't be so radical because you have children in common, for example, limit contacts to a minimum, always regulating them with the support of a judge and a court. This caution is essential to create an insurmountable barrier around your life and ensure that the narcissist cannot reach you. If you are forced to have contact with a narcissist, make sure it is short and limited to the topic of your meeting, use simple, short sentences, and do not show emotions. If the narcissist tries to hook you up with taunts or seduction, immediately end the conversation and walk away. Don't forget that by nature he loves to have even sporadic contact with the victims of his past from whom he can receive support and satisfaction.

These just mentioned are all the things you must not do if you have found yourself in a toxic relationship. In the next chapter, however, we will show you 5 fundamental steps to able to emerge unscathed and happy from a toxic relationship with a narcissist.

Chapter 10: The 5 steps to get away from your toxic partner (practical methods)

This tenth chapter is another practical one that will show you the right path, in practice, to finally be able to emerge free from your toxic relationship. In fact, these are 5 basic steps that will help you free yourself from a toxic partner who is tormenting you.

Some general defense strategies

Before talking about the 5 basic steps to free yourself from the narcissistic partner and its manipulation, let's talk about some general defense strategies. We now know that the codependency factor also depends on the relationship with the narcissistic person who manipulates, but above all on the fact that there is a victim who agrees to all of this. The important thing is, do not to accuse a possible victim, but neither self-accuse yourself if you realize that you have been manipulated and used. It is not by blaming yourself that the narcissist will stop his bad deeds. It would be much more useful, however, to apply some general defensive strategy and then, subsequently, the 5 fundamental steps.
Among these general defensive strategies from your narcissistic partner, we have:

1. As a first strategy, before starting any path of healing from a dysfunctional relationship, it is necessary to admit that you have a problem: that is, to admit that the relationship you are experiencing - although it is with the person you desired so much - is a dysfunctional relationship that makes you suffer and mortifies. If you don't clearly realize this reality, any other step risks being in vain if not counterproductive. It is also necessary to face and know the possible psychological reasons that have led to living a relationship that has become toxic or dangerous: for example, the tendency to depend on the other, low self-esteem, the continuous search for approval, a sense of inadequacy, the need to fill a void deep emotionality, tendency to cancel oneself in the relationship, etc.
2. Another really important thing to know as a general strategy is the psychological basis of a correct self-analysis, to understand what prompted us to choose that type of partner, but it is even more important to learn not to give your trust to the first one who passes by. Rather than being immediately driven by the illusion of the perfect partner and trusting, we increase the dose of trust, and when we do it, we must always grant it in minimal doses. This, rather than a defensive

strategy, is a preventive strategy, but one that requires careful work on ourselves. The narcissistic partner always takes advantage of the weaknesses of the chosen victim: the less we tell someone about ourselves, the fewer vulnerabilities that are bread for a narcissist's teeth will emerge. Even trust, in the future, always go very sparingly and you will avoid being manipulated and used by some narcissist.

3. Another strategy, immediately connected to the self-analysis above is Self-awareness: it is an inner journey, full of facets that leads us to reflect, to accept our mistakes and failures, but also to recognize our successes and create a greater climate of self-confidence. Greater awareness and security, in fact, helps us keep toxic people away, such as malignant narcissists.

4. Also, the so-called introspection (connected to a path of self-awareness) can prove useful in order to discover a narcissist. It is simply a matter of listening to your internal states and your instincts: if you are perceiving that something is not right, question yourself and give yourself the most objective answers possible. If you understand that you have suffered abuse or the simple signs indicated several times in the previous parts of the guide, then you are at the mercy of a narcissist.

5. The next step as a general strategy is contemplation. At this stage, it is important to observe the situation carefully and not just think about how to solve it. In toxic relationships, thinking about a solution becomes extremely difficult due to the presence of psychological factors different from those present in healthy relationships, the presence of dependence on the partner or other addictions and a thousand other difficulties which, if faced only with rational and logical thinking, lead always to the same conclusion: the feeling of being in a labyrinth from which it seems impossible to get out. Contemplation is instead a different attitude, calmer and more profound, which involves bringing attention inwards to one's own bodily sensations, to one's emotional state, and to the observation of situations that always cause the same automatic reactions in the couple. Contemplation goes beyond simple thinking and uses the knowledge and wisdom of the body, experience, and the sense of connection with the universe, to be able to move in the best direction. It helps to understand your values with increasing clarity, to distinguish what you really need from what is toxic and harmful and which distances us from our values and our integrity. Contemplation helps reduce the ambiguity and confusion typical of dysfunctional relationships, helping us find the right path with courage, commitment, and grace.

6. Another general strategy for defending yourself from the narcissistic partner is to acquire the ability to see things from a different perspective and try to see the situation as an outsider would see it. The different perspectives will prove to be very useful in strengthening self-awareness, further stimulating the critical and lucid analysis of a situation.

7. Finally, to avoid being victims of narcissism in the future (and this discussion will be explored in the following chapters), it is important to try to follow a path of inner balance. For a self-confident balanced person, who is aware and feels good about himself, it is much more difficult to incur such obvious reliefs as to be used as bait for a narcissist, as the person is much more confident and thinks about making thoughtful decisions, and avoid dubious attitudes and people. Therefore, work on your personal growth, perhaps with a coach or through a course, and you will see that you can implement different strategies to avoid a narcissist.

5 important steps to get away from the narcissist

Now let's see what the 5 fundamental steps can be to be able to escape from your toxic partner.
Accept reality
The first step is to admit that you have problems, for many perhaps the hardest part. We have to come to terms with the past, take note of a failure, and face guilt and related emotions, but it is a forced and necessary step.

1. <u>**Gather energy and avoid traps**</u>

Before you muster any energy needed to end the narcissist permanently you must be aware of the vacuum cleaner effect.
When the pathological narcissist feels that the relationship is about to crack, he will try in every way to suck you back in, even becoming a stalker (continuous messages on the answering machine, e-mails but also messages to friends and relatives.) The narcissist, in these situations, will promise you to change, stating that he will make an effort to make things go better but, even in this case, he will hardly apologize or if he does, they will never be deeply felt. Remember that a person with narcissistic personality disorder hardly changes and, once they get back together, will end up repeating the same dynamics and, sometimes, faced with a new crisis, could react even more violently than in the last episode of conflict.
The next step is to recall all possible resources in view of a long journey. Never underestimate this art because you risk starting without the right motivation as if you hadn't trained enough for a marathon, running out of breath halfway through.

2. <u>**Develop an action plan**</u>

The second step involves preparation and organization. At this stage, it is necessary to develop a sort of "action plan" to close the relationship. When you are in a toxic relationship, your energies are so low and compromised that it is even difficult to organize the weekend... but it is very important to think about the necessary steps you will have to take to end the relationship. Getting rid of the wrong partner is not easy because many aspects must be considered: psychological, physical, practical, and even legal, all in order to favor a transition that is as quick and safe as possible. We must never forget that similar situations can in fact precipitate and result in episodes of violence or stalking. In fact, at the moment of the actual breakage, it is necessary to proceed by implementing the appropriate precautions for the case. But remember something very important as well: when you are in a relationship characterized by abuse and mistreatment, seek help from a domestic violence center. You should also call the police if you fear for your safety. Indeed, particular attention should be paid to those relationships in which physical violence is present: in this case, predicting the partner's moves and her reactions is essential to act safely. Preparing, therefore, means considering all the possible difficulties to be faced and ways to deal with them: start contacting professionals who can be of help such as lawyers, financial advisors, social workers, and psychologists and possibly notify the police if a violent reaction is feared from the partner. It is necessary to find a place for oneself and any children or pets that are part of the family (violent men often attack pets and it is, therefore, good to think about saving them too). You need to reflect on your priorities to be clear about the things you have to keep and those you can give up: work, car or home, finish your studies, protect your children and animals, take care of your health if you are taking important pharmacological therapies (diabetes, chemotherapy, degenerative diseases...), etc. Subsequently, you have to imagine all the possible scenarios - including the worst - that could occur to your decision to end the relationship permanently: physical violence, control and theft of money, destruction of common goods, threats and stalking, involvement of third parties, public, suicide attempts or threats to harm themselves or others, etc. Imagining these scenarios must help you find - immediately afterward - a way to deal with them so that if they should occur or if you should fear their appearance, you already have a solution ready to deal with them.

3. **Action**

At this point, it is a question of putting into practice what has been prepared and closing the relationship. It is very important at what point you really want to end the relationship, having considered the pros and cons and any psychological resistances present. American author Amber Ault suggests the following questions: "Am I really ready?", "If my ex comes back crying and despairing, making promises to change and affirming his love for me, will I be able to stand firm in my decision?". In the case of a relationship based on breakup/reconciliation cycles, ask yourself if everything possible has been done to prevent relapses and ensure that this time the decision to close is final: "Have I foreseen how to do to avoid the temptation to backtrack? ". "Have I planned everything necessary for my own safety, that of any children, other family members and pets?"

Have I foreseen the most dangerous behaviors that the partner can engage in?"

Sometimes it is possible to communicate the decision to the partner, sometimes it is necessary simply to leave when he is absent, to avoid violence or dangerous scenes. In healthy romantic relationships, it is preferable and respectful to communicate the decision to end the relationship face-to-face. But in toxic relationships, to avoid aggression or dangerous behavior, it is better to choose other ways: telephone, email, letter or face-to-face in a safe place among other people.

Here are some recommendations on the content and method of communication:

- Simple and clear message. Briefly explain the reasoning for your decision. For example: "I have been unhappy in this relationship for a long time, and I realized that I don't want to continue like this. I decided to separate/leave / end the relationship / never see each other again ".

- Don't justify yourself or give too many explanations: you are not doing couples therapy but only communicating your decision. Everything you say in this stage will likely be manipulated to change your mind, misrepresented, or used against you; therefore, it is better to speak as little as possible and limit yourself to repeating the fundamental concept of the message.

- Avoid blaming your partner. In communicating, even if the other has behaved badly, teased, betrayed, or mistreated you, you need to start from your center. Preferably say: "I am unhappy" instead of: "you make me unhappy", prefer: "I feel little respected or not considered", instead of saying: "you don't respect me". This way you will feel stronger and more centered, and you will not open the door to manipulation or denial of reality ("it's not true I love you, I respect you, I haven't betrayed you" etc...). Resist the temptation to start a discussion about the why of your decision and its faults. It would only lead you to lose energy and question your decision, perhaps for the umpteenth time!

4. Keep as little contact as possible

When you decide to end a relationship with a narcissistic person, it is important to maintain a firm and coherent attitude right away, interrupting all forms of contact, and blocking emails and telephone numbers. Responding to even just one of the messages would mean giving the narcissistic person the opportunity to incorporate you again.

No contact means no longer having contact with someone who only hurts you. But it can also mean reducing it to the essential minimum in cases where completely interrupting all contact is not possible, for example when there are children in common.

An aspect that I often find is instead a tendency against putting the right distance. That is, stubbornly believing that we must see each other to talk, and at all costs lead the other to understand our reasons and his mistakes. If it is not strictly necessary (e.g., the presence of children or common property) it is better to completely cut ties, and no phone calls, messages, or emails. Narcissistic individuals know how to use any means to deceive and persuade, with the aim of rebuilding the bond. About no contact (explained in a deep way) we will deal with this in the next paragraph.

5. <u>**Metabolize the breakup**</u>

We have already seen that a codependent relationship develops between the narcissist and the victim. Both basically need each other. The narcissistic part needs to control and become the puppeteer who pulls the strings of his own show.

The insecure part of having someone close to protect him and give him validation at any cost. And therefore, although controlling, better together with someone rather than alone.

Well, yes, they both meet because they need each other in some way. Indeed, the narcissist would not have a long and easy life with another more independent personality.

The dependent on his part would be forced to try to be less dependent if he entered into a relationship with a less controlling personality.

And the game only lasts until both decide to continue playing. This tells us how much even the insecure and dependent party (recognized as the presumed victim) actually has their own responsibility for repeating this game.

In fact, accepting everything puts the other in a position to continue doing what he does. And the continuous blows delivered by the other party put the insecure and dependent party in a position to lose more and more strength, independence and self-esteem. So much so that you can't think of being anywhere else but there, despite the unspeakable suffering.

But, remember to forgive for locking the story into the past. If you want to pigeonhole the relationship you have experienced in the past, to prevent it from invading your present, try to forgive the ex-partner's shortcomings. Start feeling compassion for them, which doesn't mean allowing them to make you used or mistreated, but thinking that behind all the security that narcissists show, there is a serious relational deficit and an emotional immaturity that drives them to constantly seek the approval of others. Also, remember that narcissists are unable to empathize and understand unconditional love, everything they do serves them to fill the sense of emptiness and inadequacy they feel. After the clean-cut, you need to leave the wound time to heal, take care of yourself, listen to your emotions, asking for help from friends, family or a therapist if necessary. Never be tempted to come back again: often we tell ourselves that it may be useful to try them all, and any excuse is good to see him for this purpose so that he changes. In short, we begin a mission to the last breath, with the aim of trying to redeem the other and make the relationship work. When will you understand that there is nothing more harmful? The only real revenge is not to try to make him understand, or to try to change him, but to walk away and take back one's life. The other will never understand it and certainly won't change because you want it. Your task is not to change someone but to face reality.

So, you delude yourself and only give this character the opportunity to find new cartridges to use against you. And you will consequently continue to experience very strong and very painful emotional peaks.

The importance of no contact

One point that we really feel is of ultimate importance when it comes to freeing yourself from your narcissistic (and therefore toxic) partner is the concept or technique of no contact.

The only thing you should know is that the best way to defend yourself from a narcissistic manipulator is to avoid him and not have any contact with him/her. A narcissist cannot easily separate themselves from their extension. You will probably need to end all contact to avoid getting drawn into a toxic relationship.

All you have to do essentially is to consider cutting off all communication. This is the so-called zero contact method. To do this, it is necessary to cease all types of communication with the other person, first of all, one must no longer meet and see each other. But also stop exchanging phone calls, messages, emails, and interactions on social networks.

No Contact works and is the only real way to put an end to the game and get out of the spiral of ambivalence in which we find ourselves.

Practicing No Contact allows you to detoxify and ensure that a completely haywire system can slowly recover its normality. Moving away from ambivalence helps to refocus and get back on track. How long should no contact last? The time is necessary to detoxify, and it is not possible to establish a priori timing as it is very subjective. But certainly, when the healing process is taking root and is well advanced, we realize it, and you feel it.

Whenever you have contact with a narcissist, you feel incredibly fragile and susceptible, this is because the narcissist knows your weaknesses and frailties and abuses them in every way. When you wear yourself out and you struggle to understand his behavior, all you do is fall into his trap, he is aware that you are suffering and you need to talk and understand, so he leverages your need, torments you and humiliates you to ensnare you. As long as you have the presumption to establish contact with the narcissist, to make him understand that his actions hurt you, to hope that he will change, you will always come out hurt and a loser because his game is precisely to torment the victim and to establish a dependent relationship with her. He sees you as an object of his property and nothing more, doesn't delude yourself that deep inside he can love you because the narcissist uses the other exclusively to feed himself. The only step to save yourself is to learn to love yourself and take care of your needs by cutting off all contact with the narcissist. Non-contact means not responding to his text messages, emails, and phone calls, not checking his Facebook page, his Whatsapp status and not talking about him with people in common. Remember that the narcissist abuses you because he doesn't respect your requests and prohibitions.

But no contact does not only mean closing all direct relationships with the narcissist, but also indirect ones. This involves throwing away presents and deleting photos, blocking possible numbers of other co and social network profiles, as well as mutual friends and family. Avoid places frequented by the narcissist. The No Contact must be above all mental so stop talking about it and thinking about the narcissist. This is the only way to protect yourself, detoxify and purify yourself from the poison of narcissist. When no contact is not possible (perhaps because there are children), adopt the "detached contact", i.e., use the awareness of what happened in order not to get caught up in relational patterns and dysfunctional beliefs.

If you happen to meet the narcissist or close family or friends casually, act naturally, say hello, or ignore and walk away. Physically and mentally. Stay centered on yourself and your personal and social sphere. If you casually meet acquaintances, colleagues, or relatives of the narcissist, avoid talking about the narcissist, behave in a natural way and remain yourself so as not to allow the narcissist to exercise control even at a distance, in space and time.

Seeking or accepting contact with the narcissist after having shown up what really he is to be harming himself by acting like an addict who needs and takes a dose of poison knowing it is harmful.

No contact: what it is not

No contact is not a way to win back your loved one, no contact is not a way to get them back!

No contact works, but on condition that it is used in a functional way. That is, like a healthy moment, a healthy space for oneself, to rediscover forgotten normality, and get away from the clutches of the perverse game repeated for too long.

No contact is therefore absolutely not a way to "blackmail", it makes one feel missed, to punish, so that the other understands and therefore changes his mind as a consequence.

If we think of using no contact for this purpose, we are unfortunately off track and will only continue to hurt ourselves.

No contact rules

Practicing No Contact means not calling, not writing, not talking to each other even if you meet them and try to tell us something, whether it is pleasant or negative. It means not responding to any attempt by the other to get in touch, or to provoke us, whether written or verbal and to limit it to the minimum where he really serves.

Remaining in these cases only and exclusively in the topics of interest, for example, what concerns a child. This is one of the most difficult concepts for a person who is experiencing a sick love to pass, but the only real solution strategy that allows you to return to normal little by little.

Often the person thinks he is being bad by putting in place such closure. He thinks he can't do it, and some literally run away. And they soon return to their own expense in the harmful circuit of unhealthy love, in order not to leave their comfort zone.

A serious and well-prepared professional on this subject will be able to accompany you in the construction of this path. A path certainly not free from suffering, nor without impasse, but aimed at recovering oneself, at finally finding oneself. Keep in mind that it will not be easy but possible.

But as I always say, you need to really and firmly want it. Only those who really want it will be willing to do what it takes. No one can act as your jailer and prevent you from hurting yourself, only you and your real desire to heal can come to your aid and allow you to recover your dignity. All this together with the tools that a professional can provide, and it is possible to build together a little at a time.

The difference between no contact and ghosting

We really want to specify that this distancing (so, no contact) is very different from that attitude and phenomenon are well known as "ghosting". In fact, the no-contact technique is implemented following a breakup or, in any case, a separation agreed upon at the couple's level. It may happen that one of the two partners does not agree on this detachment, but has in any case been informed of the other's need to eliminate all forms of contact for some time.

On the other hand, ghosting is an increasingly widespread "method", which always works to sever relations with a person, but which consists in disappearing into thin air. All of this occurs in a situation that is not necessarily a crisis in the relationship and without one of the two partners having decision-making power. A person who is a victim of ghosting sees the other disappear completely from their life, without being able to contact them and without any explanation. A petty technique such as ghosting, in fact, is usually applied, as we have seen previously, by the narcissistic person determined to temporarily get rid of his victim in order to be able to find narcissistic replenishment elsewhere, to then return to seek it in the codependent from whom he has decided to disappear.

In this part of the guide, we have shown you the practical steps to take to get rid of your toxic partner. In case you follow them, we will continue to guide you precisely through the transition phase of this process in the next chapter.

Chapter 11: How to manage your psychological side during the transition

Here we are at the part of the book where aware that you are in a toxic relationship, you have decided to (rightly) get out of it! But what about the psychological aspect? You have to be very careful in this phase precisely because it is the one in which you will feel most vulnerable and prone to mistakes. But we are here to help you again!

Now it's over: what can I do?

There are numerous reasons why you could end up in a toxic relationship. Dealing with a breakup, even one with a person who has hurt you, can be really dramatic. A real mourning, must still be faced like the end of any other relationship. It can seem overwhelming to break free from a toxic relationship. Toxic relationships can be addictive, destructive, and incredibly painful, and can lead to a full-blown cycle of intimate partner violence. What's worse is that, once inside, it seems impossible to tear yourself away.

Most part of the time, toxicity builds and blinds you and when you realize it, maybe it's too late. Experiencing toxic love can negatively affect your psychology. You can doubt yourself, convince yourself that you deserve it, and feel guilty about yourself or your partner. Engaging in this self-talk can be a slippery slope that continues to negatively affect your mental health.

At this stage, you also need to accept the fact that understand and accept that the person you loved doesn't exist and stop deluding yourself that it will go back to the way it was before or that it will change. And that can really hurt! in this case, the only way to overcome this breaking stage is to seek help. Whether it's affection or professional help, what you have to do is look for someone to guide you in everything and for everything to overcome this really delicate moment.

Share and ask for support from groups of people who have experienced the same experience and can understand what the target is going through. Sometimes family and friends do not fully understand or incorporate into the error of guiding the victim or minimizing the forms of psychological and emotional violence suffered.

Once the "mourning" and the "trauma" elaborated, the narcissist's victim will live a fuller life, love more, it will be more aware of himself and what she wants from their life and relationships, it will be able to smell quickly, will be able to protect himself with determination and believe in himself.

The healing from psychological abuse according to the US psychotherapist Shannon Thomas, must go through five phases:

- ✓ Despair
- ✓ Educate
- ✓ Awakening
- ✓ The stakes
- ✓ Restoration
- ✓ Maintenance

After having overcome this phase, then there are three things you can do to get better during the transition phase:

1. Accepting that real apology will never come because the narcissist is incapable of empathy and remorse. Because? How is it possible? It accepts that it is so and enough even without understanding the reasons.
2. Don't worry about slander, the narcissist has been able to create the reputation of a good person, but he also knew how to make himself burnt around. People who know how to think autonomously because they have critical sense, will not give credit to his words.
3. Probably the victim will never know because it is in "no contact" but the narcissist collects what sows, like everyone else, will not be able to always get away with it and will be reddish knowing that he has not been able to destroy the target on which he no longer has some power. And if you realize this, if you are happy, you will have rescued yourself doubly: from the traumatic past and a possible future return. Narcissist people never come back from those who have unmasked them, they could no longer play and are afraid.

As for the objectives you need to bring at the end of a toxic relationship and in the transition phase, these could be:

- ✓ Restore your mental, physical, and emotional health and learn how to keep you in balance and in relation.
- ✓ Learn to see the positive in all the experiences that happen to you and change the future vision for yourself and in relationships.
- ✓ Explore parts of you that you did not know you have and developed a new version of yourself and attract a different partner and a healthy relationship.

- ✓ Keeping your heart open without allowing a past painful experience, prevents you from experimenting with a potentially healthy new relationship and risking falling in love with you again.

In essence, what we want to make you understand is that overcoming the end of a toxic relationship is not simple, above all because a dynamic of co-addiction has often been established among the partners. It is already enough that you made the courageous decision to move away alone, but now you feel suck. But this pain becomes your great opportunity. You should repeat to yourself this: "Even if at this moment I can't see the positive, I am sure that there is and that I will soon see it. All this is happening for me, not against me. I am loved, guided, and supported at all times ". This I just shared has become my mantra at any time of difficulty. And I assure you it works. Enter in the perspective you let something go that you never needed, and you are heading towards something much more beautiful and healthier.

Regardless of how much the relationship lasts, recovering takes time, patience, love, courage, and a good support network.

Even if you seem to live a nightmare and you are destroyed emotionally and physically, it only recalls that you will exceed this difficult moment, even if you don't think it possible. Over time when everything has passed and elaborated and you will look back, you will be smiling for all the splendid work you did on yourself.

Tips for the transition phase

However, if you have found the strength to put an end to your toxic history, in addition to asking a specialist for help, it is essential to implement a series of behaviors that do not make you fall back into the relationship. Below, to help you, you will find some useful tips to deal with this delicate transition phase:

<u>Recognize what happened and what role you played during the relationship</u>

When you just got out of a toxic relationship, you will most likely cross the negation phase. It is like developing mourning. "If I had done something different maybe he would have worked ... it was all my fault for how he treated me ...". These thoughts depend on the style of attachment and your inner child, they are natural thoughts to have, but they are also dangerous because they can lead you back to research your ex or depression. Recognize the dynamics in the relationship with it and if you need to help a coach or a therapist especially if you have an insecure attachment style.

Improvisation

Consider the possibility that there is something you could not predict about your partner's possible reactions or unforeseen complications. Be ready to "predict the unpredictable".

Always the dear no contact

We have already examined no contact and its proving to be useful even when you want to remove a person from your life, without any desire to win them back. In this case, it is implemented by those who have chosen to end a relationship, especially if the ex is still too morbid and does not seem to want to respect any of the decisions made at the time of separation.

In the transition phase, it is really important to continue on this line. You have done absolutely nothing wrong: on the contrary!

In this context, your ex-partner has been informed of the intention to end the relationship, but he continues to want to reconnect. But you are in the presence of a narcissistic person who has been used to a series of attentions for the entire duration of the relationship and who, now, finds himself with no one left at his disposal. Similarly, no contact proves to be effective in getting away from toxic contexts or in which one has been a victim of emotional addiction. And in the context of transition, you have to heal from this. The narcissist is the best way to permanently end a toxic relationship. It is a difficult suggestion to grasp and put into practice for a series of sentimental, sometimes moral reasons... but in many cases, it represents the choice of choice. You will find a lot of information on the narcissist technique on the net. The low contact indicates the minimum contact. Preferable in cases where it is necessary to maintain a relationship: presence of children, work in common, assets in common or anything else that requires shared management.

Self-esteem

The detachment from a toxic partner passes from the abatement of fear, especially toward the consequences that this choice can generate. The uncertainty that can be read in the future tends to deform the contours of a destiny that is a harbinger of new possibilities that can instead be opened up with a change of life. In this phase, the constant support of family and friends is crucial, and feeling the closeness of loved ones helps to overcome many anxieties, including suffering and the initial sense of bewilderment that the end of a relationship entails. If necessary, the presence of a specialist can also help in this phase. Loving each other and choosing each other first gives strength to this choice, giving self-esteem useful for managing the aftermath of a relationship whose continuity of dialogue could cause further damage: by clearly cutting ties, for example, one avoids expiring in uncomfortable discussions. Focusing on different activities and projects and surrounding yourself with positive people are excellent ways to cultivate self-love when self-confidence has been heavily compromised. For this reason, it is essential to dedicate time.

Release your anger

It's natural to feel anger after ending a relationship with a narcissist. You expected someone who was kind and loving to be around you when, in reality, they were indifferent to your needs and desires. Anger is an important element in the recovery process. So, acknowledge your anger. Reflect on the gestures and behaviors that triggered this feeling. Then find ways to download it in a sane way. You can cry, confide in a friend, or play sports.

Detox

Even if you choose to end the relationship, you don't come out of a toxic relationship unscathed: it's as if you really need to detox. It can be of great help to identify self-care activities and not only makes us feel better, and that gives us satisfaction. Practicing relaxation techniques can be of great help during the detox phase, where one must deliberately avoid any negative vibrations. Therefore, to rediscover the energies that lead to psychic relaxation before physical relaxation, muscle tension must be reduced.

See a therapist

It is important to talk to a therapist so that the same relationship patterns are not repeated in the future. Also, you need to try to manage your emotions in a healthy way. You must not neglect your personal needs. If you've been viewed as a narcissistic extension, especially over a long period of time, you've probably forgotten everything you want and need out of life. The intervention of a neutral party can help you not to overlook these aspects. Try asking your doctor which mental health professional you can go to. If you study at a university, your university may offer a psychological counseling service for students.

Contact your support group

Not only a therapist, but a support group can really also help you in this transition phase. It would be better to do it before leaving him or her, so as not to find yourself too much in the void, but if the decision is made you have all the time to do it. Your friends and family can help you right now, but keep in mind that they can't do your job. Dedicate only a part of your time to others and consider that they may not understand you. Surrounded only by people who really have shown to accept you and love you as you are. If it is not your case rather than receiving greater disagreement and being worse, you can subscribe to some online communities or search for groups in your country.

Don't think you'll be alone forever

To overcome the end of a toxic relationship it is essential to "dethrone" your former partner. Your mind was convinced that it was "wonderful" and the less we have something more we want it. It is the functioning of the mind. But try to focus a moment on the aspects you didn't like. Was it really so perfect? Realize that he is not the only man on earth. Even if you now seem to have lost George Clooney, try to understand that the sea is full of fish, and probably less abated than what you eat so far.

Do not regret the past

If it had to go differently, it would have gone differently. Give a positive meaning to your experience so that it can be recorded not as something traumatic. For example, observe that it helped you better understand how to recognize red flags, how to establish healthy borders, connected you to your inner child. Past is teaching you how to elaborate your emotions and what false beliefs have secretly guided you. It brought you closer to people who probably had forgotten to stay behind your partner and also made you develop resilience. In short, identifies all the positive aspects of the experience. This combined with emotional work will guarantee you are open to a healthier love.

Make your physical health, emotional and mental health

This is the time to be selfish and find love for yourself. Practice body care, make your home a welcoming place, keep a diary of emotions, objectives and daily thoughts and eat healthily. Try to create a daily routine that increases dopamine and serotonin levels in your body. At the end of a toxic relationship, these two substances are at low levels and the brain thinks that only the presence of the partner can continue to produce them. Teaches your mind that this is not the case. Practice yoga, dance, or painting. Coloring mandalas can also help you. Do things you like and make you happy, slowly they will acquire more and more value. Make sessions of Reiki or massages to rebalance the energy. Become your priority.

Healing

At this stage you have to dedicate yourself to understanding, forgiving and healing the deep reasons that led you to have a destructive relationship. If you are facing some troubles with depression, panic attacks, other major psychological problems, or behavioral or substance addictions, you only need to treat and heal these first. At this stage, it is necessary to seek the help of a professional or self-help and awareness groups. Dedicate yourself to family and friends, to your favorite activities, to taking care of your physical, mental, and spiritual health with activities such as meditation, yoga, hiking, creative activities such as painting or pottery… whatever helps you gradually get in touch with yourself and to make you.

Surround yourself with positivity

The fact of learning about self-gratify is really essential so, surround yourself with the right people too. Spend time with those who make you feel good, whether it's indulging in your favorite meal or doing whatever makes you happy. Going through a difficult time in a relationship can cause incalculable stress, it's important to remember that all emotions are useful, and we cannot eliminate them.

Stand firm in the decision

Forgetting a toxic love is tiring. After leaving someone, it's quite natural you start to miss them. This is normal. It's easy for our brains to remember the good times and forget the bad parts of a relationship. To your eyes, it may seem so tempting for the narcissist to come back into your life but remember that you came to this decision after a long and thoughtful process. Stand your ground and remember that she was made to make you and your life better.

Forgiving yourself after a toxic relationship

The experience of emotional abuse can be traumatic. It becomes very important to go through a personal path of awareness, to get out of the role of victim, recognize one's responsibilities, heal one's wounds and finally become protagonist and free to choose who to be and who to love.
Healing from a toxic relationship also means forgiving yourself. Be kind to yourself but don't become a victim of what happened to you.
You are allowed to be angry. You are allowed to have mixed emotions about the end of this relationship. But the only thing you need to recognize is which emotions are serving you and which ones are keeping you stuck. So many people have been in

toxic love relationships, just like you, and have learned to forgive themselves and come back stronger than ever.

Your self-esteem has probably taken a hit and recovering from a toxic relationship will take time, so surround yourself with people you trust. There will be many good days and some bad days, but that's okay. Bearing in mind that what has possibly been taken away from us (serenity, self-esteem, confidence in ourselves and in others) is still within us, just a little hidden and currently not accessible. And that it's never too late to move on: but sometimes it's not easy and you need support.

With these tips, we have finished our advice to better face the transition phase at the end of a toxic relationship. Now that your guardianship process has begun, we will show you, in the last part of the guide, how to move forward, forget your toxic relationship and avoid falling back into the trap of the narcissist.

FIFTH PART: HOW TO MOVE ON AND BE HAPPY AGAIN

Chapter 12: What you need to do to avoid falling into this trap again (practical methods)

Our main goal, as well as making you recognize a possible narcissistic partner and move away from him, is precisely to make your life better, and therefore make you happy again. And by this, we mean both making you live a possible new relationship peacefully and avoiding making you "fall back" into a toxic story. In this chapter, we will take care to provide you with some useful and practical advice to ensure that you no longer fall into the trap of possible other narcissists.

First things first: what not to do to prevent your current toxic partner from coming back

How is it said? Sometimes they come back. Well yes, the return of the narcissist is a great classic. Before we get into the specifics of avoidance, manipulators, narcissists, and any high-potential toxic partners, here are some helpful tips to get rid of your current toxic ex-partner for good. Because unfortunately, he will come back: you have been the narcissistic extension of him for a long time and, given the time (a lot) spent in a codependent relationship, he will still need his narcissistic supply.

Especially when we manage to cut in time (but also when the bond has dragged on too long) it can happen that the people who have messed up our lives with their toxic attitude can come back to create another bit of havoc. This happens especially with a narcissist, that person who believes that everything revolves around them and that very often creates a lot of damage in other people's lives. Clearly, all people can return, but the narcissist re-enters the scene for a series of well-defined reasons connected to his specific personality traits.

This is why it is important to understand what the moves of those who behave in this way are and what to do in these cases because it is very easy to fall into the insidious trap of revival. Let's find out together how to behave in these cases and what "weapons" to use.

So, remember that:

- ✓ The first thing you need to do is avoid getting involved in the relationship again. In any way. The narcissist does not allow his extension to slip away easily. If you're trying to distance yourself from someone like this, be aware that he or she will manipulate you into losing you. Avoid getting drawn into this vicious circle. Be strong when ending a relationship with a narcissist.

- ✓ People with narcissistic personality traits may have a tendency to want to get back in the picture. If this happens, however, the real reason is not realizing that you love the other person, but it has more to do with returning to having control of the other or at least returning to having an influence in his life.
- ✓ If you have already rejected narcissistic individuals for bad behavior towards you, do not rebuke them. It is highly unlikely that they will behave differently in the future.
- ✓ Often the narcissist pretends to want to change when he senses that someone is leaving him. He can go so far as to say things will be different this time and promise big changes.
- ✓ Remember that the narcissist only acts to satisfy his needs. He (or she) makes promises in hopes of getting what he wants, namely your attention and interest in him. Don't believe anything he says as you prepare to leave him.
- ✓ Don't try to force yourself not to think about him, not to think that you miss him, to repress your emotions or play superhero and pretend as nothing happened. This attitude will only make you bury your head in the sand, but it won't prevent you from starting a new round of waltz. Result? In a few months, you will still find yourself searching the web for "how to get over the end of a toxic relationship". And that's not what we want for you. Accept your inner world first, your weaknesses and your strengths. So, the only thing you can do is allow yourself to fall and get back up. Learn to go beyond mental dialogues, and become curious about how the mind works. Practice at least 10 minutes of meditation a day.
- ✓ Awareness of the narcissist's patterns and his own fragility in the relationship can save his or her ex-partner from the dramatic misrepresentation of the return, support her in refusing new communications or meetings and commit to definitively process the detachment. In the absence of this awareness, however, the irreducible manipulations of the narcissist can hit the target countless times, causing pain, humiliation, anger, feelings of helplessness and a series of psychological symptoms of an anxious and/or depressive type attributable, together to other indicators, to the love addiction.

How to deal with a returning narcissist?

After giving you some useful advice in the previous paragraph, let's see how to definitively answer the question of what to do if the narcissist insistently comes back to haunt your life.

The narcissistic relationship is governed by possession and not by love, for this reason, the narcissist needs to return to the victim moved by the need to reconfirm his influence over it and make sure that it has not escaped him. He can do it days, weeks, months or years after the end of the relationship, but he will always do it and, almost always, his returns will baffle the ex-partner and have a paralyzing effect on the affective life of the prey.

The narcissistic return mistook for love. Those who are sentimentally dependent on a pathological narcissist can, even after a long time from the interruption of the bond, misrepresent the return as a meditated and romantic action, as the sign of the hoped-for change that takes place and which promises a serene love to be gently abandoned after too many pains. Sadly, the perverse narcissist reserves no such thing, and while the "victim" may know about it, they often manage to notice it too late.

The strategies of the narcissist's infinite returns range from the simple unexpected text message to an invitation to dinner, from the allusively sentimental post on Facebook to the most impulsive marriage proposal in the world. These strategies can ideally be ordered considering two variables: the narcissist's commitment to return and the frequency of his actions on the ex-partner. On this basis, we have 4 types of "narcissistic return":

1. Low-effort, low-frequency return. It is the most typical "come back" strategy, exemplified by the classic text message "Hello, how are you?" which can reach the victim like a bolt from the blue. It's a low commitment because a text message costs nothing and, even in terms of content, it doesn't seem to imply anything other than a polite greeting. The low frequency, for example, a message a month or every two months, denotes that the narcissist is not in a hurry, feels he has the person in his grip and is content to verify that this is the case. On the other hand, the reactions of the "victims" to these infinitesimal inputs are often abnormal: messages such as "I always think of you" or "Evil. You ruined my life". And we don't want to mention emails or phone calls are enough to reassure the daffodil of his influence and enough to interrupt the interaction for a while. Until the narcissist's next "possession check".
2. Low-effort, high-frequency return. If the previous method didn't work, the second strategy always involves the typically narcissistic low communicative commitment, but increases the frequency of messages, also conveyed on multiple

channels, especially via social networks. Indirect provocations, cheesy photos, and prefabricated romantic texts will crowd the profiles of the narcissist, intertwined with each other with a very strong tenacity. Also, this style of "return" has excellent chances of success and is interrupted as soon as the prey yields with enthusiasm and abnegation.

3. High-effort, low-frequency return. This type of return is given by the proposal of a coffee or a walk, by a less cryptic message than usual or by a photo signed with an emoticon. For the rest, it will be the ex-partner who will do everything: reciprocate with deep thoughts, attention, gifts, and testimonials of love of disarming naivety. If this does not happen, the narcissist can reinforce the commitment and go as far as to stun the victim with declarations such as "You are the only woman I have ever loved", "I want a child from you", and "I want to marry you". These returns end in bed one-off. And then, the disappearance is guaranteed until the next round.

4. High-effort, high-frequency return. After a few texts and conversations in the middle of the night, these people are likely to go back to pretending the other person doesn't exist. Perhaps always leaving a few small traces of one's uncertain presence, perhaps by viewing stories on Instagram or leaving tactical likes on social media posts. This orbiting is aimed at understanding if the other is still controllable or if, on the contrary, he has really moved on and there is someone else in his life. It is the riskiest form of the narcissistic "return", implemented when the prey is decidedly on the run, in the middle of the release phase. Unfortunately, this modality can endanger the ex-partner more than others because the insistence of the courtship and the petulance of the messages could lead to stalking and, if the victim's refusals are ambivalent or late, lead to aggression verbal and/or physical.

When a woman or a man manages to push away a narcissist, she may come to believe that she has managed to get rid of him forever, but she is not like that at all. An abandoned narcissist tends, in fact, to return to his victim.

This is a very frequent attitude in the covert narcissist, who will be willing to swear to have changed in order to win back his woman. It happens more rarely, but even the malignant narcissist can pretend to have changed and even go so far as to apologize to regain possession of his victim.

The return of a narcissist is perhaps not the rule, but it is highly probable because it is not easy for this type of person to accept that the other has decided not to have anything to do with them anymore. It can happen even after months or even years, but sooner or later it will happen, so how to deal with the narcissist? We will always answer in the same way: "Putting him or her away from your life!".

In these cases, the solution is only one, which is to disappear. You don't need these kinds of people, so cut them off, start blocking them on social media and ignore them in real life too. Your worth does not depend on anyone, much less on a narcissist.

The methods of return, as we have seen, can be of different types and can imply a more or less profound commitment on the part of the narcissist. However, all of them have very serious consequences for the victim, who should literally do everything to learn to recognize the strategy and resist the temptation to believe the narcissist's lies again.

However, we realize (and answer to this important question) that it is much easier said than done and that a relapse phase can be useful for making the final decision and finding the emotional strength necessary to leave the narcissist permanently.

How to avoid narcissists in the future? A general reflection

How to avoid running into other narcissists if you've been there before? There could be tricks, which come from experience, to learn about this type of personality and therefore recognize them more easily. We could pay attention to a certain number of elements. For example: Does a person you just met ask you about yourself, or is he just interested in talking about himself? Or how does he talk about his exes? Does he consider them all horrible people and himself the poor victim? Or again, does he tend to pontificate, have a paternalistic tone, and have an opinion on everything?

These could be some of the signals to consider, however… wish it were always that simple. The problem arises because, no matter how head-on we understand what it is, there is a part of us that has a tendency to point to that person right there, or rather to feel attraction towards that type of person. And the attraction, you know, is much more difficult to get around.

When an attraction arises our rationality cannot do much about it, and therefore… what is necessary to do? What is really required?

Our proposal here is to let go. There is no recipe, no one-size-fits-all procedure because otherwise, everything would come automatically, and it would be one of the great discoveries of all time.

It's never like that. It's not a how or why here; on the contrary, it is an exercise of presence, a stay in contact with ourselves, with our knowledge, and with the relationship, we create with the different parts of us. And this can happen in so many different ways: what are these ways? I always say there are those that make sense to you, at that particular moment. The ones that have energy, that is, that somehow have that specific crackle of something that resonates with you, that depends from person to person and moment to moment.

Essentially it is this: getting in touch with the parts of us that react to some ancient patterns that escape the rational and what we have understood in our heads, because, of course, if this step is missing, it can always happen again... perhaps it has already happened to you. Maybe you met a person and said to yourself: 'Great, that's the right person!' because they are not like the previous ones, and then, once the addiction sets in, that person brings out new aspects of themselves, new sides which make you realize that it is actually a reproduction of previous stories.

There are so many different ways to connect with those parts of you that want to be seen, and for this reason, professional help remains of paramount importance if you are to avoid falling into the narcissistic trap again. So, all you really need is some thorough work on yourself: understand your dysfunctions, fill in the gaps, and love yourself again!

Prevention is better than cure: tips to avoid falling into the narcissistic trap

Now let's see what all the best tips can be to avoid falling into any possible narcissistic trap again. Better to go wrong once. These tips can help you avoid ongoing unpleasant relationships with people who have narcissistic disorders one more time:

- ✓ "Don't accept sweets from unknown people": that is, keep your guard up and keep your critical thinking ability trained.
- ✓ To get better you need to learn to forgive yourselves, and reconcile with yourselves: having lived through certain situations does not make you weak or wrong people. Let's remember that leaving a toxic person is never easy for anyone. The sensations that this kind of exercise produces will be perceived introspectively as a form of well-being, serenity, and tranquility. Because letting go means becoming aware that some people have been part of our history, but do not belong to our destiny. And for this reason, reconciling ourselves allows us to avoid other toxic relationships in the future.
- ✓ If these people didn't respect your boundaries early in the relationship, they won't respect your boundaries later in the relationship.
- ✓ Prick up your antennae: if the initial attitudes of "he" or "she" seem exaggerated, incredible, or rushed (you may even feel a vague sense of unease and intrusiveness) you need to pay close attention. Certainly, the initial phase of falling in love is magical for everyone, but a stable and true bond is created over time, and trust must be conquered gradually.

- ✓ Give importance to the first signs of jealousy (even retroactive towards exes) and disapproval of other acquaintances even old friends and family. Similarly, if he disposes of your time without asking your opinion, he makes commitments for you without asking you, it's not a good sign.
- ✓ Do not hope that the person will change and do not give in to their promises to cure themselves.
- ✓ Trust your belly. If being with this person makes you uncomfortable or regularly forces you to do things you don't want to do, this person probably isn't right for you. Your belly already knows this from the first few dates, so trust your instincts for once before it's too late. Love should never create discomfort or submission, remember that.
- ✓ Listen to your intuition, and the alarm bells of a potentially toxic relationship: with a partner you should always feel safe, and never uncomfortable.
- ✓ Friends and close people, who knew you before, are more objective than you: if they tell you that you've changed, that you don't show up anymore if they ask you if you're really sure that he makes you feel good and that he's the right person… Listen to them.
- ✓ If the internal alarm sounds, the relationship must be ended as soon as possible, perhaps relying on a trusted person: a close and supportive friend, a family member, or perhaps even a professional psychologist or psychotherapist who can help to understand and treat the deep reasons why one has fallen into this type of dysfunctional relationship.
- ✓ If you have understood that you are dealing with a narcissist again, the most effective weapon to get out of it is to practice no contact: no contact, in a very determined way. It is necessary to interrupt any type of communication, direct (telephone, messages, emails, etc. must be blocked) or indirect (posting a photo on Facebook or Instagram to send him a signal or make him jealous).
- ✓ Run away if intolerance is immediately taking over. This is one of the typical sensations of those who are experiencing a toxic relationship. Constant tension, the fear that at any moment, for no specific reason, the other person (whether it's a partner, friend, manager, or colleague) will stop talking or get angry are alarm bells about the fact that there is something wrong in the relationship you are experiencing and therefore you have to immediately delete this person from your life.
- ✓ It may be useful (for a short time, however) to attend groups or forums of other people who have gone through the thick experience, to seek sharing, comparison and understanding, without feeling accused; at a certain point, however, it is necessary to detach oneself and concentrate on something else.

- ✓ Get distracted, hang out with people from a different circle, and get passionate about something else: the world is big, varied, and colorful. Not everything - fortunately - revolves around "him" or "her".
- ✓ Watch out for everything too perfect: usually toxic relationships don't start badly right away; there is often an initial phase characterized by enthusiasm and positivity. In the case of couple relationships, there is the feeling that the other person is capable of giving us exactly what we need, and this often happens in friendships as well. In the professional field, things can go differently because you can immediately get the feeling that the shift manager is an irritable or unpredictable person or easy to raise his voice. In these cases, the toxic relationship can manifest itself with attempts to please or not irritate the other person. But by now you know what's wrong and so flee as soon as possible.
- ✓ Always about fake and alarming perfections, do not consider them for the positive and idealized image they project of themselves: in the knowledge phase, we know by now, narcissists show themselves to your eyes as safe, honest, and clear people, but this facade actually serves to hide a great void and deep insecurity. They are convinced that they have to "defraud" you in order to have some form of relationship with you, because - even if they flaunt cynicism, independence and lack of affection - they feel they are not worthy and do not deserve love or attention. If the person comes across as too perfect or flaunts too much perfection from the start, he or she is a narcissist. Avoid it like the plague!
- ✓ To avoid falling into any possible narcissistic trap, do not overshare personal information: in the love bombing and idealization phase, they act as a mirror for you, so you are inclined to tell them your whole life, including your weaknesses, traumas, or wounds. These triggers will then be used against you in quarrels, conflicts or purely for manipulative and abusive purposes. Also, beware of their provocative "charges"; you are not required to justify, explain, clarify, or discuss trifles or facts that never happened, especially if, as almost always happens, you have done nothing. The accusation as an "overture" and bias, for narcissists, is just a manipulative strategy aimed at control. They have no interest in your explanations. Plus, whatever they accuse, it's often what they're doing. Avoid for your own good.
- ✓ So more than mistakes and failures think of lessons to be learned. Appreciate and reward yourself for every little daily success, and support yourself even when you fall and feel bad. Everything is always fine. You're not the only one who's been in a toxic relationship, and you won't be the only one unable to get out of it. You will make it; indeed, you already made it. If you're just reading this book, it means you've already taken the first step in the right direction. It means that you want

the best for yourself and that in the future you will not accept someone who treats you even slightly below what you deserve.

How to avoid manipulations like love bombing, gaslighting or emotional abandonment?

We close this chapter with a little useful advice to avoid the typical techniques of the narcissist (a technique already explained in the previous paragraphs). To avoid this type of manipulation or abuse in a relationship, it is very important to pay attention to how you feel when you are with the other person. As we have just seen, the return of the pathological narcissist will always, inevitably pass through a more or less long series of more or less big lies.

There will be nothing honest about the return of the narcissist even if, as a good seducer he is, he will be able to appear extremely sincere and absolutely honest in staging his repentance.

In fact, to be sure of breaching the victim's heart again, the narcissist will apologize for all the harm he has done to her in the past and will be ready to swear that he has changed and that he did so by virtue of the love he feels for her or for him.

The lies of the narcissist always tend to grow in intensity as the victim resists the temptation to return to the arms of his tormentor. If a simple "excuse me" isn't enough, the narcissist will be able to come up with all sorts of ruses to get the victim's attention.

In many cases, it is completely normal for everything to seem too good to be true at the beginning of a relationship. But when displays of love become too overwhelming for you, this can be a warning sign to be aware of. If you feel that you are in or have been in an abusive relationship, it is important that you see a psychologist if you feel that this has affected you or is interfering with your daily life. What must always be kept in mind is that nothing the narcissist will do or say on the occasion of his return will be honest and sincere. His goal is always and only to obtain his interests through these techniques and then disappear. It's up to you to recognize the typical techniques and be smarter, so get away as soon as possible!

True love is about treating each other with respect.

With these tips, we concluded our chapter on how to avoid narcissists and toxic relationships in the future. In the last chapter of this guide, we will take care of showing you how to live a healthy relationship with your next partner.

Chapter 13: How to live happily in a new relationship

Here we are at the last chapter of the guide. In this section, we will show you how to live a new relationship happily, but only after having made a small introduction. However, know that, although your story has really been a disaster, it will be possible in the future for you to have a healthy and happy relationship anyway.

A small premise: listen to yourself

Before showing you how to live a new relationship that will be fruitful and happy in the future, let us give you a small introduction. This little premise is about you and starting over from yourself. This also means accepting a period of solitude to understand what you want and, above all, what you don't want from a relationship in the future. You have already suffered enough!
A little advice for you, at this time when you will surely be more fragile, is to avoid launching yourself into a new relationship
This is one of the most wrong things. The time to spend in a healthy "single time" is essential. You risk attracting another perpetrator or a partner of the same dynamic because you still haven't worked out those parts of you that led you to attract the previous one. Do yourself this favor: learn to enjoy time with yourself. The more you develop inner grounding the less you will fall back into toxic relationships. Be careful not to close yourself out of fear. It doesn't mean that if it happened in the past, it would happen again. Relationships are a risk but if you have done the job well, you have developed your secure attachment and you will have all the tools to calmly decide if a person is right for you or not. You will no longer dive headfirst, but you will have a good balance between head and heart. But that doesn't mean you won't be able to find a partner soon. The important thing is that it's not another toxic person if you want to live happily! And in the next paragraph, we will explain how to live a happy relationship with another person who is more suitable for you.

Living happily with a new partner is possible!

Ok to be alone, but will I be able to be happy again with a new partner? Will it be the right one? We are sure that, after having worked on yourself, on a possible emotional addiction and on your inner emptiness, you will have the opportunity to make better choices.

So, let's see some good final tips to live better and happier in a new relation.

The key is doing better choices

Past and present suffering must be a resource for learning. Generally, women or men who find themselves in toxic relationships come from dysfunctional families in which emotional needs have not been adequately recognized and they immediately learn to consider the relationship, or even just the presence of the love object, as the only possible way to feel good about themselves and learn a behavior model that tends by all means to recognition by the other. Then as adults, they choose dysfunctional partners who continue to deny their emotional needs and deny their worth, hoping that their love will ultimately change the other and that they will finally be loved. And this illusion, the efforts made, the anguish and despair must be the first step in choosing to give yourself a chance for a healthier future life. And therefore, opting for a better partner is capable of making you truly happy. Now that you have learned how to recognize a narcissistic person and a toxic relationship, you will be more aware of the person you decide to date and then establish a relationship with. Therefore, choosing the right person for you, who is light years away from the type of person you just left behind is definitely the first step to living a happy relationship.

Learn from the past and think love it's still real!

Ok, you have chosen a person who seems healthy, and normal, and who can make you happy, but often, the problem remains, for those who have been the victim of a narcissist, stop trusting in love. What is the way to believe that you can have a new relationship, this time a happy one? To answer this question, it can very well be said that after each separation it is difficult to start over and we often fear not being able to meet a person again, but in reality, they are fears related to the painful moment that we are experiencing and are unrealistic. In fact, when you are ready to face a new relationship, the meeting is easier than you think. The important thing is to learn from the negative experiences lived and to start from first of all having faith in oneself, in one's abilities and thinking one deserves and therefore giving oneself a chance for a better life. And in the face of new love, trust partners who are able to welcome, support and respect you. Restoring trust also means getting involved, taking responsibility for the relationship not knowing how it will go, and accepting the situation realistically, without making any effort to change it at all costs in order to be accepted.

Get smarter... and you'll be happy!

If you decide to date again, how do you not fall back into old patterns? We believe, in this case, but we have already explained to you in the previous chapter, that it is essential to understand what went wrong in previous experiences, such as our responsibilities and those of our partner, and to identify the pattern that we erroneously tend to follow. Self-awareness can certainly allow you to detach yourself from reiterated dynamics. Learning to recognize your own needs and desires will allow you to choose different partners and relationships from those in which you have always found yourself. Changing one's mental patterns is absolutely possible and a new approach can be determined, for example, in not always focusing on the same type of partner and not a priori alienating people from whom one is not apparently attracted, without fearing the unknown and therefore changing,

And finally: 6 ways to return to love after a toxic relationship

We conclude this practical guide, with some very useful methods and advice to be able to return to love in a healthy and happy way. This is a summary of what has been said so far, with some important additions:

1. Start by knowing yourself. Focus on resources and your emotional potential, to achieve autonomy, a healthy psychological balance, and a good level of self-esteem, which allow you to think you can be accepted for who you are and not for what you do for others.
2. Learn to truly love yourself. It is distrust in your worth and abilities that make you think you cannot be loved. First, develop a relationship with yourself and learn to trust yourself.
3. Don't blame yourself and don't join partners who put responsibility for the relationship on you and who convince you that everything depends on you.
4. Allow yourself to be loved and respected within a reciprocal relationship. It is essential to reach healthier ways of relating and a new way of loving that is above all reciprocals.
5. Never again settle for a partner who denies your value, who undermines your self-esteem, who treats you badly, only in the illusion of being able to fill your emotional void with him.
6. Don't delegate happiness to a partner, it means denying your value and not taking responsibility for a change.

Our guide concludes with these tips. Now you will be perfectly aware of how to be happy again after having had a toxic relationship, perhaps with a partner who really deserves you!

Conclusions

Here we are at the conclusion of this practical guide. We have already understood, from the beginning, that narcissism is not something that is so easily identifiable.

However, since it is a real disorder, diagnostic criteria, and ways in which it is possible to recognize this pathology have been established. We have also understood that there is not a single univocal manifestation of narcissism, but that it has different facets, up to presenting a real malignant model, or the worst that can happen in someone's life.

We have also tried to make you understand the presence of all the signs, not only of a narcissistic partner but of a real toxic relationship. We have also provided you with a way out: in fact, all the ways in which you can get rid of your toxic partner have been presented, as how to face a painful transition phase and how to face a new relationship in the future, in a serene way, without falling into yet other traps that would otherwise drag you into a new toxic relationship. Without neglecting a really important factor: the return of the narcissist.

As we have seen, this return is not only frequent but practically inevitable in many respects. It can happen months after the last time the narcissist and his victim spoke to each other, but also years later. Also in this case, the way out has been indicated to you: refusing all contact and above all becoming aware of the dynamics put in place by the narcissist, from the script that he continuously recites is necessary to avoid becoming victims of narcissistic abuse again and ruining one's life for the umpteenth time. Now you certainly have at your disposal all the tools, all the means, all the solutions to a toxic relationship, how to avoid such types and how to be able to believe in love again and live happily.

But the last important thing we want to underline and that it's not just us who help you in this battle: we also reiterate that the affection of our loved ones and the help of a therapist can prove to be really important in order to be able to get out of these situations. But also, to start from yourself: the foundations of a healthy and lasting love depend on the love that we give to ourselves. Without this basis, it is not possible to have a functional relationship... And we hope for you that you are the first person to arm yourself and respect you! Good luck to all!

EMPATH IN RELATIONSHIP

Introduction

In this second guide, after discussing the problem of narcissism in all its facets, we will talk about empathy and what the concept of globally mean.

We briefly introduce the concept of empathy.

Empathy is the ability to understand the feelings, sufferings, and thoughts of others. It's a process that activates when we stop focusing attention only on our thoughts and perceptions, to activate a real interest in each other.

Therefore, empathy is not just "putting yourself in other shoes", but is based on an exchange relationship, in which the individual puts his way of perceiving reality into the background, to try to understand the experiences and perceptions of others, making the other feel that the process has been completed. The term comes from the Greek 'en-pathos' and literally translated means 'to feel inside'. Empathy is the human ability to put ourselves in the place of others to better understand them. Knowing how to feel and interpret the emotions of others, understand their perspective and be able to give an emotional response as well.

In fact, empathy is, in other words, a social skill of fundamental importance and represents one of the basic tools of effective and rewarding interpersonal communication. In interpersonal relationships, empathy is one of the main gateways to moods and in general to the world of the other. The empath, therefore, has the distinct ability to place himself in another person's situation or, more exactly, to immediately understand the other's psychic processes.

Which, as we saw in the first guide, is light years away from the narcissistic subject who has absolutely no trace of empathy.

So, the empath, in particular, is a person who has an unusually strong ability to feel other people's emotional or mental states. The components of empathy were identified for the first time by the American psychologist Norma Feshbach and are the ability to:

✓ Decode the emotional states of others
✓ Put yourself in the shoes of others, thus assuming their point of view
✓ Respond in an effective way to the emotions felt by others.

The first two components are cognitive abilities, while the third concerns the affective and emotional spheres.

But is there the opposite of empathy? Yes, and we refer to the concept of dyspathy, which means the refusal or inability to share the emotions and feelings of others. The term dyspathy was proposed by the psychiatrist J.L. González to define the voluntary exclusion process of:

- ✓ Feelings
- ✓ Attitudes
- ✓ Reasons
- ✓ Thoughts induced by others.

So, it is not a synonym of indifference or emotional coldness, but of compensatory mental action to empathy, with the aim of protecting and preventing the emotions of others from creating psychic discomfort. That of the narcissist, on the other hand, is the total absence of empathy.

With this brief introduction, we are trying to make you understand that empathy is one of the fundamental ingredients in human relationships and communication. And being an empath is a real blessing: it's really something healthy and saving when the person manages to project himself into the other's situation, so you experience a deep emotional response to the other's emotion. The problem, however, is that often these subjects attract people who shouldn't.

And here we are to help you, because an empath person, no matter how fantastic, often becomes prey and then a victim of manipulators, toxic and narcissistic people. In fact, in this guide, we will explain not only how to recognize the signs of a possible empath subject (which we assume is certainly you), but also how to avoid becoming a magnet attracting toxic people.

And after reading the first guide, in which we explained how to recognize a narcissist, a toxic relationship and how to get rid of it, above all, in this second guide, however, we want to go deeper and understand the origin of the problem: the fact that probably your strength, i.e. being an empath, could represent a weakness if you continue to establish relationships with people who just want to suck up your energy to achieve their goals.

It will be a question of looking at the highly toxic codependency relationship from another point of view, namely that of the victim. We will provide you with all the knowledge and tools to understand if you are actually an empath subject, how to best use this power of yours and above all how to defend yourself from any possible narcissistic or manipulative attack.

We will also analyze the various forms of empathy and try to understand the concept as deeply as possible. At the end of reading this guide, you will have a complete picture of the situation and you will be able not only to know the techniques to avoid toxic people in the future but also to understand your point of view and make the most of your powers as an empath to make the most of the life. Because it's right that you use these extraordinary skills to live better if no one takes advantage of them... and that you can only use these skills for positive purposes and attract only the people you deserve. This is our wish for you!

FIRST PART-RECOGNISE EMPATHY AND EMPATH

Chapter 1: Understanding Empathy

In this first chapter, we will deal with explaining in more detail (compared to the introduction), the concept of empathy. How it was born, how it developed and how it is understood today.

What is empathy?

We also begin this second guide, as we did for narcissism, this time offering a complete overview of empathy. So, let's start with a definition. But before giving you this, we should say the definitions of empathy coined by scholars and researchers over the years are many and multifaceted, but in principle, they all refer to the ability to share, to know how to share the moods of others and their sufferings. Anyway, as we have already said in the intro of this guide, the term empathy derives from the Greek, en-pathos "to feel inside", and consists in recognizing the emotions of others as if they were one's own, immersing oneself in the reality of others to understand their points of view, thoughts, feelings, emotions. Empathy, therefore, represents nothing more than the ability to "put yourself in the other's shoes" by perceiving, in this way, emotions and thoughts. It is the ability to see the world as others see it, to be non-judgmental, and to understand the feelings of others while keeping them distinct from one's own. That said, we can say that empathy is a real social skill of fundamental importance and represents one of the basic tools of effective, functional but above all rewarding interpersonal communication. Think of a comfortable relationship where you can feel but also share the emotions of the other person in front of you. In interpersonal relationships, in fact, empathy is one of the main gateways to the moods and in general to the world of the other. Thanks to it, one can not only grasp the meaning of what the interlocutor asserts but also grasp the most recondite psycho-emotional meaning. This allows us to expand the value of the message, capturing elements that often go beyond the semantic content of the sentence, making its meta-communication explicit, that is, that truly significant part of the message, expressed by the body language, which is possible to decode thanks to the empathic listening.

Having given these definitions, we can very well say that empathy is a personality trait characterized by the ability to feel an appropriate emotion in response to that expressed by others, to distinguish between oneself and others while regulating one's own emotional responses. The empath is then able to be aware of the source of the emotion and to decode the emotion of others. The empath has this ingrained characteristic and, as we will see in the next chapters, has very specific skills and signals.

Empathy: historical notes

After understanding its meaning, let's see how the concept of empathy was understood in the past and how it is today.

Ancient Greece

The term empathy was used in ancient Greece to indicate the emotional relationship of participation that linked the author - songwriter (aedo) to his audience. Empathy meant them "feeling inside the other, experiencing how the other person lives an experience".
Plato and Aristotle were already aware of the process of identification that was activated in art, especially in the theatre, between the spectator and the tragic hero. In fact, the audience and protagonist suffered together, they became one. But for the Greeks, empathy did not have the meaning we attribute to it today. Ptolemy speaks of "physical passion" and Aristotle himself of "pity and compassion". Specifically, therefore, among the ancient Greeks (and by now we know that the word derives from the ancient Greek "εμπάθεια" (empátheia), in turn, composed of en-, "inside", and pathos, "suffering or feeling") the term it was used during theatrical performances to indicate the emotional relationship of participation that bound the author-singer to his audience.

Feel inside

The concept of empathy in philosophy was introduced at the end of the 19th century (precisely in 1873) by Robert Vischer, a scholar of figurative arts, in the field of aesthetic reflection, to define the ability of human imagination to grasp the symbolic value of nature. He used the term Einfühlung which, only later, was translated into English as empathy.
So, for the philosopher Vischer empathy could be defined as "the ability to perceive external nature, as internal, belonging to our own body".
In other words, Vischer conceived this term as the ability to feel inside and to consent, i.e., to perceive external nature as internal, belonging to our own body. It, therefore, represents the ability to project feelings from us to others and to the things, which we perceive.

And it is only in the second half of the eighteenth century, in Germany, that the term Einfühlung, "feeling inside", appears, which was born in full Romanticism to describe, above all in art and philosophy, the fusion between man and nature as a new perception of the world.

Meaning of empathy: definition by Edith Stein

The term empathy did not come into use until 1909, at which time the nascent psychologist already modern took its first official steps in the analysis of human consciousness however second a simultaneity symptomatic of the fact that right in the womb of that the term would have assumed, during the time, previously the phenomenon of "identification", which with the empathy began to be traced back to a precise psychological substrate, had been made philosophically through terms like sympathy or Einfühlung: the first used in a particular way by Hume and Smith during the eighteenth century, the latter adopted by some exponents of aesthetics German in the second half of the nineteenth century. Historically crucial is the theory of Einfühlung elaborated by Theodor Lipps. It will be Theodor Lipps, indeed, who in 1906 will use the word Einfühlung to describe empathy as a fundamental psychological function for emotional participation.

In other words, Lipps introduces the dimension of empathy in psychology, speaking of profound participation in the experience of another being, thus introducing the theme of otherness, which will then be taken up by the phenomenological school. For Lipps the observation of the movements of others arouses in us the same state of mind, which is the basis of the observed movement, however, this state is not perceived as one's own experience, but is projected onto the other and linked to his movement (there is no is lost in the other); it is about empathy as participation or inner imitation. Instead, in 1917, Edith Stein will take a step forward in the definition of empathy as intersubjective communication: "empathy is the paradoxical act through which the reality of another, of what we are not, we have not yet experienced or what we will never live and which moves us elsewhere, into the unknown, becomes an element of the most intimate experience, that is, that of feeling together which produces expansion and expansion towards what is beyond, unexpected".

Meaning of empathy today

But it is thanks to the English psychologist Edward Titchener (1909) that the term empathy takes on today's meaning. In fact, Titchener was looking for a word other than "sympathy" (feeling together what one feels), to indicate the human ability to put oneself in the place of others to better understand them.

The notion of empathy has been the subject of numerous reflections by intellectuals such as Edith Stein, Antoine Chesì, Max Scheler, Sigmund Freud or Carl Rogers.

And the merit of the introduction of the principle of empathy in psychoanalysis is mainly due to Heinz Kohut. His principle of him is applicable to the method of collecting unconscious material.

Therefore, it was during the 20th century that the concept of empathy stabilized: the presence of an interpersonal relationship based on the emotional response that is activated when it is perceived that another person is feeling an emotion. Always today, according to the American Psychological Association, empathy consists in understanding a person by adopting their point of view instead of your own (a concept very similar to the theory of mind) or in the indirect and often involuntary experience of the mental states of a person (a concept developed after the discovery of mirror neurons). Empathy does not necessarily imply the motivational or emotional drive to help, although its evolution into sympathy or emotional contagion can determine rescue and help actions and behaviors. Definitions of empathy can be included in a broad range of social, cognitive, and emotional processes. These processes, first, are concerned with understanding others (and others' emotions in particular).

So, at this point, we should say that empathy can be of several types: cognitive, emotional, physical, and spiritual. In common usage, empathy is the ability to give one's attention to another person, setting aside personal worries and thoughts. Relationship quality is based on non-evaluative listening and focuses on understanding the other's basic feelings and needs.

Empathy theories

Let's see the meaning of empathy, from the point of view of different theories. Let's start with the psychological one.

Empathy: psychology theory

In psychology, empathy is an emotional competence that, through the observation or imagination of other people's affective states, induces shared states with the observer. In fact, this sharing allows a direct form of understanding, precisely defined as "empathic".

It involves two different activations: emotional (feeling the sadness or discomfort of others) and cognitive (understanding the reasons for that sadness or discomfort). The lack of one or both characterizes some forms of psychopathy: in schizophrenia, for example, the affective component of empathy is lacking; in the presence of autistic sphere disorders or borderline personality traits, however, a cognitive deficit is found. Psychologically, empathy can be described as a multidimensional construct, a process that occurs when observing or imagining the affective states of others induces shared states with the observer. In fact, this sharing allows a direct form of understanding, precisely defined as "empathic".

It also involves two activations of a different type: on the one hand, an activation of an emotional type, i.e., being able to feel the sadness, annoyance, or difficulty of the other. On the other hand, cognitive activation allows us to understand the reasons for the emotional states of the other. Emotional competence, therefore, allows you to tune in to the frequency of the other; it involves the areas of affective sharing, self-awareness, and the ability to differentiate oneself from others. According to Nancy McWilliams then, at the professional level, empathy is a tool that is not only useful but necessary for the professional psychoanalyst to perceive what the patient feels from an emotional point of view. In fact, it often happens that there are many therapists who complain of not being very empathetic towards their patients, but in reality, their insecurity, fear and often hostility towards their clients are caused by not very positive affects, which arise precisely from their high level of empathy, which allows you to enter the patient's state to such an extent that you feel his feelings, to the point of confusing your own with those of others. The effects of the patients therefore often cause such great suffering to the therapist himself that it is difficult for him to induce responses of the same intensity in them. All of this is actually very positive because in this way the patient's unhappiness becomes perceived in a sincere and genuine way. It is therefore not the result of a mechanism dictated by mere professional compassion, but considering the uniqueness of the person, one authentically becomes part of his emotional experience.

A double theory: mind and heart

When it comes to empathy, is it the heart or the mind that is involved? Actually "empathizing" is a process that involves both aspects.

- ✓ Cognitive empathy: We talk about cognitive empathy as the ability to perceive another person's perspective to understand their thoughts, emotions, and actions. In fact, one senses the thought of the other and understands their point of view, even without necessarily implying an emotional sharing. So, it can be summed up with "I understand what you are experiencing". Difficulties in cognitive empathy, in distinguishing between self and other, often lead to high levels of anxiety and personal distress which can lead to an avoidance of emotionally charged situations. So often if a person on the autistic spectrum avoids emotional situations it is not because she is disinterested, but because she is too invested in

them. This is a key concept to understand some of the antisocial behaviors of Asperger (and in a good percentage also of DSA) who perceive the emotions of others, but literally do not know what to do with them because they do not have adequately developed cognitive empathy.
- ✓ Emotional empathy instead, by emotional or emotive empathy we mean the emotional response that derives from the awareness that the shared emotion comes from the emotion of the other: vicarious sharing, feeling what the other feels.

It is, in other words, the ability to feel what other people feel: our bodies connect with their moods, whether they are happy or hurt. Emotional empathy is visceral and is felt through the body. It is a faculty rooted in the distant past of evolution: we share this neural circuit with other mammals who, like us, must be very attentive to the distress signals sent by their young.

Emotional empathy operates in the oldest part of our brain, what is called the bottom-up system, and much of the neural networks used to directly sense what others are feeling are located below the cortex, in areas of the brain that "think quickly", but not in depth. These circuits bring us into harmony with those around us by arousing in our bodies the same emotional states that we perceive in others. Thanks to empathy, we understand and "feel" the state of mind of others, we perceive their emotional state and the "quality" of their experience. So, it can be summed up with "I feel what you feel".

However, despite this distinction (cognitive and emotional empathy), some researchers consider empathy as a multidimensional construct, in which there is an integration of the two components, affective and cognitive.

Mirror theory

To explain empathy, social learning theories were the first approach. The watershed in the scientific study of the phenomenon coincided with the discovery of mirror neurons: a class of motor neurons that are activated both during the execution of a task (or an action) and upon seeing the same task performed or undergone by another individual. This same mechanism also affects emotions and is the basis of empathy. Despite this, the neuronal component, although present in each of us, is not everything. The development of empathy depends on a process in which a series of bio-psycho-social factors contribute. It is therefore not an innate skill, but one that can be trained. But empathy is not just the result of social learning. Retracing the history of psychology, the social learning component is certainly important, but not the only one: only since the 80s and 90s have a series of studies been conducted which have shown that empathy is supported by a particular class of neurons, mirror neurons. These motor neurons, which we now know are located in the front-parietal area of the brain, are activated both during the execution of a task (or an action) and at the sight of the same task performed or undergone by another individual. The same process is also found with emotions. At a neurobiological level, mirror neurons are activated both in the person who feels an emotion and in those who are next to him. Not only observing, but even imagining the other in a certain emotional state activates the same neural correlate in the observer, normally involved in the first-person experience of the emotions themselves. The group of Rizzolatti and Gallese then formulated the theory of mirror neurons, according to which empathy arises from an embodied simulation process that precedes cognitive processing.

At a neurobiological level, the understanding of the mind and of the experiences of the other is supported by a particular class of neurons, defined as mirror neurons: participating as witnesses to the actions, sensations and emotions of other individuals activates the same brain areas normally involved in carrying out a first person of the same actions and in the perception of the same sensations and emotions.

At the basis of empathy, there would be a process of 'embodied simulation', i.e., a mechanism of an essentially motor nature, very ancient from the point of view of human evolution, characterized by neurons that would act immediately before any more proper cognitive processing.

Here's how the author describes it: "in this case, we can say that perceiving an action – and understanding its meaning – is equivalent to simulating it internally". This allows the observer to use his own resources to penetrate the world of the other through a modeling process that has the connotations of a non-conscious, automatic and prelinguistic motor simulation mechanism. When I see someone expressing a given emotion with his face and this perception leads me to understand the emotional meaning of that expression, The emotion of the other is constituted by the observer and understood thanks to a simulation mechanism that produces in the observer a bodily state shared with the actor of that expression. It is precisely the sharing of the same bodily state between the observer and the observed that allows this direct form of understanding, which we could define as empathetic" (Gallese, Migone and Eagle, 2006).

Empathy and psychotherapy theory

Freud (1921) states that it is only through empathy that we can know the existence of a psychic life different from ours, but he does not consider empathy as a therapeutic method, a step Kohut will make many years later. Kohut, in fact, considers empathy not only as a tool of knowledge but also as an important therapeutic tool: repeated exposure to experiences of empathic understanding, on the part of the analyst, serves to repair the "defects of the Self" of the patient. Later, in 1934, Mead added a cognitive component to the construct of empathy.

Empathy today turns out to be central in psychotherapy; on the theme of the therapeutic relationship, in fact, Aaron Beck underlined from his first books that: "the optimal qualities that the therapist must possess include warmth, empathy and openness".

These characteristics modulate the therapeutic collaboration to favor the application and therefore the effectiveness of the treatment.

Empathy is understood as the therapist's ability to enter the patient's world, trying to experience the same sensations and feelings experienced by the patient, and sharing this experience, which will increase the patient's perception of being understood and will facilitate the birth of trust in the therapeutic relationship.

Empathy: social theory

To explain empathy, social learning theories were the first approach. The watershed in the scientific study of the phenomenon coincided with the discovery of mirror neurons: a class of motor neurons that are activated both during the execution of a task (or an action) and upon seeing the same task performed or undergone by another individual. This same mechanism also affects emotions and is the basis of empathy. Despite this, the neuronal component, although present in each of us, is not everything. The development of empathy depends on a process in which a series of bio-psycho-social factors contribute. It is therefore not an innate skill, but one that can be trained. In the human sciences, empathy designates an attitude toward others characterized by a commitment to understanding the other, excluding any personal affective attitude (sympathy, antipathy) and any moral judgment. Fundamental, in this context, are both Darwin's pioneering studies on emotions and the mimic communication of emotions, and recent studies on mirror neurons discovered by Giacomo Rizzolatti, which confirm that empathy does not arise from an intellectual effort but is part of the genetic makeup of the species. In this regard see also the studies of Daniel Stern. From a biological point of view, in fact, empathy finds its reasons in the sociality of the human being, in its evolution and survival strategy: we are programmed to tune in with all our fellow human beings, to create connections and relationships, to identify ourselves with those who stand around.

Empathy and Development: Martin Hoffman's Theory

The model elaborated by Hoffman provides a description of the development of articulated and complex empathy. Indeed, Hoffman extends the definition of empathy to a wider range of affective reactions consistent with the feeling experienced by the other and places the first manifestations of empathy in the very first days of life. Furthermore, he does not consider empathy as something "unitary" but articulates it in different forms which, as development proceeds, become more mature and sophisticated (Hoffman, 2008).

Hoffman proposes a model with three components: affective, cognitive, and motivational.

According to Hoffman, empathy manifests itself from the first days of life. This consideration reflects the greater autonomy and relevance attributed to the emotional dimension of empathy: in fact, in the very first empathic manifestations, it is the affective dimension that plays the most important role, while the cognitive dimension is almost absent.

Proceeding in development, the cognitive component will acquire increasing importance and will interpenetrate more and more with the affective one, allowing the development of more evolved forms of empathy.

In addition to the cognitive and affective components, according to Hoffman, a third factor intervenes in the empathic experience: the motivational component. The experience of empathizing with a person who is suffering, in fact, would represent a motivation to implement helping behaviors. The motivating effect depends on the fact that sharing the emotion of the other, helping him, makes those who help feel a state of well-being; conversely, the choice not to comfort the other would bring with it a sense of guilt.

Empathy, in its most mature form, is therefore characterized as a response to a set of stimuli including behavior, expressiveness and everything that is known about the other. The acquisition of this function, given the high level of complexity of the cognitive mechanisms involved, has a gradual evolution, which is, in most people, fully completed around the age of 13.

Different types of empathy: get to know them

Now let's see what the different facets of empathy are. As far as the concept of empathy is concerned, in fact, it is possible to distinguish some different types:

Positive and negative empathy

Let's see a very important difference between positive and negative empathy. Positive empathy is the ability of an individual to enter into an emotional relationship with others, therefore, to participate in the joy or pain of others. It differs from sympathy (from the Greek sympathies and more specifically from syn, "together" and apatheia, "feeling", therefore "feeling together") which instead refers to concern for someone or to the desire to see that person in a state of Welfare. It's that affinity you have with friends, for example, often based on common experiences, but it doesn't involve emotional sharing, the " feeling inside " typical of empathy that certainly involves more commitment and availability. So, positive empathy means the subject's ability to participate fully in the joy of others; it is a question of rejoicing and therefore knowing how to grasp the joy of others, and being aware of the happiness he feels. In this sense, empathy in positive terms can be connected, in general, to sympathy. However, joy captured through sympathy is different, with respect to content, from joy captured through empathy. In the first case, in fact, it will be a non-original joy and therefore less intense and lasting than in the one who is closest to this joy; while in the second case, the joy captured through empathy will be of an original type, as the content of what is experienced by empathizing with the other will have the same content, even if only another mode of givenness. Instead, negative empathy characterizes those who are unable to empathize with the emotional sphere of others, since their own experience and emotions take over and hinder attention towards the other. Therefore, this barrier that prevents us from entering into consonance with the other can derive from a present or past negative experience that blocks the ability to participate emotionally.

Negative empathy refers to the experience of someone who is unable to empathize with the joy of others, transferring his emotions into his own original experience. This happens because something in him opposes; a present or past experience, or the person's own personality act, in fact, as a barrier to his ability to grasp the joy of others. The example could be that of the loss of a loved one, which prevents the individual from eliciting sympathy for the other's joy and therefore from sharing it. In this case, in fact, the sad event and the feelings of the same type that derive from it give rise to a conflict, as the ego feels divided between two parts: to live on the joy of others or to remain in the sadness that what happened determines

Difference between female and male empathy

Empathy is often considered, also thanks to numerous cultural stereotypes, as a typically feminine quality, as it allows one to best fulfill the maternal task. And the men? Are there differences between male and female empathy?

If by empathy we mean the ability to understand another person's emotions and point of view, it is a process that involves the activation of complex functions on many levels, associating cognitive and affective, but also social and cultural elements. According to some research, the measurement of empathy through self-reports could lead to responses influenced by the participants' identification of cultural stereotypes, in which women are expected to have a certain degree of empathy and morality, while for men poor empathy would be normal because it's not a socially required skill. But then how do male and female empathy differ? According to some experiments, men would be able to be empathetic only through identification, while they are less inclined to emotional empathy. This means that they empathize only if what they hear has affinities with their own personal history. So, the male gender has a different way of expressing empathy.

Are there biological bases to explain this diversity? According to a study conducted by Jack van Honk, professor in the Department of Psychiatry at the University of Cape Town (South Africa), there is a relationship between empathy and testosterone, a hormone more present in the male body that influences brain development and social behavior.

During an experiment, 16 women were asked to perform a test in which they had to understand the emotional state of some people by looking into their eyes. Women are given testosterone pills before the test had empathic abilities decreased by 75%.

Empathy and mentalization

Now let's see both the similarities and the differences between empathy and mentalization.

Let's start with some common elements: Choi-Kain and Gunderson (2008) report three aspects of empathy that unite the various definitions and conceptions:

- ✓ An affective reaction that involves sharing an emotional state with another
- ✓ The cognitive ability to imagine the perspective of others
- ✓ An ability to sustainably maintain a self-other distinction.

Empathy has been the subject of various methods of study, from the more neuroscientific ones of neuroimaging to self-report measures. The overlaps and differences with the construct of mentalization touch on various aspects. First, both involve appreciating the states of mind of others, but empathy adds sharing and concern. Furthermore, the orientation of empathy is directed more toward others, while in mentalization it is evenly distributed. Both operate both implicitly and explicitly, but empathy is considered species in its most implicit mode. Finally, the content of empathy, as with mentalization, involves the use of cognitive skills but is primarily focused on effects. For what about differences while mentalization is also the conscious or unconscious subjective experience of the other at a given moment, empathy is, beyond that, the understanding, conscious or unconscious, voluntary, or automatic, of the ultimate determinants that they produced that kind of experience in the other. Empathy is therefore a broader view of the entire process that led the other to assume one or more mental states (cognitive and/or emotional and/or behavioral). The basic mechanism that allows the empathic relationship, even if it concerns a single element of the communicative-relational sequence, is the assumption of the other's point of view (frame of reference), stepping into his shoes but discarding them, when necessary, always aware that there are two points of view, one's own and that of the other.

Empathy and emotional intelligence

Now let's see a possible correlation between empathy and emotional intelligence.
Emotional intelligence can be defined as "the ability to monitor one's own and others' emotions. This to differentiate between them, and to use that information to guide one's thinking and actions" (Salovey & Mayer, 1990); it contains within it those skills of awareness and self-mastery, motivation, empathy, and ability to manage social relationships, which any person can develop, and which prove to be fundamental for every human being. Emotional intelligence is defined as the ability to recognize and understand emotions both in oneself and in others and to use this awareness in managing and improving one's own behavior and relationships with others (Morgese, 2018).

The author who remains most influential in terms of emotional intelligence is Goleman who, at the base of emotional intelligence, identifies two types of skills, the personal one, i.e., how we control ourselves and the social one, i.e., the way we manage relationships with the other (Goleman, 1995). When emotional intelligence is not developed, one runs the risk of becoming emotionally illiterate (or emotionally illiterate), i.e., one becomes incapable of recognizing and controlling one's own emotions and has difficulty recognizing the emotions of others as well, which makes one unable to feel empathy and compassion. High levels of emotional intelligence, on the other hand, allow us to be empathetic toward others, understand them and know how to put ourselves in their shoes (Morgese, 2018).

Empathy in medicine

An experimental study carried out by the Giancarlo Quarta Onlus Foundation, in collaboration with the University of Udine, observed what happens in the brain of a patient when he listens to the referring doctor. The research was based on a sample of 30 healthy people aged between 19 and 33 years.
Through neuroimaging tests, the test showed that the doctor's choice of words and even gestures activated specific brain areas linked to the need for emotional understanding and attention, very important aspects for overcoming the depersonalization of the disease which transforms a "person" in "sick".
On one side, it is crucial for doctors to learn how to communicate empathetically with the patient. On the one hand, psychological detachment from the patient can

help to have an objective view of the pathology, but it is equally useful to try to 'feel' what the patient 'feels'.

But in the other side, the empath will therefore tend to absorb the emotions around him wherever he goes. Even unpleasant emotions can invade him as if they were his own. Places like nursing homes or hospitals can cause feelings of tiredness in these types of people. In any case, however, the assessment of the doctor's communication and empathic skills should therefore be part of his training background. Furthermore, the empathic incapacity considerably reduces the effectiveness of the therapeutic action because medicine is about taking care of people, without ever losing sight of one's humanity.

Empathy in love relationships

Empathy is a fundamental factor in couple relationships. In love relationships, the human being does not give material things, but himself in substance; therefore, the people who love to feel alive. There is a desire to merge with the other being, understanding it fully, which is just a dimension of empathy itself; therefore, empathy facilitates the involvement of growth within the couple.

Empathy can produce positive and negative effects on the couple. In the first case, it can be used to resolve misunderstandings and futile quarrels; in the second case, however, it can damage it by highlighting the differences that threaten the continuity of the relationship. In fact, empathy prolongs love when there is no disparity between partners in mutual understanding and ability to feel each other. But when a dysfunctional relationship is created, empathy represents a form of imbalance towards empathy. This discussion will be discussed in much more detail in the next sections of the guide. Heinz Kohut said that empathy is the oxygen that gives life to the loving relationship between individuals, meaning the relationship as an autonomous individual formed by two individualities in a temporary state of the fusional relationship.

The Dark Side of Empathy: Disorders and Degeneration

Empathy, we have said so far, represents something positive, capable of creating healthy relationships (even if we have already mentioned the negative empathy discourse). However, empathy doesn't always have a healthy, positive side, it can have darker sides which we will briefly review below.

Empathy and Psychopathology

Well yes, even empathy can be a psychopathological disorder.
There are two categories of very complex and difficult-to-treat disorders, with multifactorial and little-known etiopathogenesis, which predispose to even serious antisocial behaviors:

- ✓ Psychopathy
- ✓ Psychosis.

Patients with schizophrenia also show a lack of empathy and recognition of the emotions of others, but it is only one symptom among many and is rarely a problem for social security.
But empathy could be a wake-up call for the following disorders:

- ✓ In fact, cluster B personality disorders, characterized by traits of drama and impulsivity, lead to an alteration of interpersonal relationships and emotional dysregulation, which can at least in part be traced back to an empathic deficit.
- ✓ Narcissistic Personality Disorder (NPD)The distinctive elements of narcissistic personality disorder basically concern three themes: the grandiose idea of self, the constant need for admiration and the lack of empathy. Referring to this last characteristic, it can be said that often patients with narcissism are unable to put themselves in the shoes of others and to recognize that they too have desires, feelings and needs. From this comes the belief of narcissists that their own needs come first and that their way of seeing things is the only universally right.
- ✓ Histrionic Personality Disorder (IPD). A person with a histrionic personality disorder is characterized by excessive emotionality and attention-seeking. In particular, the patient manifests discomfort in contexts in which he is not the center of attention, seductive and/or provocative behavior, exaggeratedly inappropriate, unstable, and superficial emotionality, use of physical appearance as a means of attracting attention to himself, impressionistic speech, highly suggestible, tendency to view relationships as more intimate than they really are. Surely one of the aspects on which the treatment of these patients is developed is to increase social skills, including a sense of empathy, and avoiding overly seductive or provocative attitudes.
- ✓ Borderline Personality Disorder (BPD). A borderline personality disorder is a condition characterized by long-term patterns of emotional, interpersonal, and behavioral instability. The serious difficulties manifested in interpersonal relationships could be due, at least in part, to difficulties in the sphere of empathy

and theory of mind processes. New research from the University of Georgia indicates that this may be linked to poor brain activity in regions important for empathy in patients with the disorder. Other recent studies (Guttman and Laporte, 2000; Lynch et al., 2006), however, show that in borderline disorder there would be an exaggerated and hyper-affective resonance with the mental state of the other, determined by a dissociation between the affective and cognitive components of empathy.

- ✓ Antisocial Personality Disorder (DAP). The person affected by antisocial personality disorder is mainly characterized by inobservance and violation of the rights of others, which manifest themselves in an adult subject, at least from the age of 15. Childhood is usually punctuated by petty thefts, lies and fights; adolescence from episodes of substance abuse and, upon reaching adulthood, there is a manifest inability to assume responsibility, keep a job and maintain a stable emotional relationship. The way of relating to others is drastically characterized by superficiality and lack of respect for the feelings and concerns of those around them, generally, they can be defined as not very empathetic and not very sensitive to the feelings or rights of others.

Empathy in the dark triad

Let us try for a moment to analyze a possible degeneration of empathy from another point of view.
Personality research reveals a new psychological construct: empathy in the dark triad. We are talking about seemingly cold people, but who are actually capable of kindness, compassion and emotional connection.
We have already touched upon a few possible disorders above, but in general, it is assumed that the psychopath, the Machiavellian, and the narcissist lack genuine empathy. However, as we have seen from what has just been reported above, this discourse is more complex than one might think. So much so that from the field of personality, there is already talk of a new variable as interesting as it is revolutionary: empathy in the dark triad.
What is it about? It is a new psychological construct that defines a very small slice of the population. These are individuals who, although they present some traits of the classic dark triad of personality, reveal a less dark and even compassionate side. The data has attracted the attention of experts and it seems that research in this direction is destined to continue.
Some call them anti-heroes. Most of them are men who, although they display a somewhat cold demeanor and even some mastery of the art of manipulation, hide

talent, personal responsibility and even kindness. In this case, narcissists and serial manipulators can therefore be excluded.

Evolutionary psychology has advanced the hypothesis that traits of the dark triad can give humanity a certain boost. Skills such as decisiveness, the ability to lead others, making quick decisions in complex conditions or not backing down when you have a goal in mind are clearly advantageous aspects.

But what do we mean when we talk about the dark triad? It is a psychological theory, formulated in 2002 by Paulhus and Williams, which encompasses three characteristics of the personality: narcissism, Machiavellianism, and psychopathy. These traits define a clearly malignant personality in which emotional coldness, aggressiveness and falsehood stand out.

But what would you say if we told you that the broad spectrum of traits that define a dark profile also includes a more compassionate and civic-minded part? Recent studies reveal that a new personality trait called dark empathy has been discovered which, in some ways, represents the more positive side of the dark triad. In other words, dark empathy is something that could be placed in the triad. But how? Through research published in July 2020 the Universities of Nottingham and Bishop Grosseteste (UK), together with Auckland University of Technology (New Zealand), conducted a study to better understand the role of empathy in the dark triad. It emerged that: neither the psychopathic nor the narcissistic and Machiavellian personalities show dark empathy. They feel empathy if they perceive the emotional reality of others, but it is a resource they use to better manipulate. Their empathy is clearly instrumental. Nonetheless, thanks to this research conducted on a sample of almost a thousand people, an extraordinary fact has been discovered. While showing dark traits, 19.3% showed a different type of empathy, very high. They were able to connect and feel each other's reality and even feel compassion. This empathy has been called dark empath (DE) or dark empathy.

So, can empathic psychopaths exist? Are there any compassionate narcissists? In fact, the study shows that people with "certain" psychopathic, Machiavellian, or narcissistic traits may experience a dark form of empathy.

What are the characteristics of empathy in the dark triad?

This subsection serves as a discriminator to understand what an empath is not and to avoid confusion with the darker variant of empathy. So, let's examine what are the characteristics of a possible empathic subject belonging to the dark triad:

- ✓ It is mostly men. In the world of cinema and literature, they are presented as the classic mysterious or malevolent characters who reveal that they have a good heart. It is the vampire who does not drink blood, the cold, sagacious and antisocial investigator, but who always defends and takes care of the needy. The calculating thief, who leads his group and who commits a criminal act only for a good cause. These prototypical images demonstrate that dark triad characteristics can sometimes be oriented toward a noble end, hence the interest in psychology. After all, these personalities embody several traits that can be useful in certain professional careers: spies, soldiers, doctors, and even public officials.

- ✓ Extraversion and neurosis: Dark empathy is accompanied by dynamic and clearly extroverted behaviors, which make it easy to express one's feelings to others. Likewise, these people exhibit neurotic traits. In other words, they can show emotional ups and downs (anxiety, depression, phobias, etc). Very often they get trapped by their own emotional pain.
- ✓ Friendly, sociable, and pleasant in social relationships. Kindness is genuine. The person does not feign her feelings and enjoys relating to others, creating an authentic connection with them.
- ✓ Participatory leadership. One of the common traits in the dark triad is a thirst for power. These subjects like, define them and feel satisfied with their leadership. Empathy in the dark triad makes such leadership more humane. These people can bring out the best in others for the good of all. They are leaders who inspire, participate, and improve the psychological health of others.
- ✓ Empathy in the Dark Triad, a vulnerable narcissism. Another characteristic of this highly empathic personality is narcissistic-type vulnerability. He is easily offended. She understands and respects the reality of others but is strongly influenced by negative comments or certain behaviors.
- ✓ Imperfect, but brilliant. This profile tends to show great expertise in many areas. He is talented, he is a good leader, and he interacts very well with the people around him. Although, of course, he continues to display complex traits, such as a certain narcissism and clear manipulative skills.

Studies on this personality variable will continue in the coming years. Thanks to this, we will be able to learn more about these fascinating figures.

So, who is the dark empath?

When we talk about empathy, generally, despite what we have jest said above, we think of a positive quality, but a Dark Empath person can be downright unpleasant. Sure, the name is quite alluring – and if you're a Star Wars fan, you might be thinking of Darth Vader or some other leader of the dark side of the Force.
But the charm, as they say, is that of evil, at least potentially. In psychology, studies on this type of personality are increasing more and more, which has a decidedly pop name but in reality, must be taken with a grain of salt. Continuing the comparison

with the universe (indeed, the galaxy) of Star Wars, it could be said that a Dark Empath is a person who uses empathy for dark purposes.

We have seen that, on a psychological level, empathy has two essential aspects: the cognitive and the emotional (or affective).

Often, in narcissistic personalities, there may be so-called cognitive empathy (stronger than affective empathy).

When this cognitive empathy is used to do harm, we can speak of dark empathy, from which the term Dark Empath emerged. Such a personality is one who is capable of deeply understanding another's emotional state, but who exploits his or her understanding of other people to harm them. It may happen that Dark Empath people also possess one or more antisocial personality traits that we have already mentioned and that makeup what in psychology is called the Dark Triad, i.e., Machiavellianism, psychopathy, and narcissism.

While the term Dark Empath isn't exactly official in psychology, research, as shown above, is moving toward understanding whether there is an empathic version of the Dark Triad personalities. Or what is the role of empathy in the personality patterns of narcissism, Machiavellianism, and psychopathy? At the basis of these studies is the connection with some important traits (for example aggression, high professional functioning, social relationships, etc).

A Dark Empath is therefore similar to Dark Triad personalities in regard to the level of vulnerable narcissism, leadership, psychopathy and Machiavellianism, DEs have higher levels of grandiosity and lower levels of exploitation. They are poor in close relationships but have greater social pleasure than Dark Triad. These results highlight the protective effects of empathy.

So, dark Empath (DE) people therefore exist. But why can they be dangerous? Clinical psychologist, Dr. Ramani Durvasula has explained the reason why they are particularly insidious personalities. He affirms practically that "a dark empath can be more dangerous than a colder, more callous Dark Triad personality. This is because the so-called dark empath can draw you closer and do more damage as a result." The dark empath, Dr. Durvasula continued, seeks to "understand what makes (another person) work with the aim of extracting the information" useful for their own benefit. In other words, a Dark Empath uses his empathy (understood as the ability to connect with others) to hurt them more deeply. Understanding this difference is really essential for you to use your empathy in the best way and avoid the traps of toxic people.

To conclude the general discussion on empathy and move on, in the next chapter, to talking about the real subject of empathy, it is evident how empathy can be considered not only as a form of knowledge, but also as a cognitive process, an ability that can be practiced, trained, and mastered. Being able to decide in a flexible way when, how and how much to activate the empathetic feeling, depending on the situations and the person or the social context in which we interact, would enable us to avoid falling back into the two extremes of absence or excess of empathy, which it can, in turn, cause nervous breakdowns and depressions in those who experience it, which certainly do not make them more capable of helping others.

Chapter 2: Are You an Empath? (Typical signs and how to recognize if you are an empath)

Here we are at a very important part of the guide, the one that will explain to you whether you are actually an empath or not. A specific definition will be provided and what are all the signals to understand if you are actually an empath?

Who is an empath?

As always, let's start by defining what we are talking about: in this case, we will define the empath person. Therefore, we have already said that empathy is nothing more than the ability of a person to perceive the mood and feelings of another person, thus realizing an emotional harmony towards him which allows him to share his inner experiences and emotions. So, the person who is an empath is the person who has these qualities and skills. But let's define it even better. Empathy is the ability to experience an appropriate emotion in response to that expressed by others requires that a person is aware that such emotion derives from the other and at the same time is able to distinguish between self and others while regulating one's own responses emotional. But as we have said, not all people, despite being able to understand empathy, are able to put themselves in the other's shoes. That is, there are many people who feel and understand what is happening but then cannot manage emotions and communication to empathize with each other. Empathic people differ precisely in the fact that they are able to project the feelings and emotions of the other within themselves, however regulating these emotions, not like a mirror, but reworking them so as not to hurt, stay close and communicate with the other in a positive and assertive way. So, an empathetic person can be defined as a subject who is very sensitive to the emotions of the people close to him and their energy. This sensitivity occurs both towards those close to the empath every day and towards complete strangers. Empaths feel the world around them and perceive what others experience through their highly developed senses and intuition.

They understand how people are feeling and are able to understand what they are going through. So, what differentiates an empathetic person from a person who can empathize? The empath has a higher level of connectedness than the average. Empaths don't feel simple empathy, let's talk about something more: they don't need physical senses (sight, hearing, smell, etc.) to absorb other people's emotions and energies, they are instead capable of feeling and internalizing other people's emotions.

Doubts about the subject empath

Now that we have provided a definition of the empath subject, let's answer two very important questions, which will further clarify the matter.

Do all human beings have the same capacity to be empathic?

The neuronal component at the base of empathy is present in every individual, but the development of empathy depends on a learning process that can also take place in a profoundly different way. A series of bio-psycho-social factors contribute to the development of empathic competence. One of these is given by the relationships that are established during early childhood, then developed throughout life. Primary interactions play a fundamental role, above all the mother-child relationship.

Are there people who are not empathetic?

The lack of empathy characterizes, for example, the forms of psychopathy characterized by a deficit of the empathic component. Within the sphere of psychological and psychopathological disorders, we can find shortcomings in the development of this competence. On the one hand, the affective component may fail. On the other, the more properly cognitive one. For example, in severe disorders such as schizophrenia, there is a lack of affective empathy: on a cognitive level, the patient understands the mood and situation of the other, but is unable to take action, is caged and has no possibility of expressing and accept the feelings of the other. Conversely, a cognitive deficiency occurs in the case of autistic disorders or borderline personality traits: those who suffer from it perceive what comes from the other but are unable to decode it.

Why do we become more Empaths?

Although this ability, as we have seen, is a biological and genetic ability that we all have, many people fail to develop it. Therefore, empathy must be considered as a cognitive process that needs to be trained and that can improve, and not just a fact. In fact, training would allow us to manage our empathic emotions in a flexible way and in keeping with the context or the person we are facing, ensuring that we do not fall back into excess or lack this ability. But how is it possible to train empathy and what are the factors that can stimulate it or not? In general, education and the environment in which one grows up, as the experiences lived during childhood and adolescence can have a negative or positive influence in this sense. For example, a very competitive climate in the family at school, the establishment of toxic relationships or a low self-esteem could negatively affect the building of empathy.

But not only. The social context also plays a fundamental role in this sense. According to a study by the University of Michigan, college students today are 40% less empathetic than students in the 1980s and 1990s. What are the reasons? Let's look at some of them according to this study:

- ✓ Increased media exposure (including television, newspapers, movies, video games, etc): this type of exposure could make people more indifferent to suffering because it tends to normalize it. If you also include the sensationalism of today's media this indifference only gets worse.
- ✓ The role of social media: relationships that are established online, whether friendship or love, tend to be managed in a different way than those experienced in person, thanks to the ease with which it is easy to disconnect if you don't want to listen to the other's problems or simply if you don't want to hang out with him anymore.
- ✓ Competition, narcissism, and the aspiration to success that is promoted by many cultural models (influencers, reality shows, online success, etc.) mean that people are so focused on themselves and on these ephemeral and superficial values that they do not have time to devote to caring for others and empathy.
- ✓ Self-centeredness, narcissism and very often the lack of relationships in the offline world make our society less attentive to the requests of others and to the development of empathy.

Signs that you are an empath

As we have noticed, they are people who have a special gift even if it can sometimes become a burden: they are empaths, and you could be too.
Have you ever been told that you are too sensitive or emotional? Do you feel drained if you spend time with other people like they've drained your energy? Do you ever change your mood from one moment to the next, for no apparent reason and when someone close to you feels sadness or physical pain? Or do you feel raw when a person isn't sincere, or when they're hiding something from you? If this has happened to you more than once, it means you are an empath.
Sudden crying, laughter, and sensations that you are not experiencing firsthand but that you can really feel? Think about it, because if it happens to you often you are probably an empathic person. Even if it will seem absurd and not very rational, people with empathy are those who can grasp, understand, and feel other people's emotions and feelings. For this reason, empathy is a very useful social skill and above all an uncommon gift. However, this special "ability" has its downside.

For many people, all this means loading themselves uncontrollably with negative feelings, anxieties, and bad sensations in the simple moment in which others experience them.

Below we will show you what are the 14 characteristics to recognize if you are an empathic person. If you recognize yourself in these 14 characteristics then you too have this special ability.

Let's see together these typical characteristics:

1. **You are a woman, and you may probably be empathic by nature**

As we have seen before in this guide, several studies on the subject have in fact shown that women are more empathetic than men and that there is therefore a sort of gender attitude. Obviously, we must not generalize, not all women are very empathetic, as there are many men who are.

2. **You can feel the emotions of others, even when they are not present**

You can feel the emotions of others as if they were your own. This is the classic number one trait of an empath. It doesn't matter what someone else close to you is feeling, even if they think they don't show it, chances are you will notice it immediately. But more than that: you may actually feel the emotion as your own, "absorbing" it.

How exactly these works is a matter of some debate. But we know that people who have high levels of empathy also have highly active mirror neurons, the part of the brain that reads other people's emotional signals and figures out what they might be thinking or feeling. In other words, if you're an empath, chances are you can pick up on subtle changes in expression, body language, or tone of voice that others don't see, and immediately sense what that person is feeling.

Those same active mirror neurons, however, mean you basically experience the sensation as if it were your own. This can be a powerful gift, but also exhausting and overwhelming at times. Those who are empathetic are able to capture the "energy fields" of people with whom they have a strong bond and often happen to ask themselves "Why do I feel these emotions when they are not really mine?" If you're an empath, it can be difficult to get into public places, because you may suddenly find yourself caught up in an emotion that has come out of "nowhere" - or, more accurately, someone else who is in that area.

3. **The "vibe" of a room matters to you, a lot**

Perhaps unsurprisingly, empaths are extremely sensitive to the "feel" or vibe of their surroundings. When they are surrounded by peace and calm, they flourish, because they take on those qualities within. By the same token, beautiful places can be transformative for empaths, whether it's a peaceful garden, a beautiful bedroom, or the halls of a museum. Likewise, chaotic, or depressing environments will quickly draw energy from an empath.

4. In the evening you are often tired for no reason

This aspect is very common in empath people who have contact with different people during the day, feeling their sensations, they take charge of everything and in the evening, when they get home, they suffer the "emotional discharge". Because of this, they need to spend time alone and love being in nature to recharge their batteries.

5. You understand where people come from

Empathy expert Dr. Judith Orloff explains that this is the most fundamental trait of an empath, even more so than absorbing the emotions of others. In this case, empaths could learn not to absorb completely emotions, and some empaths rarely "absorb" them at all. But all empaths are capable of intuitively sensing what someone is trying to express, even when they're having a hard time getting it out. Empathy, after all, is basically about understanding and connecting with others. And that's what it means to perceive where people come from.

6. People come to you for advice

Empaths are often sought out by their friends for advice, support, and encouragement. It also helps that empaths tend to be good listeners and often wait patiently for the other to come up with what they need to say and then respond from the bottom of their hearts.
If this sounds familiar to you, you can probably understand that it can be difficult at times: people don't always realize how much energy it takes to listen and give advice, and some people take it for granted.

7. Tragic or violent events on TV can completely knock you out

If you are an empath, it doesn't matter that a certain horrible event isn't happening to you personally, you still feel it throughout your entire being. It may seem that you feel the pain or loss related to a certain event, even if you are thousands of miles away - or indeed, even if it is an imaginary event from a show. Often, this kind of reaction can be completely overwhelming.

Empaths, such as HSPs, may dislike violence or a tragic event, even if it is in a film that others find compelling. An empath person has such sensitivity that he often finds himself with feelings of pain or happiness even for people he doesn't know, scenes seen on TV or episodes told. For example, being moved even in front of a video or wanting to celebrate someone's success as if it were your own.

8. **You cannot contain your love for pets, animals, or children.**

Sure, everyone knows that babies are adorable little miracles and cats, and dogs are delightful creatures, but for you, those feelings seem to be much stronger. You may not be able to keep yourself from cuddling someone else's baby, or immediately squat down to show your love for a puppy. Some people may find your reaction "over the top" but you, how can you not act like that?
In many cases, this is one of the many benefits of being an empath. All your feelings, including positive ones, are magnified.

9. **You may also perceive people's physical illnesses, not just their emotions**

When someone is sick or injured, you may even come to feel their discomfort as if it were your own. This doesn't just mean feeling compassion or concern for them, but having actual physical sensations such as pain, tightness, or soreness in the same areas of the body. It's as if your empathic brain is not only mirroring what the other person is experiencing but also physically projecting that experience into your own body.
And that can be annoying, even debilitating. It's probably not a "gift" that most empaths like to have. But it's also at the root of why empaths are such great "helpers." Without this ability, they wouldn't be able to truly connect with someone who is hurting or get what they need to feel more comfortable. Not surprisingly, empaths are drawn to roles like nurse, doctor, and caregiver. If you have this ability to feel everyone's pain, it would be surprising not to want to be in such a profession.

10. **You can get overwhelmed in love relationships**

Relationships can be difficult for everyone. But imagine how much bigger those challenges are when you can sense every little mood, irritation, or yes, even lying from your partner. And positive emotions can also become overwhelming as if the relationship could "swallow you up." Sound familiar to you? But it's more than that. Once you cohabitate, the shared environment is also a hindrance. The "energy" of a cohabiting partner is always there for an empath and can almost feel like an intrusion. Empaths see their homes as a sanctuary where they can get away from the constant

"emotional demand" of others, and a partner who lives in that same space changes that.
While some empaths choose to remain single for this reason, others learn to adapt, perhaps reserving a room that becomes their private space or (extremely importantly) seeking a partner who respects their boundaries.

11. **You have a strong sixth sense and you recognize people who lie**

When they are able to experience the sensations of others often, empaths also understand when the person who addresses them is lying or if he is hiding something, without knowing the reason, however, but precisely as a "feeling". Sure, there were probably times when someone successfully duped you, but also times when you recognized that you were going against your instincts all along. An empath's ability to process even the smallest cue from another person means that it's nearly impossible to hide your true intentions from them. Even if you don't know exactly what a person really wants, you know if she's not being completely honest or if she seems shifty.

12. **You fail to understand why a leader wouldn't put their team first**

There are many managers and group organizers who simply don't pay attention to the needs of their team. If you are an empath, this is not just rude or annoying to you, but a failure of leadership.
In part, this is because empaths can make excellent leaders themselves, and when they do, it's always by listening to their team and uniting people around shared goals. Empaths tend to be thoughtful and attentive, making sure every team member feels heard. The result is not only to have a group of happier people but also to be able to make the best decisions by obtaining all the information.

13. **You have a calming effect on other people and the power to heal them**

It is true. Just as people seek advice from empaths, they also feel more at peace in the presence of an empath. In fact, people often unknowingly seek out their most empathetic friends during tough times.
This is something you can develop and use to actually heal people, in the sense of helping them overcome serious emotional baggage and overcome unhealthy patterns. But you can't do it if you hide your sensitivity and empathy: you have to embrace your gift if you really want to make a difference.

14. You can't see someone in pain without wanting to help them

Can you walk past someone in need without wondering how you could help them? Do you struggle to "turn off" everything that may concern you for others because "there is work to be done"? If the answer is no, not even when you're busy, not even when you're in a hurry, then there's a good chance you're an empath. And that's why empaths are such a valuable part of the human race's amazing kaleidoscope. For an empath person, others are the brightest things on their radar, and for this reason, it's quite impossible not to see and respond to the needs of others. This is exactly where an empath's healing ability comes from, and it's something we could use more of in our world.

15. You are too good

The last characteristic trait in empathetic people is that they have a big heart and sacrifice a lot for other people, this type of aspect leads them to commit themselves to any person, friend or stranger who gets into trouble sometimes being upset first from their situation. If you have found yourself in these 6 characteristics, then there is no doubt: you are an empath.
And although this great gift is so complicated and sometimes heavy to manage, know that you are special people, and you will always have an edge over the others. It is no coincidence that empathy is one of the characteristics that charismatic leaders, great women of history and well-known personalities from the entertainment world often have.

With this little test to understand if you are an empathic person, our second chapter ends. In the next chapter, however, we will talk about the typical signals to understand if you have another empathetic person in front of you.

Chapter 3: 12 signs you need to recognize an empath

Well, so far, we have seen what empathy is, who the empath subject is and how to recognize if you are or not. Having done this, in this chapter we will briefly discuss the importance of empathy in others and what are the signs to recognize if a person is empathic.

What does it mean to feel empathy?

Before indicating why it is important to deal with empathic people and how to recognize them, let's do a little review of the meaning of feel empathy.
Feeling empathy means having the ability to identify ourselves with another person, in their thoughts, in their moods, and in what makes them unhappy. It is a feeling that penetrates the folds of the intimacy of the other, perceives the anxiety from the tone of voice, the irritation from the speed of the gestures, the uncertainty from a look. Unfortunately, the pandemic has cooled the driving force of empathy, making it increasingly complex and difficult, also due to fears of contagion and our lifestyles marked by fluctuating isolation. Healthcare distrust is perceptible everywhere. When we enter the supermarket, walk down the street, the time to meet someone. The bombardment of the infection and its progress has changed our perception of human relationships, and even very cautious physical contact is considered an object of risk, high risk. Hence a creeping regression into solitude, distance, and detachment from others. Without real affection.

The importance of recognizing empathy in the others

In this brief introduction, we will explain why it is important to recognize empathy in others. Now that you have discovered that you are an empath, you may be wondering if maybe people in your social circle can be one too. Why is empathy needed?
Empathy is a very important relational ability because it allows you to implement behaviors that bring people closer rather than push them away.
Being empathetic is important because thanks to understanding each other's experience you can direct your behavior towards help instead of aggression.
To use Martin Hoffman's words, empathy is like: "the spark that gives rise to human interest in others, the glue that makes social life possible".

Empathy, we reiterate, means the ability to put yourself in another person's shoes. It's the ability to feel what other people are feeling and understand what they need - how nice would it be if others were like that too? Understanding whether we are dealing with empathetic people is certainly important for establishing healthy relationships based on understanding, communication, and mutual respect. In order to fully understand the importance of empathy, it is good to enucleate and separate the empath from other similar feelings, such as sympathy, compassion and identification, emotions that are, perhaps, preparatory components of empathy itself. Tisseron (2013) compares empathy to a three-layered pyramid or a ship with three stacked decks:

1. **Basic empathy**

The purpose of this vessel, says Tisseron, is the basic empathy common to all men: an ability to change points of view without getting lost.
Basic empathy can, in turn, be divided into two levels, on the first level we have emotional empathy, typical of children who are beginning to know the outside world, and the second, the more advanced level is called cognitive empathy and allows us to perceive feelings of others. In short, here are the first attempts to put yourself in the place of others and their thoughts.

2. **Mutual empathy**

A higher level is that of mutual empathy, that is, when we begin to think that others too can think and feel the way we do, like true "mirrors", others can identify themselves and experience the same sensations as us; we are in contact with the gestures and the identifying vision of other beings.

3. **Intersubjective empathy**

Intersubjective empathy is the highest process of the empathic hierarchy, true inner "places" of oneself come into contact as mutual changes and transformations. It is based on reciprocal experiences capable of activating real intersubjective psychological bipolarities.
The empathic process, therefore, consists in putting oneself in the other's shoes, thus feeling their emotions and expectations. Empathizing with the emotions of others allows us to competently understand the inner world of the people with whom we connect.
Freud in 1921 in "Psychology of the masses and analysis of the Ego", explains how empathic identification the first way is to connect and communicate with others in the early stages of development. For Freud, indeed, it is only with psychological

empathy that we can enter into communication with psychological dimensions other than us, but with Kohut, empathy becomes a basic methodology in therapeutic work. In fact, for Kohut, the therapist's immersion in an empathetic climate of closeness is the first step in rebuilding a SELF damaged by traumatic experiences. In fact, empathic people are well aware of the mechanisms and structures behind social relationships, and they also know very well how to analyze them. Precisely because of their intuition, listening skills and observations, they are able to recognize the feelings and intentions of others, even if they have just met them.

Having said this, one of the main disadvantages of the empath is getting too involved in the emotions of others, running the risk of becoming an emotional sponge and at the same time perhaps suppressing and not letting one's emotions leak, building emotional barriers for oneself so that others do not know their private thoughts and feelings.
Indeed, the empathic climate produces a strong reaction in the brain mirror neurons capable of activating sensations of well-being and neuro/psychological reward capable of regulating and positively modulating emotions and affective experiences.
Having suffered this empathy deficit creates distortions, symptomatic transformations, and denial of the validation of us as bearers of just rights and just needs, leaving us as illegal immigrants in the sidereal void. Therefore, it's really important to recognize people like us, who don't want to take advantage of our dislike, but who rather want to create a constructive relationship. But there is one thing to say; in love, the empath knows exactly how the other sees him: how he loves him, whether he respects him or not, and what he thinks about the relationship. Finding a partner is therefore a difficult thing and relationships often remain incomprehensible to others. People usually don't realize this kind of sensitivity; they are attracted to them and subconsciously they reveal very personal things. At a time when emotions are seen as weaknesses, this ability can also be seen as a curse for the empath. But particularly empathic people are sensitive, intuitive, grasp details, understand when people have conflicts or particular moods, are very insightful and know how to put themselves at service. Usually, an empath person experiences at least once in their life the experience of being betrayed, exploited, or judged. The classic empath must learn that empathy represents a rare and therefore precious resource, not to be underestimated. The empath person who learns to value his talent and learns to protect himself manages to accomplish great things and also uses his intuition for work. In short, in interpersonal or work relationships, empathy becomes the main and perhaps the only "access key" to feelings, moods, motivations and more generally to the world of the other. Thanks to it, one can not only grasp the meaning of what the interlocutor says but also grasp its deeper meaning, tuning in to

its own psycho-emotional "wavelength". Being able to connect with others emotionally means having power and knowing how to use it well for yourself and for others means turning a way of being in favor of good and harmony.

In the next paragraph, we will explain which signals you need to consider in order to recognize an empath person.

12 signs of an Empath

Empath people are the type of people who are particularly predisposed to absorb or feel very strongly the emotions of others or other physical symptoms. All this would be due to the very great sensitivity and the inability of these people to better metabolize and understand emotions or their feelings. In extreme cases, these people can end up with various problems, including depression. Let's see together 12 characteristic signs present in this type of person.

It must be said that these characteristics have a lot in common with what we have already shown you in the last chapter that which was about you and recognizing your empathy.

1. <u>Empaths are very sensitive people</u>

If you have understood to fall into the empathetic category, you will have been repeatedly told that you are too sensitive or emotional. As mentioned earlier regarding you and the signs to understand if you are an empath, in general empaths are people who naturally perceive other people's emotions more, and this leads them to be good listeners and to be hurt more easily. This greater sensitivity leads empaths to absorb and be conditioned by these external feelings, in fact, if an empath person is in contact with people who express negative feelings, he will assume the same state of mind. They are two adjectives, in fact, that well describe the nature of an empath. Also, empath people are open and approachable, and good listeners. If you have an empath in your circle of friends you recognize him because he is the one you turn to when there is a problem: you know that you can talk freely with him, because he listens to you, has ears only for you and knows how to dispense good advice. Be careful though, because being very sensitive it is very easy to hurt them, even unintentionally: they lack the armor that can protect them.

Their excessive availability to others leaves them without energy, which is why empaths are often both physically and emotionally tired. They need to take breaks, and disconnect from the rest of the world, to be able to recover and rest.

2. <u>They feel the emotions of others, and feel their own pain</u>

Because of their extreme sensitivity, empaths tend to take charge of the emotions of others without even realizing it. If there is no awareness of being like a mirror that reflects what others feel, life can become very difficult for them, as they will find themselves sad, depressed, and angry, without knowing why. In cases of greater sensitivity, they can even feel physical pain and feel bad if the other is sick. They are more prone to disease and have a very low pain threshold.

3. Empaths are very introverted people

It is known everyone that empaths are mainly very introverted people, in fact interacting with large groups of individuals is not easy for them. Generally, these people prefer to have stable contact with a few people at a time or with only 1. All of this naturally causes a drastic decrease in time spent in public or in a crowd. Even so, the time they spend in someone's company is limited, because contact with others exhausts them energetically.
An empath is unlikely to do well in a crowd, as this only amplifies his emotions and feelings. While they are excellent listeners, they are unlikely to tell you about them, preferring to keep their feelings and experiences inside.

4. They are loners and spend a lot of time alone

Another characteristic aspect present in empath people is the fear of being overwhelmed by intimate relationships for fear of losing one's identity. Because their energy is overwhelmed in the midst of others, empaths prefer to be alone. They are often described as loners: it is when they are alone, preferably in contact with nature, that they manage to recharge and find their balance. Furthermore, empathic people are very sensitive to hectic everyday activities, therefore, to recharge and relax, they love being in the middle of nature.
If they go out with friends, they are the ones who arrive alone in their own vehicle, so they can leave when they want, without depending on others.

5. They have excellent intuition and problem-solving skills

Intuition for empathic people turns out to be the tool with which they interpret the world and feelings, in order to understand which relationships to maintain and which ones to close.
Empaths are good listeners and are able to put people at ease, so much so that listening becomes one of their strengths for understanding and deciphering the world. They are also able to read the environment and have good intuition to understand what the other is feeling or experiencing, without necessarily having to express themselves in words.
Empath people, thanks also to their strong sense of problem-solving, love to find solutions to problems because they are great thinkers who love to explore different

topics. Furthermore, as soon as they feel worried or distressed about something, they will tend to immediately seek an answer to their crisis, to find peace of mind.

6. They are a favorite "target" of energy vampires

Perhaps you have heard of energy vampires: these are people who tend to "suck" the energy of others in a more or less conscious way. The energy, anger, or fear of emotional vampires can weaken that of an empath and thereby undermine their stability.

Hardly those who are so sensitive manage to defend themselves or put barriers between themselves and others and very often end up being a victim of emotional vampires. One of the most dangerous categories is the narcissist: the one who only cares about himself and convinces others that their behavior is the problem. In the most pathological cases, the narcissist can even convince the other that he is not worthy of being loved. To remedy such a scenario, in the next sections of the guide, we will explain to you how to avoid being prey to these toxic people.

7. They love nature and animals

Empaths are capable of unconditional love, which is why they often surround themselves with the company of a dog, cat, or other pet at home. And they can't stand the cruelty that can be done to defenseless beings. Outdoors, in the middle of nature, they find their balance: they feel particularly good near water, whether it's the sea or the lake because this natural element regenerates them.

They respect every living thing that is part of the natural world because they know that everyone has a soul and has feelings like humans.

8. They hate lies

Empaths have difficulty lying because they are very expressive, but mainly because they feel that others know they are lying. Also, they can't lie to themselves or pretend they like something they don't actually like. They typically work in creative fields (writing, dance, music, etc.) to be able to express themselves and feed their soul.

Empaths don't need to ask questions, hear the tone of voice or study nonverbal language: if someone is lying, they know it. Their sensitivity also allows them to understand the reasons that lead the other to lie malice, ignorance, to spare someone else a painful truth, etc. And it's not about intuition: it's the certainty of knowing what drives the other to lie.

9. They are creative and dreamers

They are also curious, and have an ever-expanding knowledge and an infinite imagination: empaths have a great interest in the arts and culture because they are an expressive form of emotions. They are also very expressive with language, body, words, thoughts, and feelings. Their creativity is expressed through dance, theater, or their body expressions.

One of the strengths of empaths is that they are naturally creative, have a talent for the arts, and have a wild imagination. They are good writers, artists, painters, and singers. They also need always new stimuli: empaths may find it difficult to focus for long on things that don't stimulate their mind: they are dreamers who get bored or easily distracted. Then, if left unstimulated, their minds drift away, until they detach from physical reality. This is why they are easily found daydreaming or with their heads in the clouds. They are in fact daydreamers: they often spend much of their time daydreaming. If they don't receive stimuli, they get bored and distracted. At home, work, and school, they have to do something that piques their interest, or it will be hard to keep them grounded.

10. They can't stand violence

Empath people are particularly sensitive to images, scenes, movies, news, etc., that have to do with violence, drama, sadness, injustice, etc., and will not be able to look at them.

Precisely because they tend to absorb and experience the pain of others, physical and emotional, empaths cannot tolerate violence. Not even that of the movies or that is told through the news. Consequently, it is very difficult for them to read a newspaper or watch television.

11. They are free spirits

Freedom of movement and expression are very important to an empath. Rules that are too strict, confinement for supervision or routine are all things that could make them feel bad. They feel the need to discover the meaning of life and to gain experiences to gain knowledge on many subjects. Empaths rarely conform to society's standards. The traditional family, they prefer a solitary life made up of freedom, which allows them to live without restrictions or chains. They are truth seekers, so they spend most of their time learning something new, reading and researching. They are hungry for knowledge that they try to satisfy as much as possible. An empathetic person also finds the excessive presence of noises, smells or too much talking very annoying, leading to irritation. But not only that, even some people turn out to be "difficult" to manage due to the feelings transmitted, such as narcissists or people who victimize themselves too much.

12. They have a mighty heart

Finally, the last characteristic trait present more in empathic people is undoubtedly the fact that they have a big heart and sacrifice themselves a lot for other people, this type of aspect leads them to commit themselves to any friend or stranger they find in difficulty, remaining disturbed by their situation. They are people who exude a lot of warmth and compassion, and for this very reason they attract others towards them: even people who don't know them will tend to approach and unconsciously open to them to tell details of their private life. It's easier to open your heart to an empath person because you feel understood and free to be yourself. Even animals will tend to get closer and become more attached to these people.

With these twelve signals, our discussion on signals to understand if we are dealing with other empathic subjects concludes. In the next chapter, however, to conclude the complete picture of empathy and empaths in general, we will talk about the various types.

Chapter 4: The different types of empaths there are and how to classify them

In this concluding chapter of the general discussion of an empath, we will talk about the various types and how we can classify them.

How many types of empaths?

Generally, you recognize an empath person immediately. Some signals (aw we have indicated in the last chapter) trace the personality and the approach with others. An empath is sunny, positive, knows how to listen, doesn't talk to herself or himself, and doesn't stop at the first impression of the other person. Empath manages to go beyond the superficiality of a human relationship, she delicately grasps the emotions and moods of others. Empath recognizes the difference between superficiality and frivolity. Empathy means getting in tune with people's emotions and feelings, so much so that empathic people risk being overwhelmed even by negative energies that can somehow influence them.

Empaths have a high sensitivity and usually, their aim is to help people in need. Some people open up and even tell their entire life story to an empath, likely due to their kind and caring nature.

Empath people often feel misunderstood and ignored by today's world, which uses too much logic and reasoning. The dreamer, the wanderer, the drifter, the artist, the outcast, the hippie, etc. do not understand or resonate with the modern world, so society automatically deems them as 'troublemakers' or judges them as 'too sensitive.'

However, empaths bring very important gifts and lessons to the world. An empath shows us how to take the time to connect emotionally with someone else and thereby connect with them. Empaths teach us to take time for ourselves and nurture our creative and intuitive spirit. Empathic people also represent those who don't conform to a cruel world, no matter how tempting or easy that might seem. These people are usually old souls who have come here to this plan many times and have great wisdom to share. Empaths are not afraid to be alone with themselves when it's necessary, on the contrary: it's a way to be able to feel better with others. Seen through these characteristics, empathy is a gift, but not only. It is excluded that one can learn in the course of life.

It can be developed through practices such as active listening, trying to imagine situations from the point of view of others and taking the time to really understand a person's emotions rather than immediately giving advice or making judgments. It also requires an open, non-judgmental mindset towards others, as well as self-awareness and an understanding of one's emotions.

With practice, empathy can become an invaluable tool for building strong relationships and promoting emotional intelligence. It is well known that we must, first of all, find inner well-being with ourselves, in order to then be able to feel good and in harmony with the other people with whom we interact on a daily basis.

But how many types of empaths are there? There are five types of empaths. If you identify as an empath, read on to figure out which of these five skills best describes you.

1. **Emotional empath**

This type of empath is perhaps the most common on the list. Emotional empathy happens when you feel another person's emotions so deeply that you feel the emotion itself. In other words, one can easily put oneself in the shoes of other individuals, identifying with their struggles and pain. Highly empathic people feel overwhelmed by this ability. Another characteristic that represents them is being able to feel the energy of a room as soon as they enter it.

2. **Medical empath**

It happens to those people who feel someone else's ailments and illnesses, even if the latter is thousands of kilometers away. Empaths naturally absorb the energy of other people, especially those who are close to them. If someone they love becomes seriously ill there may be a risk that they too will become ill due to the great connection, they have with the other person. A 'medical empath' may also have the ability to spot an illness within another person, simply by using intuition.

3. **Empath from places**

This empathy, as one might imagine, occurs in different places on the planet. For example, you may feel particularly attracted to a certain place abroad and imagine yourself living happily there. Or, maybe when you go to the local mall, you want to get out of it right away. Some places trigger emotions within you.

This type of empath has the ability to feel others even more deeply. They can feel out of place in moments and figure out whether it's in their best interest to stay there or not.

4. **Intellectual empath**

These types of empaths know how to understand how people's brains work. They can easily understand someone's perspective and connect with it.

You love to get information from as many sources as possible and keep learning from all nuances of your life.

5. Environmental empath

Environmental empaths feel what is happening to the Earth on a very deep level. When the Earth goes through trauma or destruction, these people begin to feel bad emotionally and experience very negative emotions. They see the Earth and themselves as a unit and just want to protect the planet and restore it to its natural order.

Environmental empaths have an intense relationship with nature, a feeling they feel at a soul level. These people like to spend most of their time in the woods or on a beautiful beach, away from the hustle and bustle of the 'real' world.

How to classify different kinds of an empath?

There are various forms of Empathy, they are essentially 3 but the most important types that are classified mixed together determine our way of being empathic.
The 3 types of empathetic sensitivity are:

1. Cognitive Empathy. We have already talked about it. It is that type of empathy that allows you to clearly understand what the other person thinks and to fully understand her point of view. It is the typical empathy used by great speakers, salespeople, and negotiators. Basically, of all forms of empathy, it is the least deep and least developed, because while there is an understanding of other people's emotions, on the one hand, there is often a lack of compassion and the desire to actually care about how other people are feeling and to want to do something to help them. We can say that Cognitive Empathy is a half-hearted, almost apparent empathy in that the understanding of the moods of others does not follow a real desire to trigger an action that is useful for the well-being of the interlocutor. Especially narcissistic, manipulative, and Machiavellian characters have this empathic typology (have you ever heard of Energy Vampires who steal your energy? This is probably their form of Empathy!)
2. Emotional or Affective Empathy: In this second type of empathy, we already know that the relationship that is created is deeper, and one is able not only to understand but also to really experience the sensations of other people within oneself. It has been scientifically proven that during this phase of Empathy, there is a real reflection of the system of neurons that activate the same emotions in our brain circuits that the person in front of us is experiencing. Emotional or

Affective Empathy is therefore a step higher than Cognitive Empathy as it allows us to understand and even feel the moods of others on our skin but not necessarily to feel compassion for them.

3. Compassionate Empathy. This last type of Empathic Sensitivity involves what is called Empathic Concern. That is, in Compassionate Empathy, all the qualities of the other two types of empathy are merged together and we are therefore able to understand the emotions of the other, to feel them within ourselves and in addition, we are also able to understand how to help the person in front of us. Compassion and the desire to do our utmost for others arise in us in order to alleviate their suffering and make us useful for their well-being. This is therefore the truest and most authentic form of Empathy, that of those who make altruism and the well-being of the community their flag and their life mission.

As you have seen, empathy is a multifaceted ability with different nuances. Have you figured out which is the one that prevails the most in your behavior? In principle, each of us has a mix of the three types of Empathic Sensitivity even if one often tends to prevail over the others and tells a lot about our way of being. We are fully convinced that being empathetic, of any form or type, is undoubtedly a great advantage that helps us find that optimal feeling with the people who are close to us, not only in our private life but in all areas.

With the classification of the various types of empaths ends our general picture of empathy. In the next section, we will deal specifically with all things, empath, and relationships.

SECOND PART- EMPATH AND RELATIONSHIPS

Chapter 5: Empaths in relationships and how it behaves

In this part of the guide, we will deal with empathy and relationships and how this subject can establish them. We will start by analyzing the various types of relationships. Later we will try to understand the behavior of the empath in every single situation.

The different types of relationships for the empath

From the point of view of the social perspective, empathy is an important emotional competence thanks to which it is possible to connect with the person more easily with whom one interacts. However, without this necessarily implying the a priori justification of behavior, the unconditional and unreserved acceptance of a certain way of doing or sharing a particular state of mind. Empathy can also be compared to an invisible "two-way bridge", which however allows you to tiptoe into the other's world, to remain there for the time necessary to understand the motivations and intensity of their emotional experience, and then return to be themselves, consistent with their own existential reality. Empathy qualifies in any field as a social skill of fundamental importance; indeed it can be said that it represents one of the basic tools of truly effective and rewarding interpersonal communication.
Let's see, in this paragraph, how the various types of relationships work for the empath.

<u>Empaths in love relationships</u>

Empathy, as we now perfectly know, is the ability to tune into and resonate with the emotional-affective states of the other. Feeling empathy does not mean totally identifying with the other but being willing to use one's emotional and thought system to communicate with the other.
Empathy is a way of communicating in which the subject puts his own way of perceiving reality in the background to try to make room for the experiences and perceptions of the other, however freeing himself from his own interpretative filters, entering the intimacy of the other person without passing judgment.

Empathy in love relationships is fundamental, it facilitates involvement, and mutual growth and allows you to resolve misunderstandings and futile quarrels. It is precisely the ability to listen that keeps couples together, empathic communication is the basis for building a solid union.

However, being able to afford to empathize with your partner means being able to calm your reactions to the point of being quite understanding of the feelings of your loved one. Being able to calm yourself means knowing yourself, listening to your needs and requirements, feeling that you can express them freely, and knowing how to calm down. Simply put, it means to be differentiated.

Differentiation and intimacy involve balancing 2 basic life forces: the drive for individuality and the drive for relatedness. It is the ability to be in contact with another without risking feeling devoured; it involves staying who you are while being close to important people.

A differentiated self is solid but permeable; it allows you to continue with your own personal development while remaining interested in the happiness and well-being of your partner.

However, empathy in love can also produce negative effects and damage the couple, highlighting the differences that threaten the continuity of the relationship; in fact, empathy prolongs love when there is no disparity between partners in mutual understanding and ability to feel each other.

According to Sternberg, there are three determining elements for a solid union:

- ✓ Physical attraction (which is not eternal)
- ✓ The feeling of love
- ✓ The cognitive factors.

"I know you and you suit me for who you are" is the most important prerequisite to be sure that the one we are with is actually the person with whom we want to share our destiny.

What are the reasons that can create instability in the couple?

More frequently than we can imagine it is our unconscious and not our conscience that governs the important choices of our life; it, as a result of needs and unsatisfied relationships from our past (father/son-a relationship, mother/daughter-o, family machinery, etc.), dominates our choices and leads us to systematically repeat the same mistakes.

Empath: relationship with parents

Already in the first moments of life, we relate to mum and dad, and it is here that we learn the relationship dynamics which we will then refer to as we grow up.

The unacknowledged child ("you are worthless, but what do you want to do", etc...) or repressed ("you mustn't do this, you mustn't go out" etc...) develops, as an adult, the most selfish aspects within the family, egocentric and narcissistic of his personality, reaffirming a strong need for autonomy and self-affirmation; when this situation continues, there is an infantile and illusory vision of the relationship, which cannot work, and over time the two partners thus begin to lead parallel lives, essentially isolated from each other, alone within the relationship.

Already M. L. Hoffman emphasizes empathy, as something that appears in the awareness of the child from the first years of life. Mother and father should also learn to be empathetic subjects, especially through sensitivity and not punishment. They should therefore be educated in the values of altruism, and openness towards others so that the child learns to understand and share the point of view of others. In general, according to John Bowlby, there is the so-called attachment theory, according to which the relational bond that is created between the child and the adult figures (caregivers), who take care of him, is innate. Furthermore, this link can be explained by resorting to the evolutionary theory, according to which the little one can survive more easily if he has someone nearby who protects him from dangers and is close to him in happy moments and in those of difficulty. According to J. Elicker, M. Englund and L. A. Sroufe, indeed, adult attachment figures not only promote positive social expectations for the child but also strengthen the child's self-esteem together with the image he has of himself.

Empath in friendship

Friendship. A beautiful word and a great feeling. An invisible bond that unites us with others. An emotional bond arises with the people who cross our path and who almost magically become fundamental in our lives. Friendship is a relationship between people who are equals who share experiences, who feel secure and who trust each other unreservedly. There are various types of "friends" and, therefore, of friendship. Let's focus on true friendship. This is a king of friendship that an empath could set. That friendship that is neither imposed nor programmed, but which is built little by little, with efforts and mutual dedication. Over time, this relationship creates a bond strong enough to resist and last for years. A true friendship knows no distances, times or even deadlines. It is a relationship in which we seek and offer support and emotional help. Friendship is based on empathy, i.e., on the ability to understand and put yourself in the other person's shoes, to suffer and rejoice with them. It is a bond that allows us to "divide sorrows and multiply joys".

A healthy and constructive relationship is based on the typical values of empathy such as sincerity, understanding, mutual affection, respect, communication, attention, concern for the other, limitless trust, patience, and the ability to listen and know how to forgive. Consistency, flexibility, generosity, gratitude, and loyalty are other values to take into consideration to consolidate a friendship relationship.

Empath at work

Empathy qualifies as a social skill of fundamental importance, in any field, indeed it can be said that it represents one of the basic tools of truly effective and rewarding interpersonal communication. This manifests itself with active listening, which becomes empathetic when you are willing to get out of your own mental schemes and disregard personal interests to consider those of the other. Therefore, empathy can be considered a strategic form of communication, a sophisticated tool of emotional resonance, a sort of "emotional radar" with which to pick up and decode the weak signals of the mind and heart, the deepest moods, and hidden thoughts. Empaths therefore as a distinctive skill that cannot be renounced for any professional and social role.

How an empath sets relationships

Now let's see what the typical behaviors of empath people are to establish different types of relationships.

Basic empathy

We have already talked about it in the previous chapter. This time we take up the discussion in terms of establishing relationships and the behavior of the empath subject. Basic empathy corresponds to what is generally called identification, i.e., the ability to change your point of view on a situation without getting lost. This quality is distinguished in an emotional component, i.e., the ability to distinguish oneself from the other - a skill that emerges early in the child - and a cognitive one, the ability to assume the other's point of view - a skill that emerges around the age of 4 and a half. This empathy, therefore, concerns the possibility of imagining what it might be like to think in place of the other. To this end, it is not even essential that the other be recognized as a human being: one can very well identify with an imaginary being, such as the protagonist of a novel or cartoon.
On the other hand, it is possible to identify with someone without even seeing them or without the other realizing it. Empathy thus defined nurtures reciprocity, supporting solidarity and mutual aid.

Mutual empathy

In this case, the ability to represent the other's world adds to the desire for mutual recognition: not only do I identify with the other, but I also recognize their right to identify with me, that is, to put themselves in my place and thus have access to my psychic reality, to understand what I understand and to feel what I feel.

This experience refers to that of the mirror and implies direct contact with the person, as well as all the expressive gestures: mimicry of the face, smile, crossing gazes, and expressive gestures.

To deny this expressive mediation denies the existence of mutual empathy. This mutual recognition has three aspects: recognizing in the other the possibility of having self-esteem as I have of myself (narcissistic component); recognizing in him the possibility of loving and being loved (a component of object relations); recognizing him as a subject of law (a component of the group relationship)

Intersubjectivity

At this level, empathy consists in recognizing in the other the possibility of clarifying aspects of myself that I do not know. This is obviously the case for those who turn to a therapist, but fortunately, it is a situation that can also be found in friendships and love relationships, where barriers fall.

It is what Tisseron (2001), a French psychiatrist and psychoanalyst, calls "maximizing empathy" by linking it to the concept of intimacy, a concept developed as a counterpoint to intimacy, i.e., exposing fragments of oneself up to that moment to a more or less vast public protected from extraneous looks, i.e., kept intimate, to have their value recognized and thus obtain validation.

In this case, it is no longer a matter of identifying with the other, nor of recognizing in the other the ability to identify with me by accepting to share my fears with him, but of discovering myself, through the other, different from how I thought I was and to let myself be transformed by this discovery. At this moment the similarities count more than the differences and the two life paths of the interlocutors are an enrichment for both.

Learning empathy day after day

It follows that each of us discovers the other and himself at the same time. This mutual discovery and the pleasure that accompanies it are the keys to the elevated forms of empathy and solidarity of which we are capable.

But, at the same time, this proximity between oneself and the other cannot fail to arouse intense anguish: the fear of being manipulated, alienated from one's own freedom and one's desire, that is, of being absorbed in the other and of ceasing to exist autonomously.

The risk is therefore to want to manipulate the other and have dominion over him for fear of being subjected to the domination of the other. In a sense, the main enemy of empathy is domination in its two aspects, active and passive.

For this reason, human beings, even if endowed with extraordinary quality, can sometimes completely strip themselves of it: it is when they fear, rightly or wrongly, being manipulated. The only way to prevent it is to develop empathy from an early age and try to cultivate it in your relationships.

Friendship empath behavior

An empath has a form of intelligence, called empathy which we know is the ability to understand the state of mind of the other, and to assume a different point of view from one's own, which is what dialogue itself basically consists of.

The behavior of the empath works in friendship and therefore becomes a way of knowing oneself through emotions, because it allows us to understand what kind of people, we are from the way we act towards others, once we understand what they feel "inside". People almost never forget, even with age, how you made them feel.

The ability to listen

The ability to listen is one of the best skills that an empath uses in general for setting his or her relationships. Anyone who can feel empathy demonstrates a particular ability to listen to others. Listening empathically doesn't simply mean hearing the words being told to us, but "entering the conversation" and being sincerely interested in what is being said, without feeling the need to intervene or interrupt. For this we go beyond the words of the interlocutor, trying to decipher the emotional sphere. Only in this way can you have a "complete" picture of the situation and act accordingly. Obviously, the more you have a close relationship with the other person, the more you can implement some gestures that make them understand our closeness. For example, especially in a love story or friendship, it will not be enough to understand why the partner or friend is sick, but it will be necessary to give advice and answers that consider her state of mind.

Another great relational skill of the empath: accepting differences

Judging someone has only one result: accentuating differences and alienating others. Since empathetic people connect with others on a mental level, understanding their point of view, situation, and feelings, they could never create a barrier made of judgments, because it would interrupt that "connection". Therefore, those who feel empathy do not judge and accept diversity, even if it is ideas or emotions that are very far from their own. He doesn't stop to take note of it but tries to understand why the person in front of him thinks or feels them, deepening the situation.

How the empathy relationship is established between parents and children

The relationship between parents and children is complex and difficult to frame in general rules. A good relationship with your children helps them on their way. Empathy, in this sense, plays a fundamental role. We can speak of empathy, in the relationship between parents and children, as the compass in the arduous path that coincides with the birth of the person.

Some people are more prone to empathy while others constitutionally have more difficulty with emotional attunement. Despite this, it is important to know that it is possible, through introspective work, to enhance empathy.

An environment capable of facilitating his physical and emotional development is essential for the growth of the child, a secure basis for creating the bonds necessary to face life. Indeed, educating based on empathy means entering into a relationship with children, trying to put themselves in their shoes and observing how they feel about themselves and the outside world. But this can only be done if we are first in an empathic relationship with ourselves if we give space and voice to our emotions if we value what passes in the relationship beyond words.

Children have this particularly developed empathic capacity and are able to perceive (perhaps not to pronounce) the emotional states of the other. So empathic communication exists in the relationship between adults and children, even if we don't always recognize it. This is particularly evident in relationships with children where, in communication, the verbal does not coincide with hearing, this is immediately felt by the child precisely through her empathy. It is therefore important that, on the part of each parent, there is constant training on their own feeling, which is what then, in communication, reaches the other beyond the verbal. In fact, emotions are breathed, perceived (if one pays attention) even very distinctly and are transmitted to the other in an inescapable "underground" dialogue. A little heard "no", a recited hug, and an inauthentic smile, reach the child as a dystonic communication with respect to what the child perceives with the emotional part. It is therefore particularly important, especially with our children, to give space, to give voice to what we feel and to try to put it into words. This creates an authentic, syntonic communication with the child in which there are no dissonances between what is heard and what is said, but it also serves to train our children to connect feeling with the verbal, without censoring the emotions but giving them the right of citizenship and speech. Especially in our historical era, in which the world is particularly centered on performance, on demonstrating one's efficiency, on playing a role, it is precious to train future generations to give value to what is not seen, to one's feeling, ultimately to the emotional world that exists within each of us. The role of empathy is central to this process, and it is with our example that children can truly access their own and others' emotions, learning to name them, to give them the value and preciousness that enriches the person and all their relationships.

Another way the empath parent can use to help their child is empathetic listening. Empathic listening is a person's attempt to experience the emotional life of another while remaining an impartial observer.

In other words, it is a question of identifying with the other, of imagining what we would have experienced if we had found ourselves in the same situation as the other while continuing however to maintain one's own internal separateness and thinking about what we have heard in order to give back to the other one useful communication.

Empathic listening requires respect for each other's times and expressive methods even if we are usually in a hurry to define the situation to get out of our discomfort, believing that admonishing or advising is enough to do this; empathetic listening is nothing more than a form of service carried out towards the weakest subjects and in particular of children and adolescents, endowed with lesser communication skills of an aware type, with less contractual power on a physical, social and cultural level.

However, empathic listening is not the exclusive preserve of psychologists who offer their services with professionalism. Empathic listening is therefore a relational modality that respects the autonomy of the other giving him the sensation of not being alone: this condition appears indispensable from the beginning in the life of the individual so that his psychophysical development takes place without problems. In the 1950s, psychologist Margaret Mahler carried out longitudinal observations to study the process through which the individual develops an identity of her, that is, he perceives himself as a separate person and different from all the others. Mahler speaks of this intrapsychic process as a "psychological birth" which is an infinitely more complex and lengthier event than biological birth. The phases through which it takes place concern the period that takes place from the fourth-fifth month of life until about the thirty-sixth, the outcomes of each period influence the entire existence of the individual. To conclude on the possible behavior of the empath in the parent/child relationship, we would like to express a final reflection on the importance it has in every human relationship, especially in an educational relationship, the recognition of the fact that all we can do for the other is to support each other to him, we can help him think of something that he could not have done on his own consider. However, we are not the ones who can find his solutions, even if the possibility of feeling our emotional closeness and our trust is what he basically needs to find them on his own. Raising and, above all, educating children is not an easy task, since by acting incorrectly, we can destroy family ties. Tons of patience, affection and goodwill are needed to promote healthy and responsible growth that allows children to develop in the best possible way and, at the same time, take care of their partner.

In this task, some skills are relevant, such as knowing how to listen to our children, learning to put themselves in their shoes, setting limits and being able to convey to them the feeling of belonging to a single group that will offer them security and protection, which is the family.

Empath and the couple relationship: how she or she behaves

The empath, within the love relationship, manages to maintain an active communication relationship. Some examples of active communication are:

- ✓ Being curious about the other, asking how they are, being interested in their thoughts and desires, and not taking them for granted
- ✓ Think about what positive aspects each partner brings to the relationship and what moments of crisis the relationship has gone through
- ✓ Ask yourself how to improve the couple
- ✓ Knowing what scares the future partner or what he regrets about the past
- ✓ Turn resentment into words to clarify and explain (to yourself first) your emotions
- ✓ Maintain a couple of planning, and set small but also challenging goals.

So, empathy for the empath is a way of communicating in which the recipient puts his way of perceiving reality into the background to try to bring out the experiences and perceptions of the interlocutor in himself. It is a very profound form of active understanding because it involves identifying with the feelings of others, freeing oneself from one's own filters of interpreting the message that comes from the other to enter intimately into what he is trying to convey to us, without any judgment.

The so-called "dyadic empathy" is what is felt within the couple and expressly refers to the feeling of empathy that is felt towards the partner. According to the researchers, dyadic empathy facilitates the couple's relationship by improving its quality and this affects both of its components. In particular, dyadic empathy makes it possible to improve the relationship as it makes the members of the couple feel not only understood but also "confirmed" by the partner, through his displays of affection and understanding. Quite different from the identification mechanism that leads partners - for example - to have the same tastes, empathy constitutes a way of communicating in which those who put it into practice decide to put their way of perceiving reality in the background to try to bring out in himself the experiences and perceptions of the other. It is a very profound form of active listening because it involves identifying oneself with the feelings of others, freeing oneself from one's own interpretation filters, from the desire to comment, to draw conclusions, to give suggestions or advice, to get into the depths of what the other he is trying to convey to us, without any judgment and, above all, without this constituting renunciation of self-expression.

From falling in love to love

To better understand what role empathy plays in love, let's think about the way a love story can be born. The first phase is that of falling in love: those who fall in love see everything positively, the defects of the other are minimized and above all they gradually expose themselves. It is with time, getting to know the partner and increasing trust in her that we let our flaws emerge.

When we move on to love by now, we should have seen almost all the "ugly" of the other, we enter a phase in which lucidity increases and therefore we establish that those defects suit us.

On the other hand, we would like the certainty that he accepts us as we are and that he understands our point of view.

Double blade in a couple of relationships?

Having arrived at the stage of love, therefore, being able to see the other for what he is, to understand and accept him without merging into him is an advantage. Starting a love relationship is not considered a good thing for an empath: this is because one must always recognize each other as two distinct people, while mutual understanding increases complicity and, above all, long-term involvement. However, empathy can also have negative implications, especially if this is present only in one of the two partners. When one member of the couple offers to understand but does not receive it, it can cause an imbalance that compromises the right balance. Empathy is a skill that must be cultivated and that changes over the course of an individual's life. The education received in childhood certainly guarantees us a predisposition, but we can learn to be empathic just as we can cease to be due to particular events such as a series of disappointments in love or traumatic events. In love, it remains important that the partners grow, even psychologically, in parallel, so that not only their needs but also mutual understanding go hand in hand as much as possible.

Mutability

Empath in love is not given once and for all, it is not fixed and immutable, but it grows with us and is strongly affected by the events of our life; however, it is necessary that the person in question, in the course of his development, has been able to experience and develop a basic ability that allows not only the relationship with others but, first of all, with himself and with the world: the 'affectivity.

Children who, in the very first stages of their life, did not receive adequate maternal care (even the banalest, such as caresses or any other type of physical contact), will hardly be able, later on, to develop an affective attitude and to feel emotions, not only towards others but above all towards themselves. Psycho-affective maturity is the result of a long and tiring process: the emotionally mature man enjoys a considerable margin of inner freedom and can love constructively, harmonizing his way of being, his needs, and finally, the fact that the other does not exist as its image, but as a reality in its own right with its own needs. The mature person is aware of his uniqueness and is equally capable of considering the uniqueness of his partner, accepting her limits without the illusion of making him change (to learn more about this concept, you could read our article Harmony in Couples).

To conclude the discourse of the empath and its relationships, therefore, we can say that empathy in love (as well as in other fields) plays a fundamental role precisely because it consists of the ability to listen to the feelings that are hidden behind the words allowing you to experience the emotions that your partner, friend or colleague is experiencing firsthand.

If a partner or friend can empathize with the other means that he manages to calm his reactions to the point of being quite understanding of the feelings of the person close to him.

With the relationship discussion over, let's move on to likely toxic relationships and why empaths attract narcissists in the next chapter.

Chapter 6: Why Do Empaths Usually Attract Narcissists?

Let's move on to a really important part of our guide: after talking about relationships in general, however healthy, let's move on to discussing the fact that empath represents a sort of "bad luck" for narcissists.

Empath and narcissist: a sad combo

Before discussing why the empath attracts the narcissist let's analyze an even more general aspect that concerns the fact that often the empath and the narcissist (or the manipulator) form couples.

To confirm that narcissism and empathy represent a sad pairing in fact, a recent three-phase study carried out by researchers at the University of Surrey and the University of Southampton shows that, if supported by behavioral indications on how to take another's perspective individual, even narcissists can feel empathy for the suffering and needs of others.

It is known and widely documented that narcissists have some lack of empathy. Tendentially self-centered and full of themselves, it may seem difficult for them to be able to get so in touch with the other to understand their thoughts and share their mood.

Yet a recent three-phase study by researchers at the University of Surrey and the University of Southampton shows that, when supported by behavioral cues on how to take another individual's perspective, even narcissists can feel empathy for the suffering and needs of others.

Subjects with subclinical narcissism were selected for the samples, selected based on the results of the Narcissistic Personality Inventory (NPI; Raskin & Terry, 1988) which they had voluntarily completed online.

Participants were then divided into two groups called low-narcissism and high-narcissism, indicating lower or higher levels of narcissism than the average non-clinical population.

In the first experiment they were asked to read the story of the breakup of a relationship and the empathic reaction was recorded through a self-administered questionnaire of 12 items adapted from Davis' Interpersonal Reactivity Index (IRI) (1983).

True to expectations, the high-narcissism group showed little empathy for the protagonists of the story, no matter how bad the situation.

The main problem is that narcissists - who know human weaknesses very well because they already had to learn to defend themselves as children, focus on the illusion of invulnerability in which they have no real need for the other - focus on the weakness of self-esteem of the 'empath to generate in them the desire to reach a False Self, which does not exist, which the empath has not requested and which is nothing more than a mere projection of the False Self of the narcissist on the other, a vulgar desire to transform the empath into a bad copy of himself. Emotionally dry and unstable people only try to ensure a constant supply of emotional energy and attention, without however giving anything and replacing, if anything, their emotional and affective deficiencies with some greater formal and economic availability in this type of relationship.

Once the addiction is generated, the empath will be obsessed with making the other happy. He will always be intent on behaving in a way that cheers him/her up, not irritates him, or relieves him of various chores that usually sadden him/her to the point of ruining your day.

The empath wants to give the narcissist a better life than he has had or to be his equal to her.

The passive-aggressive strategies with which narcissists exempt themselves from taking responsibility in relationships deserve a separate chapter, but in short, they are enclosed in this magic formula: "if you force me to do something that I don't like and that bores me, I will put you my face and I'll ruin your day, or I'll make it so bad, that believe me... you won't ask me again.

So, very often, the people with whom narcissists come into intimate contact and with whom they establish a relationship are characterized by deep empathy and at the same time by deep emotional wounds which in most cases are still bleeding. The relationship between a narcissist and an empath becomes a perfect fit in which each of the two satisfies in a destructive and dysfunctional way affective and emotional needs of which they are either unaware or do not know other ways to satisfy them. The result is emotional carnage that can last anywhere from a few days to a lifetime.

Why this attraction?

Between a narcissist and an empath person, the attraction is irresistible, yet in a story of this type, there is never a happy ending because it has all the characteristics of a toxic relationship. From the beginning, an unhealthy dynamic is created, of power games, escapes, and frustrations: all stuff that has nothing to do with true Hexian love.

The first problem the empath has to deal with is their difficulty in accepting the fact that not all people can or want to be helped and that they are not compatible with everyone. The empath is also mystified by the fact that the narcissist, especially in the love bombing stage, tends to be very compliant and seemingly capable of identifying and meeting emotional needs. Even later, when the relationship stabilizes, the narcissist alternates moments of aggression and violence with others in which he seems gentle and fragile. Precisely this alternation of behaviors induces the empath to hope for a change in the narcissist, but this illusion locks him into a real trap, that of the expectation that the narcissist can love. The fundamental difference between an empath and a narcissist is that the former feel the thoughts and feelings of others to understand them, while the narcissist intuits the feelings and thoughts of others to manipulate and use them.

An empath often bonds with a covert narcissist who displays listening, understanding, and helping skills, sensitivity and keen intuition not realizing that these behaviors are an imitation of empathy and understanding but in reality, the sensitivity of the narcissist is addressed only to himself. Intolerant of criticism, he does not tolerate any judgments and contradictions to which he reacts with aggression or self-pity.

Narcissists are often intuitive and intelligent people; they are able to evaluate and analyze situations and behaviors but are not endowed with any propensity to put themselves in other people's shoes. The big mistake the empath makes is to imagine that even the narcissist shares attention others with him, the narcissist on the other hand doesn't understand emotions but uses them to figure out how to manipulate others.

This type of relationship can be a very painful combination, especially for the empath because the narcissist has an ancient wound: something, in childhood, caused a sense of worthlessness, so he is in a constant and desperate search for approval. Everything seems great at first, but as the relationship continues, it becomes toxic.

In this case, the empath is a healer and by easily stepping into someone else's shoes, they will bond with a narcissist trying to repair and resolve the damage and attempting to eradicate their pain. When the narcissist realizes that he (or she) has lost the ability to control the empath, he will most likely go looking for the next victim. The possibility of bonding for these two types of people is simply impossible. The heart of the narcissist is closed, and that of the empath is open: in short, a perfect recipe for a huge disaster.

Despite being totally different, however, they can't help but attract and chase each other in a relationship of co-dependency. "The narcissist and the empath are opposites like day and night, it is true, yet it is a very frequent relational dynamic with a high rate of attraction. Empaths are very sensitive to the emotional experiences and feelings of others, while narcissists are very good at manipulating others to get their own needs met. Furthermore, narcissists are people with a strong hunger for attention and empaths are always ready to help and feed anyone. A perfect fit that, however, will only bring suffering to the empathetic. To better understand the dynamics of the codependency relationship, we refer you to the first guide.

Why empathetic people are attracted to narcissists?

Let's see in this subparagraph, the question from another point of view, namely that of the empath. In fact, we wonder why empathic people are attracted to potential narcissists (and disturbed personalities in general), who, unlike them, are incapable of empathy.

Empaths are attracted to narcissists - and in general to emotionally unstable personalities - because - compared to the average population - they are in touch with their emotions, and they know how to recognize and understand them intimately, at the very moment in which the other is experiencing them.

Empaths know how to identify with each other's pain and compared to simple compassion, they manage to feel that pain or that joy; they observe and are able to perceive every detail of the internal reality of the other person in front of them, so have a natural propensity for unconditional love. Empaths are, practically, in love with love and know how to relate to each other, even when the other is not available to connect emotionally.

But empaths know how to glimpse that emptiness, that wound, that pain for a profound lack of love and are convinced by strong idealism and optimism that love can heal any wound and that their love will be able to fill the enormous emotional and self-esteem of the narcissist or emotionally unstable person in general.

What an empath does not know, however, is that a narcissist or an emotionally unstable and immature person enters a relationship (stable or less stable) with the only intention of procuring vital energy without giving anything in return; for this reason, he first puts on a mask of an ideal of love to enter the relationship and once the conquest phase is over, he will put himself "at rest", starting to deny himself and refuse to provide even the slightest attention, which one would expect in a couple of relationships. The intent of emotionally immature and unstable people is to be admired, to receive the attention and care that, in all probability, were lacking in childhood and that the empath feels obliged to provide.

To achieve this, narcissists deceive the empath by claiming they can no longer give in that relationship, not so much because they lack the capacity, but because the empath has not behaved well. Narcissists push the other to constantly feel guilty, in order to raise their emotional performance levels: "You have to give me more and then I when I get what I deserve and desire, will repay you by behaving as I did at the time."

How do narcissists make their empathetic partner codependent?

In the next paragraph, we will give you an overview of the various stages of the toxic relationship between the narcissist and the empath. Here in general, we can tell you that the first phase of the ideal behavior of the narcissist is the tool with which pathological dependence is instilled in the empath because it constitutes for him one of the highest forms of emotional repayment that exists.

In fact, the narcissist, with his magic mirror, will show the empath the best image he could have of himself, and the empath - often the victim of self-esteem based on the recognition of his qualities from the other (seeking approval) - will fall into the trap of believing that "only through the eyes of the narcissus will he be able to see himself as beautiful, worthy of love and esteem".

In the wake of this basic emotional blackmail that sanctions the union, the empath, often insecure and/or suffering from some abandonment wound from childhood, will delude himself that he can achieve the gratification and gratitude of his partner if he always gives moreover.

For this reason, he will tend to cancel himself, to shape himself on the other, on his needs and he will find himself in a position of co-dependence, just as a child, he felt in the presence of an absent and unaffectionate parent, who no matter how hard he tried she never considered him worthy of a gesture of affection.

The narcissist at that point is already comfortably seated in an armchair to "suck with four straws from his heart" (narcissistic supply).

In fact, the narcissist convinces the empath that their story is special, that it is only thanks to him/her that he/she can experience those wonderful sensations.

The 11 stages of a toxic relationship between a narcissistic person and an empath

To understand even better what the dynamic is created between them, and why empaths attract narcissists, we have established what are the different steps of this attraction.

Phase 1: the Attraction

Narcissist favorite prey items are empaths. These two figures are looking for each other because each of them has something that the other lacks. The narcissist is in desperate need of care and attention, and this makes the empath feel "indispensable" because they are always ready to nurture and help anyone. Despite this apparent exchange of needs, the two figures never complement each other, because they are unable to satisfy their mutual hunger for love.

Phase 2: the Illusion

As the relationship deepens, the empath begins to feel strong and unconditional love, while the narcissist has no intention of returning that love but is good at hiding it and pretending to reciprocate. The empath is convinced that he has met the love of his life. The narcissist feeds on this illusion, but his only goal is to have control of the situation in his hands. He really just needs the empath to love himself and satisfy his ego.

Phase 3: Manipulation

The narcissist's goal is to bring down the empath's self-esteem. He will instill doubt in him, so much so as to start making him doubt himself. Feeling increasingly insecure, the empath will begin to feel gratitude for having the narcissist around. This will cause an addictive dynamic, where the narcissist will take control.

Phase 4: The Game of "Victim" and "Perpetrator"

The narcissist, taking control, will assume the role of the victim constantly in need of help from the empath. The latter increasingly in love and grateful, will do everything possible to please and make the narcissist happy. Thus, will begin a manipulative vortex with no exit.

Stage 5: Failure

The empath goes to great lengths to heal the wound of the narcissist. He feels her strong need for care and attention and would like to fill his voids. In reality, the narcissist is unaware that he has a problem, he thinks he is immune to love, so no one may be able to save him, not even an empath.

Phase 6: the Trap

The empath is trapped, he is not happy, but he is also unable to rebel. The whole relationship is centered on the narcissist and his needs and wants for him: he will start to bring all the talk to him, so only his problems will be bigger and more important. The empath will enter a dead-end vortex of manipulation and control by the narcissist.

Stage 7: The "Suffocation"

As the manipulation continues, there comes a time when the empath begins to feel suffocated, oppressed, and increasingly unhappy. Sensing the change, the narcissist tries to make him feel guilty and accuse him of being selfish, triggering an escalation of ever more excessive demands for attention.

Stage 8: The Empath's Escape

The empath is confused, he begins to feel bad and not up to the person he has next to him, his mental balance is in the balance. He withdraws into himself and will take some time to clarify within himself. In this phase it is very important not to push away friends and family, to confront one's loved ones, it can be useful to return to reality and perhaps have the strength to ask for the help of a specialist.

Phase 9: Acknowledging the truth

By working on himself, the empath finally realizes the bitter truth. He sees the narcissist for who he is, he understands that not everyone who says, "I love you", truly loves and that "I need you", can also have both a healthy and an unhealthy meaning. The empathic realizes, at this stage, that the narcissist will never change.

Phase 10: the Painful Awakening

The now-aware empath understands that he can never heal the narcissist. It is a painful awakening, but a necessary one to break free from the narcissist's terrible manipulative cycle and control. Ending a relationship like this is not a failure, but a positive step in regaining control of your life. It's important to remember that being in an unhealthy relationship with someone so toxic will never be good. This form of psychological abuse adversely affects mental and physical health.

Stage 11: The End of the Relationship

Once the story is over, the narcissist will carry on as if nothing had happened. He won't even remember what it was like to experience the love and care of the empath. He will find a new victim to satisfy his needs, repeating the same script. While the empath will certainly have a more difficult path to face, he will emerge stronger, wiser and more cautious in dispensing care and love.

From everything that has been analyzed in this paragraph, we can very well deduce that the relationship with a narcissist is nothing short of harmful for an empath. This is why you need to be very on guard against this type of subject and defend yourself. For defense strategies, we refer you to the next chapters of the guide. In the next section of the book, we'll talk about your "powers" and how to best use them.

THIRD PART-ABOUT EMPATH POWERS

Chapter 7: "Power" of empaths. Let's know better

What does mean empath power?
The main power of empath, we can say that it is the ability to get in tune with the person with whom you interact and serves as an interpersonal communication tool.
According to the theory of mirror neurons, which we saw in the first chapter, empathy arises from a process of embodied simulation, i.e., a mechanism of an essentially motor nature, very ancient from the point of view of human evolution, characterized by neurons they would act immediately before any more properly cognitive elaboration. Proceeding in development, the cognitive component will acquire increasing importance and will interpenetrate more and more with the affective one, allowing the development of more evolved forms of empathy.
Having said this, the great power of the empath lies in the fact that thanks to empathy it is possible for him or her to perceive the bonds. Four essential qualities of empathy derive from this power:

- ✓ Perspective: The ability to put yourself in the other person's shoes or recognize that that point of view represents their truth
- ✓ Refrain from judging: not easy, since most of us like it
- ✓ Recognize emotions in other people e
- ✓ Communicate it to him

The power of the empath, in essence, is being in touch with other people. Because the truth is that an answer can rarely make things better: what makes things better is the bond. And the empath has a superpower when it comes to strong and lasting bonds.

The power of empathy: what mirror neurons are and how they work
We mentioned above that the superpower of empathy alludes to the fact that it allows the empath to create connections and bonds. But all this derives from the real power of the empath: that is, the ability referred to the mechanism of mirror neurons.
This type of neuron was discovered by Professor Giacomo Rizzolatti and his team in the motor cortex of monkeys. In a laboratory situation, they observed that in

monkeys there is a motor neuron that is activated both when the animal performs a motor act and when it observes it in others.

Following this evidence, these neurons have also been found in humans, in various brain areas (not just the motor one) and for this reason, we tend to speak of a mirror mechanism: that is, "the ability to transform information from the outside world, or of actions coming from the external world (emotional or otherwise), into motor acts of the individual".

These neurons enable experiential knowledge: that is, what other people do resonates with something we know how to do too.

Mirror neurons and relationships

But why do we believe that this mirror mechanism is the basis of empathy and its power and therefore of the skills that allow it to relate to others? When we observe the actions of others, we are not only able to "see" the action, but we perceive its intention. The "how" a person moves a leg allows us to understand if he is taking a step forward, kicking a ball, or defending himself from an object that is about to hit him. That is, we can understand the intention and respond appropriately. This occurs for motor acts, as well as for emotions.

At this point, you might ask yourself: but if empathy is in our brains, how come we may be more sympathetic and feel closer and more moved by the death of Kobe Bryant and his daughter Gianna, compared to the thousands of children who die in Syria? Empathy is the basis of social life and allows us to feel others, but other factors enter into its functioning: cognitive, cultural, educational, and media, which influence each other. By now it is known that the more similar we feel to others, the more we will be able to have empathy, and basically, an American NBA star is more similar to us than a Syrian child, just as we feel a rabbit closer than a crocodile. The cultural and educational aspect modulates our perception and the values we have to define how close or not we feel to others (living beings, plants, rocks...).

Being an empath is already a superpower

Many of us already have a "superpower", which is often ignored.

I'm talking about an ability resulting from millennia of evolution - a masterpiece of nature - which today allows us to dominate the planet and have no dangers to worry about (if not ourselves).

It is found in our brain, thanks to the activity of special neurons, which allow us – more or less – to read the minds of our fellow human beings.

It's called empathy. Empathy being the that great ability to understand the mood of those around us represents the tool (and therefore the power) that people have to perceive changes in the mood of others. Knowing what the person in front of you is experiencing, you can pronounce the right words (or make the right gestures) to bring the other "on our side" and convince him to do what we ask of him. Imagine being a policeman who has just caught a man about to kill his lover, perhaps because the latter has just left him.

The criminal, discovered, takes the woman hostage, and orders the policeman to let him escape, or he will make a massacre. A good policeman should be able to use the right words to get the other guy to release the hostage and put down the gun, avoiding a fight before it even starts. And avoid tragedy. Just as in real life your 'empath superpower will allow you to help your friend, colleague, or partner in crisis and restore harmony (as well as probably save their life!).

The other powers of the empath

It does not just mirror neurons or the ability to create relationships that are typical powers of the empath. The empath is also capable of crushing conflicts before they even arise.

You would be wrong if you thought that empathy could only be useful for those who have to negotiate for work or to create a cooperative relationship.

Even when you have to get the other residents of your apartment building to pay their dues, you need empathy.

Even when you need to figure out why your co-workers aren't doing their best, you need empathy.

In short, it really serves everything.

The empath also has the great power that allows him to do many vital things outlawing violence as a weapon of conflict resolution.

First, it is what our human nature is based on and what has allowed us to build an advanced society. The ability to put yourself in the other's shoes has at least reduced the violence that characterized ancient societies. Imagine living in the city of Babylon, which existed 4,000 years ago, where all citizens had to follow the so-called "Code of Hammurabi".

It is a list of 282 laws that King Hammurabi had engraved on stone blocks 2 meters high and erected in every corner of the kingdom.

This Code was based on the "Law of Retaliation", which is a principle according to which if you wronged someone, the sentence you had to pay was identical to the wrong or damage you had caused. Summed up in one sentence: an eye for an eye, a tooth for a tooth.

Good. Imagine walking quietly through the streets of Babylon when you hear a woman screaming.

A thief has just ransacked his shop and ran past you, taking a small road on your left. You decide that you want to do a good deed and then you set out in pursuit.

You turn the corner, and you bump into an old man, who falls hard to the ground and breaks his femur. The guards, who have seen everything from the nearby square, approach and lift you up to bring you to trial.

It turns out that the old man you brought down is not a mere person, but he is an awīlum, i.e., a citizen by right (a sort of nobleman).

Belonging to the most important class, you don't get away with a simple fine, but the penalty must also be corporal: they break your leg. Yet a shred of empathy would be enough to understand that your "crime" was not voluntary, but involuntary (and therefore give you all the extenuating circumstances you deserve, such as having tried to help another person). As Jean Decety, a psychologist at the University of Chicago, points out, over time empathy has been the engine that pushed human behavior toward morality and justice, to prevent us from slaughtering each other. And the power of the empath also lies in his very strong sense of justice. Empathic (Nonviolent) Communication invites us to look for solutions in which both people "win". In fact, it invites us to translate judgmental thoughts into important values and needs. Instead of saying what's wrong with us and with others, we learn to express ourselves honestly and respectfully by saying what we care about and becoming more assertive (empowerment). We also learn to listen with empathy to words and behaviors that would otherwise be difficult to accommodate. We become increasingly aware that through unpleasant words or behaviors, others are only trying to express important needs and values. And they do it in the best way they know how, which is through the language of judgment learned from our culture. When we begin to listen to each other through the filter of needs, we begin to recognize the humanity in ourselves and others.

To conclude this chapter, we can say that our brain is an extraordinary machine.

We often underestimate its potential and forget that we represent an exception in the entire currently known Universe, consequently we tend to underestimate our potential. And the fact of being an empath and training his extraordinary powers will allow you to then be able to use them in the most unlikely situations, such as when you have to face a conflict with your partner or even just to better understand your moods. And in the next chapter, we'll tell you how.

Chapter 8: How to defend your fears and feed your power

After having illustrated what the powers of the empath are, let's see how it is possible to increase the scope of these powers, but also how it is possible to defend one's fears.

What are the fears that hinder empaths?
Our empathy (and consequently the ability to communicate effectively with others) can be hindered by several factors:

- ✓ Our role - if we are the head of a team, we think we have to maintain a certain position and that we cannot use empathy, confusing it with "becoming friends" with our colleagues; actually being a leader and exercising empathy mainly means understanding what people feel and thanks to this being able to communicate with them, inspire them, motivate them
- ✓ Fear of other people's emotions - sometimes we think that what others feel can "infect" us and make us weaker or make us feel bad, but being empathetic doesn't mean getting sucked into other people's emotions: it has more to do with knowing how to manage them effectively without being overwhelmed by them
- ✓ The fear of being vulnerable – being empathetic does not mean finding compromises and giving up our worldview; entering into a true empathic connection with others opens up an effective channel of communication but does not require us to abandon ourselves.

Below we will explain how to defend ourselves from these factors and then strengthen our power as an empath.

Dear empath: defend your fears

Dear empath, by now we know that you are an extraordinary person with powers that can only improve the lives of those around you who are lucky enough to have dealings with you. But that doesn't mean you're immune to fears. Having fears is human and makes us even more inclined toward others. A situation that frightens the empath and from which one should defend oneself is the so-called emotional contagion. In fact, there are empath people who absorb the emotions of others and the environment like a sponge: we speak of emotional contagion, and it is the way of transmitting emotions between people. Absorbing emotions from the environment or other people takes place at any time of the day: the emotional signals that the people around us emanate can be captured and transformed into the perception of emotion. This is one of the powers of empaths, but also the innate characteristic that allows us to read the moods and intentions in other people's moves and thus allows us to protect ourselves. It is a bond that was formerly linked to survival. We can therefore say that this mechanism of absorption of emotions is a predisposition of all human beings, even if there are people who can perceive and make their own surrounding emotions like real sponges, or highly sensitive people or PAS, and others who are unable to feel any kind of emotion, namely psychopaths.

Now it must be said that empathy and emotional contagion have common roots because both are based on a marked sensitivity and perception, but in reality, they differ in some respects. In fact, empathizing means understanding the other person's moods, and putting yourself in their shoes. This leads empath people to feel and acknowledge the feelings that the other person is having, but not necessarily to make them their own.

In emotional contagion, on the other hand, the emotions that the other feels become one with the emotions that the person feels without being able to get rid of them anymore. You absorb what the other feels and take it away with you.

Now the problem occurs when the negative energies are absorbed by the empath, and it is from this that we need to defend ourselves. In fact, emotional contagion can occur with both positive and negative emotions. In fact, emotions also have the task of communicating to others how we feel, sometimes this happens consciously (for example when we expressly tell a person what we feel), other times even if communicated unconsciously through non-verbal language (facial expressions, body positions, etc. ...), are equally perceived by others potentially triggering an emotional contagion. in order not to create a mechanism that, rather than made up of powers, is made up of fears.

In fact, highly empath people, when they enter an environment, can therefore easily perceive the waves of worry, sadness, or anger that emanate from the people who are there. This means that these people are more likely to absorb the moods of others, becoming sorts of emotional sponges. In general, this aspect is not a serious problem in itself: just learn to manage it, set limits, and try to focus on your feelings. However, it could become a problem when we find ourselves next to toxic or passive-aggressive people, who do nothing but pour out their feelings on us or use us as a scapegoat for their negative emotions, and we do nothing but absorb and swallow all these negative feelings. If we are very focused on ourselves, we risk not being able to tune in to the emotions of others and therefore blocking the emotional contagion.

This also happens when clinical conditions occur that affect mood and emotion, such as depression or anxiety. Finally, there may be specific cases in which emotional contagion is perceived as dangerous for the person, leading to the raising of cognitive barriers for defensive purposes. These defenses can be momentary and voluntary, such as when you are emotional and avoid looking at the other person crying to try to contain your tears, or involuntary and persist over time. In this case, the support of a professional can be useful for rediscovering one's internal emotionality and facilitating the relationship with the other.

The courage of empathy

We want to digress for a moment and talk, more about fears, about a real high power of empath, or courage. To be authentic in our empathetic attitude we need to leverage a determining factor: courage. Triple courage. Opening through the doors of empathy is an unconditional choice, without waiting for counterparts, and therefore contrasts naturally with the distrust we carry around with us towards others. The other, whoever he is, can scare us, and put us at a distance from a naturally empathetic attitude. Then there is the habit of regulating human relationships, even the most intimate ones, those that should be most full of affection, with force. And empathy is a choice that excludes the use, or even worse: the abuse of force, this too is a choice of courage. To be empathic, the ego, the superego of narcissism, must be deflated, which is not easy. Usually, one tends to cultivate one's hypertrophic self by showing oneself to be "nice", with that artificial sympathy that has nothing to do with the naturalness of empathy. And even bending narcissism to empathy is a gesture of courage.

How not to let fears take over

"If you know how to smile with those who smile, cry with those who suffer and you know how to love without being loved back, then, my son, who can contest your right to demand a better society? No one, because you, with your own hands, would have created it!"

Already in the 15th century, with this aphorism, the Christian monk Thomas of Kempis underlined the importance of the concept of empathy in aspiring for a better society. The term empathy derives from the Greek en-pathos "feeling inside" and indicates the ability to consciously experience the emotional states of others and identify with them until complete sharing and closeness.

This important human gift, which makes personal relationships meaningful, intense, and authentic, is called emotional empathy. It is a skill that makes sharing possible and not criticizing, listening, and not advising.

Central elements are the suspension of judgment which facilitates a free and calm communication of one's emotions (allowing the relationship not to be conditioned by fears of receiving criticism), and deep listening which expresses sincere interest and favors feeling understood and welcomed even if imperfect.

This is how the suspension of judgment and deep listening feed the sense of intimacy, strengthen social ties, and promote cohesion by producing positive effects that reverberate on people's psychological and physical well-being.

The added value of emotional empathy is evident in all interpersonal relationships, for example in the relationship between parents and children and especially in adolescence.

However, empathy is a complex concept with many facets. What happens, for example, if there is an excess of empathy? What can its effects be? Given the positive aspects, we would be led to think that, in relationships, empathy is never enough. The more there is, the better.

Unfortunately, this is not the case and for hyper-empaths everyday life can become difficult.

Instead of living their daily lives lightly, hyper empaths are weighed down by excessive involvement in other people's problems that trap them in a paradoxical situation. They forget their feelings and needs because they are convinced that in the relationship everything must be aimed exclusively at the well-being of the other. The hyper-empath's commitment is all-encompassing, personal projects and goals remain on the sidelines without awareness of continuous personal renunciations, until the total weakening of one's energies and resources.

Another problem could be anxiety: since empathy is closely related to compassion and concern for others, the heightened emotional awareness and social sensitivity in empathy may consequently be associated with anxiety, particularly when empathizing with individuals experiencing distressing situations. On the other hand, even greater anxiety could translate into greater concern for others, especially how one's actions might affect others. This is because being empaths seeing others in difficulty causes us distress, and helping them relieve it. Rushing to the aid of a person in need makes us feel like better people, endowed with values and high morality. Conversely, if we deny our help, we feel selfish and selfish we consider those who refuse to offer help to others and often generate feelings of fear related to anxiety.

To reduce these fears and negative feelings, especially if they lead to episodes of real panic, the only solution would be to try to mitigate them through a path of personal growth. Whether through a coach or a psychotherapist, the journey will also help you feel better about these feelings of fear. Only in this way will you be able to stem your fears and only use your empath powers to the fullest.

Feed your powers: some good tips to "train" your empathy

In this important paragraph, we will explain how to strengthen your empathetic power and make the most of it in any area of your life.

Can empathy be trained?

Before talking about the empathic power to apply in relationships, let's briefly answer this question. Fortunately, everything about us is trainable. Empathy is defined as a soft skill, also required in the world of work to improve performance and relational skills.
So, empathy is one of the most appreciated soft skills in the world of work (and not only): it is thanks to empathy that we are able to feel "closer" to each other and we are able to understand their feelings and point of view in a certain context. An empath person feels the emotions of those around them and has the ability to tap into those same emotions within themselves. In essence, empaths "become" the person they are empathizing with as if truly experiencing their emotions. A training process includes emotional literacy courses, which are important from childhood. They include games - such as role-playing games - which stimulate the development of empathy, or discussions related to facts that happen, in order to circulate their feelings. On the one hand, it is therefore possible to understand the situation, on the other, one is encouraged to bring one's feelings into play.
Indeed, the power of empathy can be trained and applied in all fields. Here, we will look at the main ones.

Feed your empath power in a love relationship

Let's start with one of the most important fields in life, love. Is it possible to train the empathetic power to improve or establish an excellent couple relationship? Of course.
Among the ways to feed empathetic power in relationships is to activate an emphatic relationship.
So how do we manage to activate this faculty or power? According to Goleman "Empathy totally ups to attention: to tune in to another person's moods we must catch the signals of his emotions, whether they are vocal, facial or otherwise." If we are attentive, if we observe, if we dispose ourselves towards the other with a spirit of openness and sharing, we also have this natural mechanism on our side which helps us to establish a better and certainly more effective interpersonal relationship. Learning to value the para-verbal part of communication, tone, volume, timbre, and speed of the voice represents an excellent way to relate effectively to the interlocutor.

If we use a high tone with someone who has a low tone, if we are fast with someone who has a slow pace, and if we use an inappropriate register, we make our way of communicating with those in front of us dysfunctional. The secret is to follow the same rhythm and play the same music. As in a concert, the out of tune of orchestra player sounds bad, so in interpersonal communication, a out of tune makes that concert unpleasant and not very harmonious.

Since empathy is the ability to "feel" the other by listening to oneself, another important way for the coach to enhance one's ability to create an empathic relationship is to develop self-awareness, the ability to " look at the interaction from above", without getting lost in your own thoughts and feelings. It is a specific competence of the coach that allows him to suspend his own involvement to observe what is happening, it is the so-called "third eye", using which the coach can have an intense awareness of the interaction without being completely reactive.

Another great way to use the power of empathy in love relationships is optimal conflict management. Thanks to the emotional and cognitive connection that this ability allows us, we are able to resolve conflicts peacefully. By understanding others, it will be easier not to get carried away by impulses. So, as we know so far, empathy is necessary above all to manage conflicts, which arise mainly due to a misunderstanding. In fact, each of us interprets what happens through our own personal "lenses", with which we filter information based on our own prejudices, beliefs, and values. If we are too focused on ourselves, we are not able to really understand others and correctly interpret what is happening. To train empathy we must therefore learn to "see beyond" behaviors. Here's how we need to use this power to improve our relationship as a couple.

Start with yourself and train yourself to recognize the emotions "behind" your behaviors: in this way, you will learn to do it with others as well and this will allow you to communicate effectively and build better relationships.

What I'm trying to make you understand is to focus on understanding what connection there is between what you think, what you feel, and what you do.

- ✓ Think of a situation where you responded in a way that you didn't find particularly effective. Write in detail what happened and what behaviors you have implemented.
- ✓ Now ask yourself what kind of thinking generated those behaviors. For example, if you had an argument with a co-worker and yelled at him (behavior), what triggered your reaction? The thought that triggered it could be "he never listens to me and never does what I tell him".

- ✓ Finally, ask yourself what emotion triggered the thought and, consequently, the behavior. Focus on how you really felt and try to dig as deep as you can. I bet you will discover interesting things.

You can do the same exercise to try to better understand the behavior of your partner. If he or she has acted in a way that you didn't like or that hurt you, ask yourself what thoughts and emotions prompted him. You will find that this new perspective will help you connect more easily with others and will improve your relationships as well as the way you communicate.

Finally, there are 2 cognitive and emotional factors typical of empathetic power that need to be strengthened for a fruitful and lasting relationship.

1. **Awareness**

A conscious couple grows together and indeed puts growth before anything else because they know that this is the only secret to keeping the relationship alive. Even if growing up is scary (because it pushes us towards change, therefore towards the unknown), the couple struggles to expand, even if this may mean overcoming the relationship. Precisely for this reason, the relationship is kept alive and so is love in the couple.

An aware couple faces current and previous problems because they know that in this way, they can access a new and more evolved level of the relationship. Anything can be overcome when we take it upon ourselves to face it.

The conscious couple works in the name of love, that is, they strive to live in it every moment and every stage. Love must be "acted out" as a daily exercise, as a first response to every gesture and every question. You don't have love, you practice it.

2. **Emotional sharing**

A powerful tool for knowing the emotions of others and maintaining stable relationships is a form of "emotional contagion", an ancestral mechanism that allows, even unintentionally, to imitate a wide range of behaviors to promote understanding and empathic communication.

This sharing of attitudes and behaviors can facilitate life as a couple because it facilitates understanding and the relationship.

The term "compassion" should be understood in an almost religious sense, not as a synonym of "suffering" or "pity" but as mental closeness, as a maximum and shining spiritual contact that leads to a commonality of intentions and profound thoughts.

Here we enter an area far from everyday life and where few exercises of silence, respect, suspended thought, and kindness. It is a world of meditation for two where words lose their importance and where contemplation and concentration become the building blocks for cementing a love relationship.

Increase the educational power of the empath

Instead, let's see how to apply the typical powers of empath at an educational level. The effectiveness of empathy in the coaching relationship (of any kind) is manifested through several aspects:

1. Suspension of judgment
2. Building a developing relationship
3. The development of emotional skills

Let's examine them in detail.

1. Suspension of judgment: the main advantage of empathy is that, by putting ourselves in the shoes of others, we learn not to judge. Empathy is free from criticism, judgment, or evaluation, there is no right or wrong, no directives are introduced, and the focus of attention is exclusively the inner emotional experience. As a coach or a teacher, the suspension of judgment serves to free one's mind from any preordained solution, in order to avoid a manipulative relationship towards the goal that we like best, rather than to support the result of a free choice of the training.
2. Building a development relationship: one might think that good communication, knowing how to ask "powerful" questions, and being able, through practice, experience, and craft, to apply this technique are sufficient in a Coaching or Learning relationship. Certainly, in many cases this happens, even with satisfactory results, but with a relationship based on empathy, a relationship of value, one has the possibility of having access to the reality experienced by another human being in the place where this is happening i.e. in the other. This helps us to understand, to feel who we are dealing with, but maintain the necessary lucidity not to be emotionally involved in the face of their emotions and to be able to take the right distances that allow us to exercise the task we have undertaken towards them. The empathic relationship enables the teacher to put himself at the center, to feel listened to and supported, to share his inner experiences with his coach, feeling welcomed and respected. This favors the focus on his obstacles and the ability to draw more fully on his resources, in other words, it supports him in the growth of his awareness and in the identification of new and more effective behavioral strategies.

3. The development of emotional skills. Empathy is also the basis of what Goleman calls "emotional intelligence", that is, the ability to recognize our feelings and those of others, to motivate ourselves, and to manage emotions positively, both internally and in our relationships. It is the intelligence of the heart, which favors "feeling" over "understanding". The coach must be aware of the mechanisms of distancing or approaching emotional contact, with himself and with the coach. As a coach or a teacher, we have to stay in contact with our self intentionally, otherwise, our automatisms take us away from this dimension and we miss what is going on in the helping relationship. If we want to govern the relationship, we must, first of all, be aware of what is happening inside us, in contact with our sensations.

Train a Culture of Empathy in a work environment

In a constantly changing world, developing a strong power of empathy is increasingly essential to observe reality from the right perspective and understand what people care about, what they aspire to, what drives them, and what bothers them. And this power can very well be applied in the workplace.

In fact, observing needs and defining insights under an empathic lens can lead to solutions that meet both the functional and emotional needs of people (who can be potential customers) and between colleagues and the relationship with one's superiors.

However, it must also be said that, in work, empathy must be managed, as in personal life, an excess of it causes wounds, disappointments, and dissatisfaction. However, there is a way to be able to take advantage of it and benefit from it for yourself and for others.

What is needed to control empathy is above all the awareness of this gift, knowing for sure that one has it, and recognizing the "symptoms" that it brings, therefore it is essential to know oneself, to know one's defects and strengths, get to know our character in depth, in such a way as to then distinguish our emotions and those of others. It is also called emotional intelligence because it is not a technical and measurable skill, but your feeling, a predisposition to put yourself in the shoes of others and to understand their state and needs, without however being overwhelmed by them.

Managing empathy is essential to work serenely and creating constructive relationships with customers, colleagues, partners, with all the people with whom you find yourself interacting.

One way to train and strengthen the power of empathy in the workplace could be the building of a corporate empath culture. Creating a corporate culture based on empathy means making a connection with others and with oneself a consolidated habit, this requires the presence of a set of values and agreed on practices present in the same organization. To do this, you need to start evaluating and working on a number of factors such as:

- ✓ The motivation that employees have towards a greater commitment that puts their customers at the center and the related benefits.
- ✓ The ability of work teams towards a more empathetic attitude also through programs that help develop this soft skill.
- ✓ The attitude that employees have is to be focused on people and their needs.
- ✓ The working environment and social norms are close to caring for others.

After considering the initial factors, it will be essential to take a holistic approach with the aim of transforming your organization through empathy. A transformation that passes through 4 main phases.

Step 1: Train empathy like a muscle

Creating a corporate culture based on empathy is certainly no small task, for this reason, it is initially necessary to form the skills and habits necessary to maximize conversations, observations, and sensory experiences, everything must be monitored and traced to evaluate improvements over time.

Step 2: Connect consistently

Apply empathy to connect with real people, in real life, on a regular basis: find the ones who can best represent your target audience and start building a real relationship with them. In-person interactions provide more opportunities for observation, but also require sustained engagement or the ability to be reachable at different times of the day in order to reveal unexpected behaviors and emotions.

Step 3: Take action

It's time to get down to business: bring the thinking, openness, and resources of your organization to the fore and make sure you tackle real and meaningful problems. Convert experiences based on the development of empathy to find new implications to respond to with business solutions. Create human-centric ideas backed by a detailed action plan.

Step 4: Develop an ecosystem of empathy

Gather everything you've learned and share it internally with staff to maximize the value of your program. Organize all the learning and keep it in a management and sharing system capable of communicating with the company's digital and social channels, a way to systematize everything that has been learned, receive feedback, inspire collaboration, and form collective knowledge.

In conclusion, a business plan based on empathy can lead to innovations both in messages and in the language of communication in the broadest sense: from packaging design to color palettes, from promotions to investments up to aspects concerning Corporate Social Responsibility. The development of empathy can certainly give new ideas and points of view to the company, guiding the experimentation of new organizational models capable of giving life to decisions and actions relevant to its success.

How to enhance the power of empathy and use it for relationships in general

Now, to end this practical chapter, let's see what the 10 things are to do to increase empathy and allow you to create any kind of constructive relationship.

- ✓ **Understand your own emotions**

To improve empathy, you need to start doing it with yourself, i.e., increase your self-awareness.

The better you understand your feelings, the more you will be able to understand the feelings of others. Pay close attention to your emotional state, noting which situations change your emotions, and what gives rise to positive and negative ones. Use what emerges from your own emotions as a starting point for understanding the emotional responses of others.

- ✓ **Ask people to talk about their feelings**

To improve empathy, sometimes a direct approach is preferable. Ask people what they are thinking and feeling. You often think you know or understand, but assumptions can give rise to misunderstandings and prejudices. Also, people are sometimes just imagining what they think they feel when they talk about their feelings.

- ✓ **Interact with various types of people, even with those you don't like**

To improve empathy, try to get to know people of all ages and ethnicities, with different sexual and social orientations, and with different levels of physical ability or health.

The more types of people you get to know, the more experiences you will have, and the more you will see things in a different light.

- ✓ **<u>Try to see things from another point of view</u>**

The first thing to know if you want to understand how to be an empath is not to get stuck in your positions: try to see things from other points of view. When you do, you'll realize that other people are probably not mean, rude, stubborn, or unreasonable, but are probably just reacting to the situation with the knowledge they have and their experience.

This is also important for empathizing with people who have different ideas than yours. A good way to bring different beliefs into a conversation is to say, "That's interesting, how did you develop that idea?" Or "Tell me more". You will show interest and the person you are talking to will trust you.

- ✓ **<u>Recognize (and accept) the perspectives of others</u>**

Being an empath also means recognizing the perspectives of others and accepting them positively. Once you sense the reason others believe what they believe, acknowledge it. Important: acknowledgment does not equal agreement. You can accept that people have opinions that differ from yours and that they may have good reasons for having those opinions.

- ✓ **<u>Don't advise unless it's asked for</u>**

Resist the urge to fix the problems people tell you about. When you give them advice, the result it produces seems to minimize their feelings. Usually, what people want is to have someone listen to their concerns.

- ✓ **<u>Give attention to others in a sincere way</u>**

You sincerely care about others. If you don't genuinely, do it, people notice, as it's impossible to feign empathy. If you manipulate people, they commonly eventually notice through your body language or the events that follow as a result you will forever become unbelievable in their eyes.

- ✓ **<u>Smile and encourage people</u>**

Talking about how to be empathetic, we cannot fail to mention a smile. Smiling is a gesture that implies a certain openness and willingness to listen. The part of the brain responsible for this facial expression is the cingulate cortex, which is an automatic unconscious response area. Since smiling puts a few chemicals in the brain, it activates reward centers and also improves health. Don't be afraid to show your smile and give sincere compliments to another person, conveying your closeness. Encouraging people can be as simple as nodding their approval as they speak in a meeting. This simple gesture, along with using their name, can have a big impact on relationship building. For example, if you believe that a colleague of yours has done a good job, do not hesitate to compliment him and point out how brilliant he was in resolving that issue in the company.

- ✓ **Learn to listen**

The characteristics of the empathic person merge with the ability to listen actively. What does it mean? It means that if you want to understand how to be an empath, you have to start by understanding how to listen. There are several ways to listen:
- ✓ Listen with your ears: what is being said and what tone is being used?
- ✓ Listen with your eyes: what does the other person's non-verbal communication convey?
- ✓ Listen to your gut: do you feel that the other person is not communicating something important?
- ✓ Listen with your heart: What is the other person feeling?

Truly listening can be a challenge. Sometimes we are just waiting to give our opinion. Make an effort on this aspect and really concentrate on the needs and message that your interlocutor wants to give you: he will feel important, and a bond of trust will be created that is difficult to scratch.

So, the most reliable way to know what others are thinking and feeling are to listen to them when they speak. People feel more understood when they are allowed ample space to state their opinion. When you talk, they don't talk, so just by talking less, you can greatly improve your empathy.

- ✓ **Don't be afraid to appear vulnerable**

Very often, in our conversations at work (and beyond), we fear vulnerability because we are afraid that others may perceive us as foolish or weak.

According to some communication experts, vulnerability helps us connect with others because it communicates that we are human; it shows our weaknesses, wounds, and fears. This creates a feeling of humanity that gives the other person something to connect with and empathize with. Simply thing to remember **is** never to be afraid to ask for help. Asking for help shows how vulnerable you are, and vulnerability often leads to a greater sense of connectedness and relationship.

Below we will show you three steps to practice being more vulnerable (and increase your empath power) in your professional interactions:

- ✓ After listening carefully to the other person, try to think of a time when you were in a similar situation. For example you may have encountered a problem with a project that was stalled due to misunderstandings in the team
- ✓ Remember what you felt in that situation. Maybe you didn't handle the confrontation well, so you felt apprehension and anxiety
- ✓ Express these feelings to the other person, then share what you've learned in the process.

With these tips ends our mini guide on how to increase your powers as an empath. In the fourth section of the guide, we will explain to you how a narcissist acts to subdue an empath but also the defensive strategies to stem possible toxic partners.

FOURTH PART- DEFEND YOURSELF FROM NARCISSIST

Chapter 9: How a narcissist approaches an empath to submit

In this ninth chapter, we will see how the mechanism of approach and submission of the empath by a narcissistic subject takes place.

A Trap for the Empath: The Narcissist's Approach

Even if a narcissist and an empath act completely differently within a relationship, however, we have seen in previous chapters that most of the time they have at least one thing in common: the search for something they are missing.
Empath people - but in this case, the term "pleasers of the narcissist" would be more correct - look for someone with empathy and swallow their feelings very frequently and consider other people's emotions more important.
They tend to appear altruistic and humble and for this reason, their generosity is often exploited, and it is bread and butter for the narcissist who, having identified his victim, in this case, the empath, will implement a series of strategies to make him "take the bait".
So, the narcissist chooses "preys" with particular characteristics that fully reflect those of empath people: these are sensitive people, who have a propensity for self-sacrifice, and are therefore used to putting the needs of the other at the center, neglecting their own and so they are ideal for putting the narcissist's needs first. The latter senses these characteristics from afar, as well as availability, human warmth, empathy, elements that constitute his emotional nourishment, characteristics of the prey that feed the narcissist's ego, because they make him feel important, and therefore he will try, through techniques we can say "standard" to conquer the empath.
Narcissists are often intuitive and intelligent people; they are able to evaluate and analyze situations and behaviors but are not endowed with any propensity to put themselves in other people's shoes. The big mistake the empath makes is to imagine that even the narcissist shares attention others with him, the narcissist on the other hand doesn't understand emotions but uses them to figure out how to manipulate others.

But let's see together how this approach phase unfolds:

The first phase of conquest or standard approach of the narcissist foresees the objective of creating a total pathological dependence in the empath and therefore his future submission. Then use all the tools that create for the empath one of the highest forms of emotional retribution that exists. This technique is known as love bombing in which the narcissist, with his magic mirror (mirroring), will show the empath the best image he could have of himself (because of his low self-esteem or his problems solved). With this approach, the empath will fall into the trap of believing that "only through the eyes of his toxic partner will he be able to see himself as beautiful, deserving of love, affection and esteem".

In the first phase of love bombing, the narcissist will attract a whole series of flattering actions, behaviors, gestures, and words towards the empath with which the narcissist initially romantically "bombards" the prey to woo and seduce her.

In this idealized and idealizing phase, the narcissist, therefore, shows himself as the ideal partner: he is filled with gifts, compliments, punctual and frequent love messages, surprises, and perhaps blatant and sensational attention. He literally worships his partner, putting her or him on a pedestal.

It is in this sick mechanism that the empath will fall into the illusion of reaching the gratification and gratitude of his partner if he always gives more.

In the second phase, he will tend to erase himself, to shape himself on the narcissistic partner, on his needs and he will find himself in a position of co-dependence.

In fact, the narcissist convinces the empath that their story is special that it is "them against all the rest of the world", and that only thanks to him/her who is able to experience those wonderful sensations. Due to this strong adrenaline rush, the empath is now trapped, as he will enter a vicious circle that will be really difficult to get out of.

How a narcissist subdues the empath: from the traumatic bonding to hoovering technique

Before talking about the submission of the empath let's make a small premise: at the basis of this perverse relational mechanism, there is low self-esteem which leads the empath to fall many times into the narcissist's trap (hoovering) during which he is sucked into the relationship pushed from the hope that the narcissist has changed. When the empath realizes that their relationship is based on expecting some calm and less emotional violence, then the realization can arise that they deserve more than begging for love and hope to live with some peace.

To fulfill his spell, the narcissist mainly uses two psychological strategies, love bombing and traumatic bonding (or intermittent reinforcement tactics).

The intermittent reinforcement tactic is perfect for generating emotional dependence, expectations, and subjection.

An example of a traumatic bond would be a sudden moment of tenderness after hours of criticism and belittling. A message with sweet words after violent accusations. An unexpected gift after days of punitive silence. In the context of a relationship where the narcissist subdues the empath, all of these situations are displays of intermittent reinforcement, put simply, when we know that the reward after our behavior will be certain, we tend to work less for it. Conversely, when the moment of reward or the certainty that we will get it is unpredictable, we tend to repeat this behavior with more determination and enthusiasm, in the hope of the final result. The intermittent reinforcement technique is typical in an abusive relationship with a malignant narcissist. In the relationship, abuse is expertly mixed with periodic affection at unpredictable moments. Intermittent reinforcement works because our "rewards" (e.g., a hug, or a show of remorse from the abuser) are given sporadically during the cycle of abuse. This forces us to work harder to nurture the toxic relationship because we desperately want to go back to the "honeymoon phase" of the abuse cycle. So, intermittent reinforcement literally may cause an addiction to the unpredictability of the total abuse cycle. This effect also works on a biochemical level: When pleasurable moments are few and far between, fused with cruelty, the reward loops associated with a toxic relationship are strengthened.

Love bombing together with traumatic bonding place the "victim" in a particular configuration: for what she receives, the victim begins to feel indebted to the narcissist. If the "victim" has a previous history of love addiction, she will most likely experience gratitude for the crumbs bestowed by the manipulator. The result? The traumatic bond works like a glue that cements the relationship and prevents the partner from leaving.

Emotional ups and downs can be addictive because the highs are fueled by dopamine, which induces euphoria, whereas when the victim experiences the lows, they lack the energy and clarity to figure out what's going on because all they want is "another dose", experience the height of the "highs" again. This is the main mechanism that keeps the victim hooked.

Intermittent reinforcement creates a climate of doubt, fear, and anxiety that forces the victim to constantly seek approval from the manipulator who has the power to relieve her distress. When the victim finally gets the attention, she wanted (through flattery, sex, and seeing that for some time the partner has returned to being the lovable person he knew), the traumatic bond will consolidate and continue cyclically, to the bitter end, like a real addiction.

Hoovering is that manipulative technique, based on messages or calls, which the narcissist uses to create feelings of guilt to suck in his ex.

This technique seems to take its name from the famous American Hoover and turns out to be a real trap, into which to make one's victim fall again.

In this regard, it must be said that it cannot be used immediately, since the narcissist knows that it can appear even months later, or even years later. In fact, it is enough for him to use a message of false emotional closeness (e.g., my twin I miss pampering you) or concerning things that the other likes or even messages concerning future events to find the best way to recover the partner.

In short, getting rid of a narcissist completely can sometimes be really difficult, even if apparently, we seem to be free again. On the other hand, how surprised: the narcissist has a continuous need to feed his ego and have confirmations.

It is with these two means that the narcissist works his magic and secures the subjection of his momentary object of desire.

The teaching that can be drawn from the relationship with a narcissist is that his love is just a great illusion and that the only way to start loving yourself is to leave without expecting anything from him. This dynamic confuses and debilitates the empath, if he doesn't have a full understanding of his own or others' abilities, he won't be able to see that not everyone is like him. An empath will always put himself in other people's shoes and experience their feelings, thoughts, and emotions, forgetting that other people may have a different agenda from him and that not everyone is sincere.

The narcissist's agenda is manipulation, often being in a position to take control over others. The empath's agenda is love and care. The more love and care an empath offers, the more powerful the narcissist will be.

When a narcissist sees that an empath is hurt, he plays on that, and the main intention will be to leave the empath in a despondent state and that is how he keeps the empath in submission to his will. The sadder an empath becomes, the better the narcissist will feel. The empath will begin to frantically seek love, validation, and acceptance from the narcissist and every cry for help as such will confirm to the narcissist the desperation he feels within. A bitter battle can ensue.

As the empath focuses solely on the pain, trauma, and destruction, he becomes obsessed and can no longer see where the damage is coming from. Instead of looking outward and seeing the causes, the empath will turn everything inward to blame themselves.

Any attempt to authentically communicate with the narcissist will be futile. But not only that, but being extremely charismatic and manipulative, he will have the power to turn things around. A narcissist will blame their pain on the empath, as well as make them feel responsible for the pain they feel.

An empath will know they are in a destructive relationship from now on and will feel so insecure, unloved, and unworthy that they will place all the blame on the narcissist. Emotionally exhausted, lost, depleted, and debilitated, the empath will struggle to understand what happened to the once loving, caring, and charismatic person to whom he was attracted. If a narcissist wants to change that is fine, but it will never happen at someone else's expense. When he realizes that he has lost the ability to control the empath, he will most likely go looking for the next victim.

However, if an empath chooses to be with a narcissist and refuses to take responsibility for what goes on, he or she is making a decision. An empath cannot let his self-worth be determined by a narcissist, he should trust and believe in himself to recognize that he does not deserve certain words and attitudes.

The more powerful the narcissist becomes, the more likely the empath will retreat into a state of victimhood. Then, a big shift will occur – the empath will also take on narcissistic traits because they are hurt and will continue to fuel this dynamic in closeness to the narcissist. Before long, another vicious circle will set in.

And it's time to break this cycle. In the next chapter, we will explain how to defend yourself against any possible manipulative technique of the narcissist.

Chapter 10: How to protect yourself from a narcissist (practical methods)

Let's summarize the situation

The empath tends to be naive and has incredible difficulty understanding the fact that there are people without scruples, ethics, good feelings, and morals. So, he will try in every way not to notice the discrepancies between the fabulous character played by the narcissist and the real, horrible being that transpires here and there as the relationship with the narcissist progresses.

The empath tries desperately to keep believing in the existence of that wonderful person, or else all of his or her beliefs will prove wrong, and the world will collapse around him.

Meanwhile, the narcissist blames his misdeeds on the empath, who he feels doesn't give him enough love and adoration and who knows what else - otherwise, he argues, the narcissus would be serene and still be the wonderful person he was in the early days.

The empath believes it and takes all the blame for the problems of the narcissist and the relationship. He then becomes convinced that in order to heal the situation, he or she must give, give more and more, until he is totally drained.

At this point, the empath typically ends up on the verge of suicide or self-destructive behaviors, and the narcissist gets rid of them as soon as he finds a fresh and "juicy" new victim.

Moral: If you're an empath, stay away from daffodils. Even more so if you have a history of codependency or narcissistic parenting. Read, inform yourself, learn how to recognize them and how manage them, learn to take care of yourself, and above all dedicate your empathy to worthy causes.

Not everything and everyone should be helped; channel your gifts of sensitivity and compassion into a suitable job, your family (as we will explain in later chapters), or into volunteer work, instead. And practice discerning and saying no. In the next paragraph, we will explain to you how to protect yourself from narcissists.

Protect yourself from narcissist: how to do it

In this paragraph, we will explain to you what some practical techniques are to defend yourself from a narcissist. We know by now that, being an empath, you are a quintessential victim of such a toxic person. The time has come to interrupt the sick mechanisms and deal only with people who enrich us and make us happy.

So, let's see together what the best practical strategies are to defend yourself from a narcissist:

Counter-manipulation

A first practical defense strategy is counter-manipulation which, mind you, is not a means of communicating by reacting, but a way of not communicating at all, of not entering that vortex of predefined thoughts and actions (patterns) that we know well and that make us suffer or simply empty us. We need to learn to have ready answers, without offending, without being aggressive, but placing ourselves in a detached way, without adding to the message, the emotional connotation that could imply underlying meanings or further irritate the narcissist/manipulator causing the conflict. The main rule, therefore, consists in observing our emotions and giving up the impulse to react, behavior in an instinctive way, even if what the manipulator says is inexact, sadic, cruel, or ambiguous; we must not give in even if we feel offended, deceived or provocative. This action implies a painful forcing of spontaneity, but it teaches you how to control yourself (in various situations) and requires you to learn to operate a sort of emotional avoidance, which is the second defense strategy that we will see later.

Emotional avoidance

Avoidance is not repression (involuntary inhibition) but rather "a voluntary and elaborated oppression" and allows you not to lose touch with your truth, learning however not to share it with those who use it against you and therefore to defend yourself from suffering constant and lack of energy (emptying). It is important to give up spontaneity with this type of person, even though they appear to be emotional, real, and impulsive; in fact, this truth is granted only to them and not to you. Your truth is just information that the manipulator will use to defend himself, attack you, or make you feel guilty later on. Unfortunately, manipulators do not have the maturity to understand, to learn from experiences, or to emotionally process their experiences; they don't have the empathy to understand that that sentence, that criticism bothers you or hurts you, but they only learned that if I do A I get B and until now every time they provoked you, humiliated you, etc. They got into a conflict and finally a heated confrontation, through which you have learned who they are not and would like to be. For this reason, it is better to avoid them.

Indifference: always the best weapon

Dealing with a narcissistic person can be devastating. To protect yourself, it is essential to respond with indifference. Furthermore, for the narcissist himself, his own personality can greatly compromise the quality of his professional, social, and relational life.

It is rare for narcissists to understand that they need help. This mainly happens when she suffers a loss or defeat precisely because of his attitude or when the personality disorder occurs together with depression, alcohol, substance abuse, anxiety, panic, or insomnia. But it's really rare, so you have to run away and ignore this person before he can hurt you!

If you recognize it, you avoid it

What better defense strategy than "prevention is better than cure?
How to recognize a narcissist? We explained it to you in detail in the first guide. To refresh your memory we tell you that, usually, it is a person who has a great sense of self and exaggerates his talents and achievements. He cultivates dreams of success, ideal love, and unlimited power. He tends to monopolize every conversation and puts down people he deems inferior. He always wants to be recognized as a superior being, even without something justifying it.

He demands constant admiration and is unable to recognize the needs of others and their emotions, he manifests a great lack of empathy. Conceited and arrogant, the narcissist tends to get furious when he doesn't get the special treatment he would like.

The average narcissist is also very good at keeping people tied to himself especially the empaths, often alternating moments of great dedication (especially at the beginning of the relationship with the love bombing) leaving plenty of room for idealization, with moments in which he literally disappears, to create a kind of addiction. Here, if you recognize that the person you are dating has these characteristics, run away immediately!

Prepare yourself right

A narcissist is first and foremost a manipulator. This means that when the empath tries to leave him, he will try in every way to stop you. Not because he really loves you, but simply because your choice will put at risk his self-esteem and the high opinion, he has of himself. So, you become bad. You should only know that discussing it is useless and you would only risk having second thoughts and falling back into his net. So, what you have to do is simple: get ready! Before telling him it's over, find a place to go, collect all your things, and become aware of your choice.

You have to be brave and convince yourself that even if you feel bad now, things will soon get better.

Turn inward to support yourself

I want you to understand that a narcissist is a false source. Were you or are you trying to get kindness, decency, understanding, validation, amends, support, and humanity from this person? But every time you try to get it from this person, they just attack you harder.

This is pushing you into the final act of letting go which is partnering with yourself, restoring power and truth to your essence, and granting you kindness, decency, support, and humanity.

At first, this seems awful. Having suffered the trauma of narcissistic abuse, you feel anxious, disintegrated, and dissociated from yourself to the point where being alone with your trauma can feel downright unbearable.

Indeed, your very essence now feels broken and terrified. And it needs you, your loving kindness, and the support that you have sought outside of yourself but that only you can give yourself.

When you turn inward with integrity, dedication, and love saying, "Honey, I'm here for you. I am so sorry that I tried to get outside sources to love and heal you. I love you; I will hold you and help you heal and I promise I will never leave again," as traumatized as he is, he will begin to calm down knowing that you finally show yourself.

This is the beginning of your reconciliation with yourself.

If we reveal what we lack, we will be at the mercy of others

Narcissists, approach us, as we have seen, and try to promise us what we most desire. Therefore, the more they know about our needs, the more they can use this information against us.

Narcissists are also expert explorers of our insecurities. For example, if we feel awkward about doing something or have doubts about our abilities, they will teach us and bully us about our most ridiculous behaviors in exchange for money. In most cases, these are useless solutions.

Among the various narcissist, there is also "the eternal victim". This form of manipulation is more complex because it does not initially seek an economic benefit. This is a person who exposes all his complaints about her, venting about everything he would like to say to other people. Later, it makes us feel guilty if we talk about our problem. The eternal victim always experiences the worst of every situation. She is always the most damaged, grieving, and also strongest person. If we complain too, instead we show a lack of empathy or maturity. We have no reason to complain or be heard even when it's our turn. Manipulation in these cases is about getting unlimited attention from us. Although there are different forms of manipulation, they are all based on the same idea. At first, narcissists leverage our feelings to get something we don't want to share. To avoid falling into their trap, we must be very cautious, be less trusting of others and avoid revealing our weaknesses.

Resist the narcissist's nastiness

There are some specific challenges along the way when detoxing from a narcissist.
Number three is vital. Leaving a narcissist is different than the usual heartbreak of ending a normal relationship. Many toxic bonds have been attached within you for the narcissist to extract their narcissistic supply.

The truth about narcissistic supply is it doesn't need to be physical. There is no need for this person to see you in person. Indeed, the narcissistic supply is psychic and parasitic. If you be afraid and have pain within you, which the narcissist has been able to activate, then he or she is feeding on your emotional energy.

This is what narcissists thrive on – the fear, dread, and helplessness of others. It is their source of food, of energy.

The malice of the narcissist lies in activating the things that trigger you and lead you to be narcissistic supply again. The narcissist knows you intimately, and knows what actions work on your accusations, apologies, memorabilia, and feelings, appealing to your compassionate side, standing in for you, and even stonewalling or ignoring you for long periods. He knows the actions that will keep you emotionally and psychically hooked.

People ask me, "What will the narcissist do next?" My answer is, "Exactly what will trigger you emotionally in a negative way or keep you in a state of obsession."

Knowing this will help you. Because it is understood that the narcissist's game plan is to keep you hooked and unable to detox.

Whatever is triggered is the very thing you can turn inward to detox within yourself, rather than falling into malice.

Don't try to have a conversation with him/her

Talking to a narcissist you want to leave is futile. Hoping that everything can be concluded quickly and without aftermath as well. Don't be fooled by his ability to seduce you this time, but he tries to be very dry and quick. Let him know you're leaving and don't want to hear from him anymore. Your answers must be short and concise. Don't get lost in small talk because it will only wear you out.

No-contact is key to leaving a narcissist

After leaving it, try to respect a fundamental rule: no contact. We talked about it a lot in the first guide. In this particular defense strategy, we tell you that you will no longer have to hear from the narcissist who has managed (in this case) to submit to you. Surely, he will try to look for you, bombarding you with calls and messages, between flattery and threats. The truth is that he's not sad because he misses you, but simply because he can't stand losing, and the fact that he left you makes him question his strength. He blocks his number on the phone, if necessary, delete it from social networks, and cut off any possible contact. For a while, you have to disappear to "detoxify" from a relationship that has never made you happy.

Let go

Easier said than done, you say! And I agree, it is.
I want to tell you from the bottom of my heart, "letting go" is the first powerful step to detox.
What does "letting go" really mean? It means acknowledging that this person is destroying you and can't stay in your life, so you need to detach.
Letting go is a powerful act of self-love. It's hard because everything inside you is screaming at you not to. You want justice. You want recognition. You want to hold this person accountable. You want him to pay for the damage he has done to you.
I understand all of this, and it is completely justifiable. Yet, holding on brings more toxicity and poison into every aspect of your life. It embeds you with the narcissist, as he or she draws his or her narcissistic supply from you, continues to punish you, hooks you, and sucks more and more of your life force.
This is why whenever a narcissist tries to retaliate with a comment, an insult, an accusation, a "poor me" victim statement, a tactic to trigger you, and smear and hurt you, you have to say – "Enough! But know that your "Enough" is not "spoken". Sometimes mere words are counterproductive. Especially with narcissists – this just fuels them with extra energy and attention.
Actions mean much more than words. Your "Enough" must be "I will not participate with you anymore". Any word, message, acknowledgment, or response to the narcissist is a narcissistic supply. It feeds him with the emotional attention and energy that allows him to continue to hurt.
So how do you prove "I won't be participating with you again"? By doing just that… by no longer participating – and then continuing with the next steps of your life.

Healthy self-esteem

The best remedy to protect ourselves from narcissists is to enjoy self-esteem. If we are sure of ourselves, it will be more difficult for us to be moved by reasoning based on emotions. In this way, we will be able to decide whether a request makes sense or not.

In addition, it is important to reflect on and analyze our relationships. Do they enrich us in any way? If the relationship we have with someone does us more harm than good, why do we keep talking to this person? The best thing to do is to get rid of all those who use us regardless of our feelings.

If one of the things we want for ourselves is to be happy without causing harm to anyone, let us not feel bad if we slam the door on someone who is harming us. If we notice that someone is trying to manipulate us, let's move away without hesitation.

Ask for help

You cannot erase a narcissist from your life and defend yourself from others without the right support network. Asking for help is not a mistake, on the contrary, it will allow you to face a difficult test with the awareness that you are not alone. Probably if you've been linked to a narcissist for a long time, he will have driven you away from friends or family, but that doesn't mean you couldn't seek them out again. Get help from your parents, a sister, and your circle of friends. Tell what's happening to you, the realization you've had, and seek refuge in their affection. They certainly won't back down. You have so many people who love you and are rooting for you: you just have to believe it! If the story has left deep wounds and you feel a very deep unease, consider doing therapy: there's nothing wrong with it, and working on yourself will allow you in the future not to end up in other unhealthy relationships.

Give yourself time

When a relationship ends it's always painful. If the story you're closing was about a narcissistic person, everything gets even more complicated. What you need now is time. Don't delude yourself: at first you will feel bad and the desire to run to him and throw your arms around his neck will be very strong. But you have to resist. In the first days, perhaps months, you will feel confused and sad, but over time you will realize that you made the right choice.

After this practical chapter, the next one will talk about managing emotions.

Chapter 11: How to govern your emotions and keep them at bay

Poor emotional management often leads us to misrepresent many inner realities. We see emotions as choices on a menu that each of us can choose or discard at will (today I feel broken, but I decide to show happiness). Internal dynamics don't work like this: emotions cannot be postponed; they do not die but are transformed: into psychosomatic illnesses and mal de Vivre. But it often leads us to make bad choices, such as entering a relationship with a narcissist. In this chapter, we see how to manage our emotions and keep them at bay

Some good ways to govern your emotions
In this paragraph, we will show me which are the best techniques to manage and govern one's emotions. Let's see them together:

<u>Emotional regulation</u>

The first tip for anyone who wants to avoid being constantly manipulated or victimized by a narcissist or any emotional vampire: really work on your emotions.
Emotions are drives and instincts with precise goals and objectives. Putting them aside means closing the door to an inner reality that, if well understood, managed, and oriented, would allow us to obtain greater well-being. Hiding emotions, on the other hand, means giving shape to a malaise that underlies a series of psychological disorders.
Because hiding emotions is not healthy and can have an immense cost, it would therefore be better to learn to work on your own well-being.
Emotions are one of the greatest gifts that life offers us: they are the most multifaceted, colorful, and unique way to experience the full spectrum of our humanity.
When we have a healthy relationship with our emotional experience, we can appreciate what each emotion has to offer, from sadness to joy. If, on the other hand, we find ourselves overreacting to situations or withdrawing from ourselves, then our relationship with our emotions needs to be healed.
Emotional regulation is really important to avoid falling into the trap of toxic people and definitely improve your life.
Emotion regulation becomes even more fundamental, especially for you as an empath.

It is a question of implementing a whole series of strategies and behaviors by each of us, to regulate the emotion felt in a given moment. Because being able to regulate emotion, such as fear, makes us less "bait" in the eyes of a narcissist.

Emotional regulation is a concept, it can be defined as multidimensional, which has the following characteristics:

- ✓ Use techniques that make us more willing to experience emotions (whether they are positive or negative)
- ✓ After experiencing emotions, strategies of awareness, understanding, and acceptance of the different emotional states take over
- ✓ After that, it is necessary to actively engage in achieving a certain goal, in response to emotions (whether they are positive or negative)
- ✓ At this point, we learn the flexible use of strategies that are always adapted to the context to be able to regulate the intensity and/or duration of the emotional response.
- ✓ Finally, the displacement of the dysfunctional emotion will take place.

So, we have said that the solution is not to repress, ignore or hide emotions. You should know that this emotional energy is there, present, and still alive. The secret is to let it flow. To better understand how to manage our emotions through regulation, let's try using three simple metaphors.

- ✓ The well. If you choose to leave your emotions at the bottom of the well, you will become ill. Water that stagnates for too long goes bad and takes on a bad smell. Avoid giving life to this image, the classic way of hiding our inner reality.
- ✓ The tsunami. You must know that, if you choose this type of strategy, maybe you will end up hurting others. Emotions can sometimes turn into a cyclone, a tsunami. They are thrown so angrily at others that everyone is the loser.
- ✓ The mill. A mill allows water to move, to flow in harmony. The movement is smooth, nothing stays compressed. The water is fresh and does not stagnate. This is the best image for managing your emotions.
- ✓ Heart-shaped water drop. It is therefore a question of learning to channel all our emotions appropriately. We have to move with them, start saying what annoys us, react at the right moment, and be assertive and agile in the face of daily pressures. Essentially, making our emotions a perfect and harmonious engine for our lives, and not a gear that blocks and traps us.

If a person becomes really skilled in controlling his emotions through these strategies, he will be able to hide them from a possible narcissist chasing them in order to dominate them and use them for his shady plans. So, take a path of personal growth in which you will be able to learn to manage emotions and not show your weaknesses. This is a fundamental step to reveal as little as possible about you. The only way to defend yourself from the attacks of a narcissist who wants to feed on your empathy is to try to keep your distance by showing as little as possible. Because they mostly play on guilt and emotions, to succeed in their intentions.

So, this is all about you

Detoxing a narcissist and being more capable of governing your emotions is not possible when looking outward to try to understand or anticipate what the narcissist is or is not doing.

Yes, initially, learning about narcissism helps understand the phenomenon. However, if you get stuck endlessly studying narcissistic traits and trying to detox, you won't heal.

There is only one way to effectively detox from a narcissist; turning inward to make the emotional detox center around meeting your essence and healing yourself.

To do this effectively you need to connect with the triggers that have clicked inside you on an emotional level and that the narcissist has activated. This keeps you bonded to the trauma and is how the narcissist was able to psychically attach themselves to you to suck your life energy.

It is impossible to stop the narcissist from doing this, but you can detox these parts of yourself so that you are no longer unconsciously holding on to the other end of the stick that is holding you down. Then it will end. Taking back your power means letting go of "what happened to me" narratives, turning inward with self-love, devotion, and the desire to deeply heal and to contact your essence, saying, "What part of does she require my healing and support never to be vulnerable or infiltrated by people like this again?"

What you will find, as you do that dedicated inner recovery work, is that the narcissist fades into the background, the symptoms of your trauma begin to melt away, and you will be excited about your evolution, you are leveling up and increasing in health, power, strength, optimism and the ability to rebuild in empowering and positive ways.

This is inevitable if you make this experience all about your healing, and less and less about them.

Stop handing over power

As you heal your inner world, become aware of where you have been given power.

Keep healing and empowering yourself, make sure you are not handing over any emotional energy, keep healing any internal parts that are firing up, so you remain calm, clear, and powerful, and be clear in finalizing things.

Be calm, clear, powerful, and whole – heal until you become "anti-fear". This puts you in your most powerful position.

You will also love your newfound and activated boundaries throughout your life. No longer will you just "indulge to move forward" (now you know how bad it ends!).

This is the time to forge your truth and values and live aligned with them and see how your life will move to support you in a healthy way.

Detox Your Life

Narcissists are toxic. And we are more susceptible to them when we are toxic.

Surely, after narcissistic abuse, we have unhealed and unresolved inner wounds that require healing and detoxification. There are also other aspects of our lives that we may not have realized are unhealthy.

Things like addiction to smoking, alcohol, junk food, overwork, bingeing on social media, shopping, gambling, or drugs. Perhaps we have avoided and abandoned love, respect, and self-care by indulging in toxic behaviors that may give us some relief at the moment, but ultimately end up doing more harm to ourselves.

Maybe we're used to complaining, judging others, and being incredibly fair with the ways we highlight the horrors of the world. Of course, this is understandable, but if we continue to cultivate the internal chemicals of toxicity, we remain susceptible to toxic people.

We should start by saying, "I will never accept a lower level of love than I have for myself."

Letting go of destructive and life-damaging people is a powerful way to raise the bar of our self-esteem.

A good emotional cleansing

Emotional cleansings are a systematic and conscious practice to purify undigested and harmful emotions, freeing us from the illusion of not deserving happiness. This sort of emotional detox thus brings us back to our natural state of deep joy. The idea behind an emotional cleanse is not to free yourself from what you might consider negative emotions, but rather to purge those that have been stagnant and stuck, leaving you free to process and experience all aspects of your emotions in a healthy way. Just as a food detox can help you digest food better; an emotional cleanse can help you digest your emotional experiences. Emotions can get stuck due to trauma, unhealthy attachments, or resistance to certain moods, usually because we don't have the tools to manage them. How do I know if I need an emotional cleansing? The easiest way to figure out if you need an emotional cleanse is, to be honest with yourself.

You may think that the purpose of emotional cleansing is to get rid of all that is "uncomfortable" - pain, guilt, sadness, and stress - so as not to leave these emotions unresolved, but this is not the case. We need to process our emotions correctly, from the most pleasant to the most painful.

In fact, every single emotion has its own value and teaches us valuable lessons that contribute to our wealth of life experiences, wisdom, and personal growth. Weakening them, numbing them, or driving them away will only delay their benefits.

Emotional cleansing works exactly like this: you don't need external tools or aids, it's a 100% internal job which, like shadow work, requires us to deeply accept our limits before we can overcome them.

It is about taking the time to observe, acknowledge, accept, and finally let go of our limitations regarding emotions that we have never faced.

There are many emotional cleansing techniques, and everyone can find their own. Below we have outlined 4 key steps to undertake this important inner work.

There are, practically, 4 emotional cleansing techniques.

1. Observe. The first step of emotional cleansing is to create an observation space to be able to work more clearly with our emotions. An important part of this step is noticing what sets you off and what areas you become particularly reactive in your life. Spend a few days observing and writing down your daily emotional reactions, without judgment, and notice any sort of recurring patterns. Behave like a scientist doing research and refrain from labeling or criticizing your behaviors. At this stage, you are just observing.
2. Improves responsiveness: once you notice what your sympathetic nervous system is triggering (that "fight or flight" feeling), you can start to find ways to calm down. Only from mental calm can we begin the hard emotional work that awaits us. You can get to this state through exercise (if you notice you have excess energy), yoga (if you feel depleted), meditation, mindfulness, or a sound bath. You can also create your own "safe space" in your mind by conjuring up a place (real or imagined) where you feel perfectly safe and without threats. Notice how your body feels in this space. You can take refuge there when you feel anxious or uncomfortable.
3. Look within yourself. The difference between self-reflection and self-awareness is very evident in this passage: self-reflection, which is the one described in the first step, is a mental process. Self-awareness, which we want to arrive at in this

passage, is instead an emotional process. The process of looking inward requires you to bridge the gap between your emotions, stand up to your inner bully (ego), and make yourself vulnerable while allowing yourself to experience your emotions naked and raw. The way to bridge the gap between spiritual ego and emotions is to engage in healthy dialogue with yourself, such as noticing the sensations of your body as feedback for respectful self-inquiry, asking yourself questions about your past and history, talking to your inner child, and showing them empathy and understanding.

4. Release. This last step is about creating a relationship with the present moment, releasing fear, and creating healthy inner boundaries. The release process is not about eliminating reactivity, but about transforming it into something new. Recognizes and releases reactive sensations to create a sense of security, stability, and strength. The key here is to be open to emotions, in whatever form they come. When you lower your levels of responsiveness to the emotions and experiences they bring you, you will be more willing to experience the depth of what you are feeling, which will allow you to have an authentic experience of your life and a deeper connection with the people who surround you. You will be more intrigued by the emotion you feel and more eager to investigate it rather than letting yourself go to the spontaneous reactions it arouses in you.

Give strength to your life

Your continued inner growth empowers your life. Narcissists are reckless, always believing that their life is someone else's fault, and refuse to take any personal responsibility, heal, learn from their mistakes, or grow.

Narcissists self-avoid, they self-relinquish their inner triggers, they self-medicate with external attention and things, and they never go home to heal and become whole within themselves.

If you do not strive to be self-involved, self-devoted, and committed to your inner development and growth, this can leave you on the ledge of unconscious energy where you will unknowingly continue to seek out other non-wholesome people to try and fulfill you.

Water seeks its level. This does not mean that we are bad people, rather it means that they are unaware of the truth – "I am the generative source of my life experience, and ONLY I have the power to change this by healing and changing myself".

When you are committed to changing and healing yourself from within then you are no longer on the trajectory where a narcissist can pick you up and feed on you.

Rather, you will be in the body, connected to your intuition, appearing authentic and capable of ferreting out narcissists without fearing them. You will also have realized that all the previous toxic people in your life no longer have power over you they can no longer manipulate your traumas and unhealed fears.

Keep your emotions at bay: how to do it

The thing you must always remember is that it's not emotions that have control over you, it's just the opposite. If you learn to recognize and manage them, you can also use them to get better and become strong mentally and keep them at bay.
So, after having shown you what are the best ways to govern emotions, here are some very useful tips to be able to keep our emotions and our empathic powers safe instead. Let's see which techniques will help us in this regard:

From fear to self-confidence

Start with this: fear keeps you safe. Prudence keeps you calm. But sometimes it doesn't allow you to experience, to meet new people. Maybe it's related to insecurity and like anything that makes you feel uncomfortable, you often pretend you don't feel it. If you're at a crossroads and your fear is holding you back from making a decision, try to write down the beauty that could come from the leap into the void. Seeing it written, black on white makes all the difference. And it erases the feeling of making a mistake, which isn't always true.

Strong borders

Empaths are more sensitive to their environment and the emotional energy of others. Often, they assimilate the energy of the environment exactly as a sponge does.
If this aspect is not taken into consideration, it can influence your will, decisions, habits, and behaviors. This means that personal, energetic, mental, and emotional boundaries have been compromised.
This is not good. You can choose which way to take your life. In a sense, you must be alert and at the same time relaxed at the doors of the various levels of your being, not fearful, but simply seeking the knowledge of "what is".
If an empath can't maintain the "healthy" boundaries of the emotions of everyone they interact with, along with all their problems and all the "noise" from the internet and media, they will be greatly challenged. Negativity will penetrate and consume everything, and this will no longer be able to stop.

Communicate your needs

Just as an empath or highly sensitive person, if you want to grow and thrive, you need to understand what our needs are communicating to us in life.

If we don't communicate our needs, then negativity can build up in our lives and make things too busy. We begin to live a life created by others rather than ourselves.

Take your time and space

When Leonard Orr, the same boy who came up with "emotional energy pollution," visited a guru who claimed to be extraordinarily old, he found him sitting alone in a giant spiritual hall with all the visitors watching in awe devotion over 30 meters away. He managed to ask the sage a question, asking, "What is the key to living to a ripe old age?"

The guru replied, paraphrasing: "I keep being away from other people."

It is important that you frequent healthy communities and social environments. It is one of our basic needs as human beings and people. However, sometimes, we also need to carve out our space and healthy detachment from others to enter ourselves again.

Pay attention to what you throw out

Empathic people tend to be highly intuitive. Energy and intuition are very often associated with the ability to detect the feelings and intentions of others.

This can have spiritual and healing benefits, but it can also have a potential setback.

It is necessary to live according to your intuition. Develop a call-and-response relationship with your intuition. Use it to guide others.

Empaths very often feel the pain of others, they enter it. But they have to be very careful about the repercussions it can have on their state of mind.

Cleaning

Do an energy cleaning even in the environments where you live or work.

Empath people need to purify themselves of the negative energies they assimilate.

You need to cleanse the negative energy and emotional energy pollution you take in, just like when you take a shower to wash. Then you have to process the emotions under this "energy". As you do so, try to understand what is the lesson that you need to learn, since this has occurred in your life for a very specific reason and purpose.

<u>Protect yourself from future energy implications.</u>

Here are some ways to cleanse yourself and protect yourself:

- ✓ Grounded with feet on the ground
- ✓ Hot bath, using candles and crystals
- ✓ Use essential oils
- ✓ Prayer and meditation, white light visualization
- ✓ Use natural herbs, such as white sage or incense
- ✓ To be grateful

All of us are in a constant quest to better ourselves and not try to cast or project the negativity of the world back into ourselves and onto others.

In essence, an empath person can embrace incredible adversity, rise through it, and transform it. To go from negativity to positivity, to demonstrate how amazing it is to be able to do this and how extraordinary it is.

By having a way to plug yourself into the emotional energy of the world, you play an important role. And like all good things, this one takes effort, love, and attention to nurture it.

To conclude this chapter, we can say that regulating and keeping our emotions safe teaches us the importance of processing and understanding our own emotions rather than reacting to them (thinking, agitating, staring, remembering).

Even if you feel like you don't know how to express them, even if you feel that negative emotions are far superior to those that make you feel good, don't give up because you can win this little battle to gain self-control from your emotionality.

Interestingly, as we process and digest all of our emotions, our ability to empathize with others dramatically improves. As a result, we can care for others without clogging our emotional flow. This is an extremely important skill to have in a world we are so often exposed to trauma and tragedy in our daily lives. Everything, as always, starts with us. Ending this speech, in the next chapter, we will explain how to reject evil emotions coming from a narcissist and other toxic people.

Chapter 12: How to Repel Narcissists' Evil and Vampire Emotions

We saw in the last chapter that emotions govern you, motivate you, and push you to change or to stay as you are. You are an empath made of flesh, bones, and emotions: you just can't ignore them, even if sometimes emotions play tricks on you and it seems to you that fear, anxieties, and frustrations take over. Yet the way to control emotions is there, so you become mentally stronger and regain control. And above all, avoid narcissists. In this chapter, however, we will deepen the discussion and show you, after making you understand how to keep your emotions (positive, of course) safe, how to reject the negative ones that come from toxic people such as narcissists, manipulators, or emotional vampires.

How to Avoid Absorbing the Evil Energies of Others

For you who have now recognized that you are an empath, endowed with empathy, and therefore you take full charge of the affairs of others without resolving your own, emotions such as anger, fear, frustration, or sadness are energies. You can absorb these evil energies from other toxic people without realizing it. If you tend to be an emotional "sponge," it's important to know how to avoid absorbing the negative energies of others. Especially those of emotional or narcissistic vampires. Anxiety, depression, and stress can convert you into an emotional sponge that absorbs all your defenses. When you least expect it, you resonate with other people's negative feelings.

Below we will show you some practical techniques to avoid absorbing the evil energies of others.

Find out if you're touchy.

The people most likely to be overwhelmed by the negative energies of others are the "empathic" ones. Here are some factors of this type of people:

- ✓ People tell you that you are very sensitive, without intending to compliment you.
- ✓ You feel miserable and suffer from a feeling of suffocation in the presence of many people.
- ✓ Other people's anxiety, fear, and stress transfer to their bodies in the form of physical pain.
- ✓ Talking too much, noises and smells unleash your nerves.

- ✓ You need to stay alone to recharge your energies.
- ✓ You are a generous person, spiritual, and a good listener.
- ✓ You tend to always have an "evacuation plan" to get out of situations quickly.

Look for the source

Ask yourself if this negative energy is coming from you, other people, or both. If the emotion, fear, or anger, is yours, then deal carefully with its causes. If not, try to locate its generator.

Move away from the possible source

Move away from anyone who is generating these negative energies at least 30 meters. Don't worry about offending people. If you're in a public place, move if you feel like someone is "infecting" you with their depression.

Focus on your breathing

This exercise will allow you to connect with your essence. For several minutes breathe out the negativity and breathe in the calm.

Protect yourself

A good way to do this is to visualize a blanket of white light (or any color that you think might impart power) around your body. Think of this light as a shield that prevents all negative energies from entering you.

Manage emotional overload

Don't be indebted to your ability to absorb other people's emotions. Tackle it with these strategies:

- ✓ Learn to recognize people who can lower your energy. It is easy to identify them: they are the ones who like to criticize, play the victim, control, or are narcissistic.
- ✓ Consume high-protein foods before experiencing stressful situations, such as going out in groups.
- ✓ Try never to depend on third parties to resolve difficult situations: always remain in control.
- ✓ Keep your private space in a house shared with others and demand respect.

Look for positive people and situations

Call some friends who can always see things from a positive perspective. Spend time with a colleague who knows how to listen. Hope is contagious and serves to lift the mood.

Create and maintain a refuge to disconnect

Use a poster or picture of a waterfall or forest to look at in times of stress and anxiety. Even better if you have your sacred loci where you can take refuge and meditate while regaining access to your resources. The Floating tub represents the ideal place to reset, recover and improve yourself naturally by accessing the resources of your mind: beyond the reduction of stress, physical recovery, and being isolated from the negativity with which others can charge you and negatively affect your well-being, the state in which your mind will find itself when you practice Floating will allow you to regenerate both physically and mentally, recharge yourself with positive energies and start a self-healing process.

Let a "kitty" choose you as your owner.

It is known that cats can absorb negative energies. it is no coincidence that if you are stressed and worried you will certainly attract the attention of your cat who will try to come on your lap. Yes, let's face it because that's exactly how it is. From an energetic point of view, the cat can be considered an energy transformer, able to help us heal and feel better: its innate tendency is to absorb the negative energies that accumulate in our aura, in our chakras, or the environments and transform them, transmute them: it is not uncommon to see a cat curled up in the arms of its Human when this is not well. If it suffers from emotional discomfort, the cat will tend to curl up at the height of the stomach, the seat of the solar plexus, the chakra it manages emotions with a "lower" energy frequency, such as anger, frustration, anxiety, fear, i.e., energies of less high quality than the energies of the Heart chakra, were, for example, Peace, 'Love, Understanding. The cat's task is precisely to absorb and transform these energies, making them less heavy. The same thing happens if the discomfort is a pain: in this case, not the cat that doesn't abandon its two-legged companion, lying down on it or in any case seeking strong physical contact.

The cats are also great experts in Feng-Shui, the ancient Chinese discipline that teaches how to improve the quality of the energy of the environment, and how to harmonize it. The subsoil is crossed by energy currents that can affect our health and the cat proves to be extremely sensitive to the underground energy networks, capturing the electrostatic and magnetic fields, which is not possible for humans; for this reason, it is important to pay attention to where they like to spend their time: if a cat tends to sleep in a particular area of the house, it means that in that point there is no negative energy that can disturb it, and if it does not disturb it disturb either do we. Due to their peculiarity of knowing how to transform energies, they can stop above the pathogenic nodes that annoy human beings so much without being disturbed by them, they do it with awareness, reaching the point of looking for these points because in this way they electrostatically charge their hair which cleans better and thoroughly.

Neutralizing a narcissist or an emotional vampire: 5 tips

In general, before showing you these five tips, the secret to neutralizing a narcissist (or a manipulative person) is to analyze the truthfulness of what she or he says or does, without being duped by the magic that he or she usually emanates.

Neutralizing a narcissist or an emotional vampire is not easy at all, as he is a bewitching person who enjoys significant social support. It counts on several characteristics that manage to "enchant". Also, he doesn't see himself as a narcissist, but as the product of a spell.

Initially, for example, the narcissist receives the admiration of others. He is a tireless popularizer of his successes, which he even tends to inflate beyond belief. If for most people the ego is the main point of reference, for the narcissist it is even more so.

These people often occupy leading positions. If so, they will often exert their bewitching power in a very direct way. In that regard, they surround themselves with people who adore them so that they can control it more easily. However, there are ways to neutralize a narcissist.

It may be easier than we think. All you need is a good dose of character and determination. Let's see 5 tips that can limit these subjects from your empaths.

1. **No, the magic word that can neutralize an emotional vampire**

The narcissist or manipulator always wants to hear yes, and that others share his point of view in all respects. The submission of others grants him a form of control. It means that her influence and his power over others are intact.

The word "no" is therefore one of the tools to neutralize a narcissist. Not agreeing with him or distancing himself from his statements inevitably compromises the idea he will have of us. In this way, in his eyes, we will pass on the side of "ignorance", as we are unable to see reality.

2. "I don't believe you, prove it to me!"

Narcissists and serial manipulators tell lies often and in different ways. Sometimes magnifying or belittling people and situations, others invent episodes from scratch to be able to praise themselves or denigrate others, or create simple fantasies.

If you are in the presence of a narcissist and you find that he is lying, do not shrink from questioning his claims about him. Ask him for proof of his words. List the topics that make you doubt the veracity of his statements. He'll probably react by walking away. In any case, you will have made him understand that you are not willing to take every single statement he makes at face value.

3. "You are not superior to others"

Implicitly or explicitly, especially the narcissist wants to demonstrate that they are superior. He always implies that he (or she) knows more or that he does it better, that he can think bigger and that he always fares better than those around him.

We must remind him (or she) that, although able to do, say or think with greater dexterity, he is not superior to others for this reason. Let them understand that anyone, with good preparation and in the right circumstances, can stand out in their area of expertise. And that if we excel in one field, there will surely be another for which we are not suited. This, after all, is part of human nature.

4. I don't fear you!"

The best way to neutralize a narcissist is to not be afraid of them. These people take hold of the insecurities and fears of others. They are always careful to discover the weaknesses of those next to them to hit them. They don't spare low blows, trying to highlight other people's weaknesses, in order to make others feel more insecure.

Not tolerating their attacks and questioning their claims is one way to show that you are not afraid of them. Let the narcissist take offense. Not letting his low blows land is the best way to neutralize him. A narcissist doesn't know how to deal with someone who isn't afraid of them.

5. "Don't change the topic of discussion!"

Narcissist always wants to have their way. If arguing, he realizes he is wrong, and in order not to agree with his interlocutor, he will change the subject. If he makes an obvious mistake, he will try to divert attention to something else. They are generally very adept at manipulating situations.

If you often deal with a narcissist or emotional vampire, you need to stop him from grabbing at straws or confusing you with his roundabouts. Bring the conversation back to the main topic. He'll probably never admit his mistake, but he'll understand that he can't manipulate you.

Neutralizing a narcissist or any other reason, to conclude this chapter, we have seen that it is not easy. Courage, wit, and determination are needed from you to be an empath. However, it is worth trying because it is equivalent to not being a victim of manipulation and to having healthier social relationships. Narcissistic person, manipulative with their own evil energies or who tries to suck in the energies of others, does not feel good about themselves, and in order not to admit it, they try to use others. Don't let them do it to you.
In the last section of the book, there will be a section dedicated to what really matters to the empath and where he needs to focus "his powers".

FIFTH PART- WHAT IS IMPORTANT TO ENHANCE YOUR POWER

Chapter 13: What to Focus on? Family or relationships

We are at the last part of this guide, the one in which we invite you to focus on what really matters not only in your lives but which is needed to improve your powers as an empath. Let's start with the aspects you need to pay more attention to.

The importance of empathic communication

One of the points on which you must invest your resources and your powers as an empath is precisely Empathic Communication.
Empathy must be transmitted to the other, an empathy that is not expressed, it is simply an inert attitude, the effect of which on the quality of communication is rather small. In this sense, empathic listening implies an interrelationship with a person in difficulty, unable to solve a certain problem correctly and efficiently in a unit of time. Empathic listening is challenging because perception can make you focus only on the feelings in the situation itself, rather than the speaker's feelings. A good empathic listener will remember that people don't always seek advice – often they just want to hear it, and optimal empathic listening means being open and not judgmental.
So, empathic communication occurs when a person focuses on listening and on the willingness to understand the other not only in the concepts he expresses but above all through active listening which also includes emotions. The deepest empathy absolutely includes taking an interest in the emotions of others.
Communication can also manifest real empathy disorders, such as the lack of empathetic communication, or that form of communication centered on the other and not always or in any case on oneself, on one's problems or states. Being interested in others is a form of empathy and empathetic communication is above all based on active and deep listening.
Empathy, in this case, being the opposite of distraction, of judging listening, of not listening is the access key to improving and having any type of healthy relationship. Empathy is pure listening. Empathy requires attention and concentration on the other, so both the body and the mind must be present, sharp, and ready to catch every word and every meaning that emerges. Distraction makes empathy impossible. Your empathy is a superior, extremely advanced state of a human relationship. We

could define it as knowing how to put yourself in the shoes of others to feel and perceive what they feel.

Empathy is neither good nor bad, and in fact, psychological empathy can also be used to understand how a wanted man, a killer, thinks, and what his next move will be (strategic empathy).

In general, in daily and professional human relationships, empathy is positive and is also a rare commodity. As Jeremy Rifkin points out: "Empathetic consciousness is based on the awareness that others, like us, are unique and mortal beings. If we empathize with another it is because we recognize their fragile and finite nature, their vulnerability, and their one and only life; we experience their existential loneliness, their personal suffering, and their struggle to exist and develop as if they were our own. Our empathic hug is our way of sympathizing with each other and celebrating her life".

Empathy is rare because it requires the subtle ability to tune in emotionally and understand the most hidden, emotional, and personal levels of our interlocutor's experience, rather than the numerical or object data he exposes to us. It also uses metacommunication (literally "communicating about the communication itself"), for example, it fearlessly asks for the meaning of a term that it does not understand, or, on the few occasions when the listener speaks, he will do so to explain concepts that serve the communication process itself. And this great communicative power will be exploited to improve your relationships. Let's see how this can be done in the next paragraph.

Family or relationship: what and how to focus on?

To answer this question, we tell you that rather than focusing on just one type of relationship, try to use your powers as an empath to improve your relationships in general.

Obviously, it must also be said that the choice of which type of relationship to focus on is also subjective. It's up to you to prioritize what goes on top.

And, in this regard, empathic communication for deep sharing between human beings can create real connections, both within the family context and in that of friendship and love. As a famous quote says: Listening without bias or distraction is the greatest gift that you can do to another person. (Denis Waitley)

Empathic listening is of impressively rare quality. In fact, active listening is an intentional act, in which we are committed to grasping both what the other explicitly refers to us and what is implicitly communicated. We can say we met him the last time a person dedicated an hour of time to us without telling us anything about him or her, to listen only to what we had to say, asking us questions to better understand, not just our own information, but our emotions. Well, if that happened, it was probably a coaching, counseling, or therapy session. It rarely happens in daily life. Daily life is so full of external distractions and "internal noises" of the mind, that empathic listening usually has no place in it. And you can train this great power to improve your relationships.

We are in the midst of the digital revolution and the number of sources and stimuli we receive daily is greater than we can manage. Research by the University of Michigan analyzed how college students today are 40% less empathetic than students in the 80s and 90s.

The great danger of this phenomenon is that we isolate ourselves more and more and see the muscle of empathy atrophy.

How many times do we see a group of kids who don't talk to each other but who are all bent over their smartphones? Or adults at dinner who instead of talking are attentive only to look at the latest notifications. This is why empathic listening becomes very important to improve our relationships, whether they are family or otherwise.

Moments of high-intensity listening are sometimes encountered in life, in true friendships, or between true companions at work, but it is not certain that the attention is always entirely and only centered on one of the subjects, as is the case in empathy. And after all, if specific courses are needed to learn empathy, it is because school, academic training, and books, are always very focused on giving information, rather than teaching how to listen.

Anyway, empathic listening has three stages:

- ✓ The aim is to clarify some things (saying "if I'm not mistaken…")
- ✓ Find the basic idea with the same words as your interlocutor
- ✓ Check and paraphrase the feelings of the other ("it is correct to say that…").

At the same time, we must say that effective empathic listening requires two fundamental skills:

1. Perspective adoption, which is the ability to understand a situation from another person's perspective and empathic concern
2. The ability to identify another person's feelings and then experience those feelings for yourself.

The principle of empathic communication is based on understanding the communication partner and, respectively, on finding ways in which the transmitted message can be understood by him.

No way: empathic communication is the most important communication skill for building relationships. But empathic communication involves learning empathic listening. Of the four ways of communicating, reading, writing, speaking, and listening, few people benefit from listening education.

Empathic listening does not imply an approving attitude; implies a fuller and deeper understanding both intellectually and emotionally of the interlocutor.

Empathic listening is also based on a series of essential rules, presented below:

- ✓ Every word should be perceived before decoding the message.
- ✓ The emotional state and feelings of the parties are perceived before classifying their point of view.
- ✓ Identify the barriers that have appeared in communication.
- ✓ Encourage dialogue
- ✓ A concise message is encouraged, followed by a check that it was received correctly. Otherwise, the details are identified.
- ✓ Eye contact with the dialogue partner is maintained.
- ✓ Much attention is paid to intonation, gesture, and facial expression, considering that, in many situations, visual memory overrides auditory memory, which can greatly distort the message.
- ✓ Open and direct questions are asked.

Another thing you will need to focus on and work hard on is the most difficult component of empathic listening which is certainly the suspension of judgment. If someone says, "I threw away the wine" or "I threw the garbage bag out the window", it is practically impossible not to judge negatively. But the "suspension" of judgment means "suspending it", not "making it disappear". Suspend it so that we can better understand what, where, how, and why certain things happen. If we didn't do it, we would have lost a large part of the information that could have come out instead. And for this, work better on this power to have healthy and lasting relationships, which enrich your life for the better.

Tips and exercises to train empathic listening

Empathic mirroring is one of the most used techniques to authentically connect with your interlocutor. Here are 4 tips to train empathic active listening:

1. Repeating the interlocutor's words, using formulas such as "you are saying that...", "in other words...", "so in your opinion..."
2. Mirror the emotions of the other: starting from the signals that come from non-verbal communication and which signal the emotional state of the interlocutor, it is possible to show understanding with sentences like these: "I seem to perceive your concern", "I see you a little ' angry" and so on
3. Ask for explanations: asking questions that underline a genuine interest in the other's words helps to express our involvement, as well as to clarify some fundamental points of the speech
4. Formulate considerations: express one's thoughts, explicitly clarifying that it is one's point of view. The use of sentences like "in my opinion", "I argue that", and "the way I see it" can be always useful for this purpose.

Among the exercises on empathic listening, here are also some examples of questions to ask yourself when listening to someone:

- ✓ What emotions are the others communicating to me?
- ✓ What is his nonverbal communication to me?
- ✓ How do his words make me feel?

There is also another famous method, namely the Gordon method to be able to train active listening and conflict management. Gordon suggested using the now-famous I-message technique, consisting of 4 phases:

1. Talking about yourself: describe your negative emotions starting from yourself, using the formulas "I believe...", "I feel...", "I think..."
2. Describe in detail the behavior of the other that creates discomfort
3. Motivate why the behavior of the other creates discomfort for us
4. Express your request to the other.

Here's an example: "I feel angry when you yell because you stop me from speaking. Therefore, I ask you to lower your voice and listen to me".

With these tips, you can improve your empathic communication and focus on creating (or fixing) the relationships that interest you most. Active listening allows you to consolidate the relationship between those who communicate, increasing mutual respect and acceptance.

Here are some examples of the benefits of active listening:

- ✓ Accept your own feelings as natural and human.

- ✓ Lower emotional tensions, the sense of threat, and anxiety.
- ✓ Facilitate the perception of problems and their resolution.

There are also many specific applications of active listening in various sectors including work and professional. It's up to you to decide where to apply them.

Summarizing everything we have explained in this chapter, we can say that empathic communication can also have pathological traits, above all when the ability to take an interest in the mental and experiential processes of others is lacking, empathic communication suffers and, more generally, the quality of communication suffers relation. In coaching, counseling, leadership, and any type of professional interview, empathic communication can make the difference between poor communication and deep, authentic, and rich communication. Thanks to the fact of focusing on this point, you may decide to establish various types of relationships with which you have established your priorities.

In the last chapter of the guide, we'll talk about how to boost your empath powers even further while avoiding the negative energies of toxic people.

Chapter 14: 10 practical ways to release all the power while avoiding narcissists

Here we are at the last chapter of this practical guide. After having explained the various characteristics to understand if you are an empath, what your special powers are, and how to avoid falling into the traps of narcissists and manipulators, we will show you what are the best methods to be able to increase these powers even more together with the fact to avoid any emotional vampire.

Release Your Power While Avoiding Narcissists: Ways to Protect Your Own Energy

Before talking about how to increase one's powers as an empath, let's see if there are, first of all, ways to protect one's energy, while trying to avoid toxic people.
The empathic person tends, in fact, by now as we well know, to absorb the energy of others.
This can cause problems in your life.
It is therefore necessary to protect yourself from unwanted energy.
Let's look at some ways to protect yourself.

1. Shielding. Shielding is a way of blocking unwanted vibrations from others or the environment.

It uses the power of the subconscious mind to form a mental shield that blocks negative energy from entering. The shield is imagined to be deflecting negative particles.
Shielding requires the faith of the empath to negate negative energies. So, you must proceed in this way:

- ✓ Close your eyes and breathe deeply until you are relaxed.
- ✓ Make sure you start with a sense of balanced energy.
- ✓ Imagine yourself inside an egg-shaped bubble or shield.
- ✓ Negative energies are repelled by this mental shield of yours.
- ✓ Notice your steady energy at the end of the day.

2. Energy cleansing. Performing an energy cleanse is as easy as imagining yourself taking a shower. It takes your intent and your imagination to communicate with your subconscious mind. So, apply the following energy-cleansing technique:
   - ✓ To clear your energy, use your imagination to activate your subconscious mind to clear the energy around you. First, breathe deeply. Close your eyes.
   - ✓ Imagine that the light cleanses your body, or the water cleanses your energy field.
   - ✓ You can also imagine taking a shower of light that sweeps away all negative energy.

3. The detachment. Detachment is about emotionally walking away from the situation.

Allow yourself not to become those emotions and understand that those emotions are not you.

Become the observer and observe the situation. Observe your emotions. Even if they continue to be heard, they don't affect as much.

4. Meditation. By understanding how to control your mind, you can control your energy.

When you are in control of your energy, it is easier to avoid being thrown out of balance by negative influences. You can also practice compassion. By changing the negative energy into compassion, it removes the negative feeling and transforms it into love.

5. Redirect Energy. Energy goes in, energy goes out. When there is no outlet for incoming negative energy, we tend to absorb it and hold it within us. This method consists of allowing one to feel the negative energy of the person and then holding it in the capacity in which he can hold it.

Then release the energy. You need to be aware that you are holding unwanted energy and that you wish to release it. Pack all of your energy into a ball and then imagine the ball flying away from you in the air.

6. Distance yourself. If there's nothing else you can do, distance yourself from the person you feel is making you emotionally unstable. Excuse yourself and leave.

7. Finally, one of the best things you can do is to cleanse your energy with intention and white sage. It is recommended to practice cleaning with sage when there has been a bad discussion in the room, when sick people have stayed there or when you feel unwell, or you understand that you have been "sucked in" by external negative energies. How to do it? Proceed like this:

- ✓ Make sure the area you want to clean is well-ventilated.
- ✓ Keep all doors in the house open and a few windows as well.
- ✓ It is best to clean and tidy the area you want to treat.
- ✓ Take your bunch of sage and light the end, then gently blow out the flame while allowing the bunch to continue to burn and emit smoke.
- ✓ Keep a bowl (not plastic) under the bunch of sage to prevent the ash from spreading on the floor.
- ✓ Set your intention: This is the most important part.
- ✓ Think about what you want to achieve with this fumigation, for example, cleaning and healing, or filling the environment with positive energy.
- ✓ While the sage is burning, it's important to express gratitude for the help the plant is giving you.
- ✓ Now go around the whole house, preferably clockwise, trying to get the smoke to all corners and on all the objects you want to purify.

In this very simple way, the energy of white sage brings cleansing, protection, and blessing to the space where it is burned.

Smoke can also be used to purify one's energy field by swirling it around. Start at your feet, allowing the smoke to drift around you and up your body to the top of your head.

As you move the smoke around you, hold the intention for clearing the negativity, and gently sweep the smoke upwards. In the end, thank you for the cleaning received.

When you're done, wash the ash out of the bowl.

Always remember that, beyond just lighting the sage and letting it smoke, your intention is powerful. Sage is considered the most effective herb for energy cleansing and really leaves a sense of peace in the treated environment and in oneself.

Apply the technique or techniques that you feel are most suitable for you.

10 best ways to enhance your empath powers

After explaining some useful techniques to get rid of negative energies and channel only the positive ones, let's explain how to make the best use of your powers of empathy.

If you are an empath, you may feel somewhat "cursed" by some special powers. Cursed because often in life, you have only attracted toxic people who wanted to benefit from these powers and your beneficial energy. The truth is that empathy is a gift, and you have the power within you to transform it into a great power that you can only use to fulfill yourself in life and establish fruitful and healthy relationships.

Now that you know how to avoid toxic people, however, it's time to turn your special traits into superpowers.

Here are 10 ways to activate the empathic power within you:

1. **Recognize that you are an empath**

If you are an empath, compassion is your calling. You were "marked" from birth to anchor light on planet earth. Acknowledging that you have come here to fulfill this mission is the first step in letting your inner light shine.

2. **Recognize and avoid toxic people**

To increase your powers as an empath you must develop some sort of radar toward the narcissist. To do this, you can consult the first guide and then review the strategies indicated in this book in the previous chapters. By neutralizing the toxic person, you can focus on yourself and work on your power as an empath.

3. **Trust your intuition**

As an empath, you are very sensitive. Whether you can read people's minds, receive psychic imagery, pick up smells, or sense a feeling in your belly, learning to trust yourself and the messages you receive will help you avoid "energy parasites" and cultivate positive, healthy relationships.

4. **Don't play the victim**

Empaths often lack self-esteem. After some time, your need to be loved can turn into a true victim toxic mentality. This is commonly seen in those spiritual relationships where the 'guru' takes all the resources and the 'devotees' are drained of self-esteem, money, and more.

5. **Set boundaries**

Once you can recognize the "energy parasites" who consume you, put limits on the amount of time you spend with them or decide not to hang out with them at all. Notice how you feel when you are with them and how you feel afterward. Soon you will be able to go away forever and recover your precious energy. You'll also have a lot more time on your hands to do something you love.

6. **Meditate**

Empaths need time to recharge. Meditation is a great tool that only takes a few minutes. This is great for taking your power back when you start to feel a sensory overload. You can also spend time in nature as a form of meditation or visualize yourself in a protective bubble where dark energy cannot reach you. Do this several times a day.

7. **Breathe**

Develop a breathing practice where you sit and breathe mindfully. As you inhale, think about clarity and power. As you exhale, think about exhaling negative energy. You can also say, "I'm breathing in power, I'm breathing out stress and negativity." Do this several times a day to get rid of any stress built up in your body.

8. **Transmutes negative energy**

As an empath, you absorb a lot of negative energy wherever you go. Employ useful ways to transform negative energy in real-time. For example, bring plants into your workspace to help absorb any negative energy. You can also try crystals which are natural energy modulators. Surround yourself with beauty. Try to speak positively in a difficult situation. Even finding humor in a serious situation when possible, can transmute negative energy. Another thing you can do is start each day with a gratitude affirmation to boost positive energy.

9. **Love yourself**

As an empath, your life purpose is to take care of yourself. That's all you're asked to do! Listening to your thoughts and emotions means self-empathy. Take time each day to honor your feelings and embrace your sensitivity. Recognize that you can be vulnerable and strong at the same time. Celebrate whenever you listen to your intuition or do something that helps you become happier, stronger, and healthier. Remember, when you live to your full potential, you can truly transform the lives of others. When you fully embrace your empathic nature, you will be finally able to experience great joy. You will see the big picture on a deeper level, a level filled with beauty. And you will be able to fill your energy cup by directly aligning with "Source".

10. **Australian Flowers**

Fringed Violet and Angelsword are the essences of choice to give you the necessary energy protection so that you can always feel strong and full of energy. We have just seen how the lack of psychic protection causes you to absorb everything in the energetic sea around you like a sponge and makes you feel tired. Fringed Violet and Angelsword give you much-needed psychic protection and release negative energies held in your energy field. This way you will feel centered and energized.

With these practical techniques, we conclude our discussion. Now that you know how to raise and release your power as an empath, you can start improving your life, avoid toxic people, and really start being happy.

Conclusions

In this guide we have taken care of analyzing all the aspects concerning empathy: from the description of empathy, we have gone on to show what are all the typical characteristics of an empathetic person. We then stopped to understand what the powers of an empath are and how they can be used to establish healthy and lasting relationships.

In the midst of all this, we have not forgotten to show but also to apply the appropriate resolution techniques, for one of the major problems that afflict an empath: attracting narcissistic aims.

With that done, after figuring out how to get rid of all the toxic evil energies of the various emotional and narcissistic vampires, we have explained how to release your powers and improve the different relational fields of your life.

Now we are quite sure that you have all the knowledge, tools, and ways to make you're being an empath a rare, excellent quality that will only allow you to be happy, get rid of negativity, and surround yourself with equally happy and fulfilled people.

This is nothing but our wish for you! As we wish you in the first guide, we wish you good luck and... may you make the most of life because you deserve it!

Printed in Great Britain
by Amazon